Island Possessed

Island

Possessed

🔥🔥🔥🔥🔥🔥🔥🔥🔥🔥🔥🔥

Katherine Dunham

The University of Chicago Press

Chicago and London

This is a book written with
love, dedicated to my husband,
John Pratt, and to the Republic
of Haiti, explaining, I think,
many things about this author
and about that island.

Published by arrangement with Doubleday, a division of
Bantam Doubleday Dell Publishing Group, Inc.

The University of Chicago Press, Chicago 60637
The University of Chicago Press, Ltd., London

All rights reserved. Originally published 1969
University of Chicago Press Edition 1994
Printed in the United States of America
01 00   6 5 4 3 2

ISBN 0-226-17113-2 (pbk.)

Library of Congress Cataloging-in-Publication Data

Dunham, Katherine.
    Island possessed / Katherine Dunham.
        p.   cm.
    Originally published: New York : Doubleday, 1969.
    1. Haiti—Social life and customs.   2. Voodooism.
    3. Dancing—Haiti—Anthropological aspects.   I. Title.
    F1916.D8   1994
    972.94—dc20   93-46117
                                                            CIP

⊗ The paper used in this publication meets the minimum
requirements of the American National Standard for
Information Sciences—Permanence of Paper for Printed
Library Materials, ANSI Z39.48-1984.

Contents

EDITOR'S NOTE

Katherine Dunham first went to Haiti in 1936, when she was granted a Rosenwald Fellowship to study primitive dance and ritual in the West Indies and Brazil. A graduate student in anthropology, and already a successful dancer and choreographer, she found in Haiti endless variations of her two interests. For more than thirty years, she has returned again and again, and as one reads *Island Possessed*, understanding grows as to why and how Haiti is indeed her spiritual home.

She learned of the bloody history and chaotic politics of the island in the early days of its independence and met many of its leaders. She recognized patterns of culture and behavior which are found in areas of the New World that were strongly influenced by the African slaves brought from the Old World. She came to know well the Haitian peasants, the backbone of the country, and developed a deep and abiding affection for them. She soon realized that the strongest influence, the unifying and vitalizing force, was vaudun, or voodoo, and she was initiated into the first class, or group, of vaudun, the lavé-tête. Much later she returned to find herself an honorary member of the second degree, the canzo or trial by fire. The first initiation ceremony, and her own thoughts and reactions during it, make up a large and important part of this haunting memoir.

Through the years Miss Dunham has taken her dance company around the world to innumerable countries, has received awards and decorations in many places, has produced, choreographed, and danced in films, on Broadway, and in opera as well as the recitals of the Dunham School and the Dunham company of dancers, singers, and musicians. She has written many articles, some short stories, and two books, which were published in America, in Mexico, and in France.

Several years ago she bought a historic plantation, Habitation Leclerc, once presided over by Napoleon's sister Pauline. In recent times she has not returned to Haiti often, preferring to spend more time in her home in Dakar, Senegal. It was there that, gathering, sifting, and reliving her memories of Haiti, she wrote *Island Possessed*.

1969

Book I

1

It was with letters from Melville Herskovits, head of the Department of Anthropology at Northwestern University, that I invaded the Caribbean—Haiti, Jamaica, Martinique, Trinidad, passing lightly over the other islands, then Haiti again for the final stand for the real study.

When I arrived in Haiti, not long after the exodus of the Marines, there were still baptized drums hidden in hollow tree trunks and behind waterfalls. President Sténio Vincent paid deference to "folklore" for the sake of the growing interests of tourists in the island, but an air of secrecy clothed all the serious ceremonies and it was not the policy of the first government after the Occupation to sponsor young women visitors in investigations that might verify to the world outside what has been a crucial problem to Haitian statesmen since the independence: the irreconcilable breach between the thin upper crust of the Haitian élite—who would have liked to be rulers of the land, participating in the revolution only to get rid of the French—and the bubbling, churning ferment of the black peasants, who really were by numbers and by historical content and character and humanness, I was to find, the true Haitian people.

Being a "first" on the scene helped. Seabrook with his *Magic Island* had been a great handicap because the élite were offended, not so much by the text, which, compared to much that has been written about Haiti, isn't so vilifying, but by the illustrations—grotesque impressions not only of the peasants, which wouldn't have mattered, but of the élite. Officially, Seabrook was not to return to the island and I believe he never did, though that might have been his own decision. Harold Courlander had been there and Melville Herskovits had just published the first serious and sympathetic study of the people and their social structure. They were white and male, these writers. Of my kind I was a first— a lone young woman easy to place in the clean-cut American dichotomy of color, harder to place in the complexity of Caribbean color classifications; a mulatto when occasion called for, an in-between, or "griffon" actually, I suppose; most of the time an unplaceable, which I prefer to think of as "noir"—not exactly the color black, but the quality of belonging with or being at ease with black people when in the hills or plains or anywhere and scrambling through daily life along with them. Though the meaning of the word negritude has never been completely clear to me, here in the country of the conceiver of the concept, reflecting on my early years, I know that I must have practiced, preached, and lived it. Léopold Sédar Senghor, President of Senegal, has interpreted and reinterpreted the word negritude over the years, but unlike Aimée Césaire, who coined the word, he has never rejected the word itself. Senghor in his book *Liberté #1—Négritude et Humanisme* defines negritude as " 'unite pluraliste' which remains the ideal of humanists today."

For myself, I insist upon the meaning of negritude as the effort to create a community of men, who happen to be black but must belong to the world around, no matter what kind or color. It is a word I feel to be redundant in most of its uses. Especially for English-speaking people it is hard not to feel undertones of nationalism and narcissism, and I do not admit to a spiritual or cultural poverty in black people which would make it necessary to coin a word or system of thinking of oneself outside the human division.

My first stop-off at Haiti on the way to Jamaica, Martinique, and Trinidad had been brief. It was June, the summer rainy season and the season for honoring ancestors. I stayed just long enough to be escorted about the countryside by Price-Mars and René Piquion, to be entranced by starched white suits and old-world courtesies, to be stunned by dirt and poverty, to deliver some of the letters from Melville Herskovits, but not the one to President Vincent, about which I was shamefully remiss, delivering it only at the end of my return stay of a year. I have never known if it was shyness, the spirit of independence, some political attitudes slowly but surely forming, or a protective sixth sense that kept the letter among my "valuable" papers. Perhaps I was afraid of being drawn in another direction, away from sources and into superficialities. And in that case this book would never have been written, so many things would never have happened, and I would, more than likely, not be embroiled in the sorcery and sociopolitics of Africa.

I had time to receive a few callers, to look over the sparkling bay from the hills of Pétionville, and to fall deeply in love with the possessed island without knowing why. I had as a base then, as later, during my long stay, the tiny one-room cupola on top of the Hotel Excelsior—a Bemelmans' dream.

Of my first day in Port-au-Prince I have two memories. One is the pink sugar-cake cathedral that never ceases to draw attention whether the voyager arrives by sea or air. It is set as a sort of pale coral vaginal opening leading into the mountains, to Canapé Vert and Pétionville and La Boule and God knows where else I may not have seen. Scattered around this Delphic beauty without rhyme or reason— except to torment tourists—the slums of Port-au-Prince extended at that time from Pont Beudette to Carrefours—

that is, what might be called the suburban area from the left of the bay in the center of which the cathedral nestles to the extreme right which follows the other protective arm of the bay, in the direction of Source Leclerc, which I was to know later. There is a magnificent royal palm grove just on the ocean, the truly painful beauty of which sheltered ordure, yaws (skin syphilis) infested parents and babies, stray cats too clever to be caught, skinned, and eaten, pigs holding bones together with skin (how do they find the calcium to produce the bristles that fringe their bony razor-backs? Some people say by rooting in graveyards). The slums extended past "cribs" run by my now dear friend Madame Nadier, past the swimming pool and tennis courts of caste- and color-restricted Club Thorland, past the mud huts of Carrefours, then well south on to the uncharted roads to the next city of any size, Léogane. They were slums unequaled in parts of the world which I have known since then, and they are hard to rival in Lima, Peru, of not so long ago, the favelas of Brazil, massed sampan river housing in Hong Kong, or the clusters of tin and paper huts bordering a bridge on the road to Rufisque, just outside Dakar in Senegal, West Africa.

I was in the Hotel Excelsior by personal introduction of Dr. Herskovits. It was just the right address for a young woman not yet placed sociologically or socially in the community she had invaded, but who was, more than likely, in the Moreau de Saint-Méry scheme of things, to be classed as mulatto and élite because of the letters of introduction she carried, her serious appearance, and her quantities of baggage. She was without question scholarly by credentials, excess of apparatus, and dress peculiarities—dress more casual even than for Americans, unless they happened to be tourists from the weekly boats, and these didn't enter into the scheme of Haitian thinking or recognition, except as they affected the economy through sightseeing and at the Iron Market.

The Hotel Excelsior still dominates one side of the Champs-de-Mars, which then was a dusty square with a tiny bandstand in the center, a statue of Simón Bolívar to one side, and a few cement benches lining the walks here and there. Poinsettia bushes pushed their way out of the dust as they could, and at times they blossomed. The Hotel Excelsior was owned by the sisters Rouzier and, I believe, still is, or at least by their heritors. The Rouzier sisters were indisputably mulatto and wore rice powder to accentuate an already eggshell color. They were the essence of respectability. I am sure that on more than one occasion they must have been baffled, distressed, and scandalized by my behavior and by the range of my associates. Often they must have regretted ever having accepted me into the place. However, their morbid curiosity and avidity were too great a combination to contest and in the end were my best insurance for a long lease on my top-floor perch.

To begin with, I was never very communicative, because of either shyness or intellectual snobbishness. In some ways this faded aristocracy of Haiti, forced to earn a living, yet still remaining genteel, reminded me of relatives I felt myself to have outgrown. In other ways, it exuded a social fatigue that I felt inimical to the vitality I didn't yet know but felt burgeoning all around me. There were occasions, however, when loneliness forced me to recognize a real concern and kindliness behind the façade requisite to status-holding in such communities. Later, when in the plains or bush on long trips, I was to miss the Rouzier sisters and to feel the separation from these friends who had become the respectable side of my Haitian family life. Looking back, I realize they had much to contend with.

In those days the first social regulation in Haiti was to stay closely knit to your own color or degree of black-white blood-mixture grouping—which was actually a caste, being exclusive, endogamous, inherent, nontransferable, immutable. The immutable part I found to have an escape clause,

expressed in an old Haitian proverb: "Mulatre pauvre—neg';
neg' riche—mulatre!" or, a poor mulatto becomes a black,
a rich black a mulatto. Of course, this was true only on the
surface. In a last analysis the Rouziers, though obliged to
resort to innkeeping to save the family silverware and pre-
serve the antimacassars, would never really be "black" in
Haiti; and daughters of families I have known, who were
educated in books, and rich, I have seen sit out dance
after dance at fancy dress balls because they were just too
dark of skin color to make the social grade and fell behind
the mulatto standard in features and hair texture. In the
eighteenth century, Moreau de Saint-Méry, the most descriptive and perhaps unbiased of the historians and chroniclers
of Saint-Domingue, notes the forty gradations of mixtures
recognized at the time of his writing between black and
white, with sometimes Arawak or Carib Indian blood thrown
in. Haiti of today recognizes the following: mulatto, marabou, griffon, black.

When the exact degree of blood mixture had been forgotten or could not be determined, as in my case, or in the
cases of Haitians expatriated and married abroad for generations, materialities of money and manners entered in, along
with those intangibles that make up a large part of all such
judgments, even those considered scientific and rational.

It seemed best to give the Rouzier sisters and the few pensioners of the Hotel Excelsior time to sort out my position
in this complex caste system in order not to run the risk of
upsetting them, as I had the immigrations officer who came
to meet our homey little Royal Netherlands Lines boat, as it
dropped anchor in the bay of Port-au-Prince that June morning in 1936. The pilot boat was guided by a coal black officer
in a stiff white uniform, striking, if for nothing else than his
color scheme. The boat at anchor beside us was white too,
bouncing on blue water so transparent one had the impression of being able to count the scales on the striped and
coral and blue fish that streaked through it. With the pilot

were two lieutenants of the Coast Guard—which I was to know as "élite" as I learned more about the Haitian social system—and a seedy, almost mulatto type, who would be a "griffon," with spots on his face, artlessly covered by talcum powder. This only accentuated the spots, which were so placed and of such a texture as to have been unmistakably yaws. That much I knew but tried not to disclose the fact that I was aware of or had heard of this peculiarly Caribbean skin disorder. This was a typical immigrations officer, whose kind I have met in three fourths of the countries of the world. Passengers of any sort represent geographic freedom, and most of the petty officials having to deal with them go to their graves seeing only the saloon or upper deck of a ship, the interior of a plane, or a cubbyhole to one side of a dock or airport assigned for the examination of papers belonging to those passengers enjoying the freedom of travel. The sound of an incoming plane, the creak of ship planks, the smell of cargo and oil, of passengers, ship's food, bilge water, and even unwashed toilets must set up a hunger hard not to satisfy. I had no reason to be ill at ease, but I knew that if I were to have trouble, this particular petty officer would be the one to cause it, and joyfully. Condescending, resentful, suspicious, sadistic, he took minutes to settle in a chair at one of the dining saloon tables, minutes to adjust his pince-nez glasses, minutes to dawdle through the passports and other identification of the few of us who were remaining in Haiti—a Dutch family, an English couple, two Jesuit priests, two sisters of charity, an American photographer— to judge from his equipment—and a perspiring student of "dance and anthropology" wondering what to do next, now that the first stage of the great adventure was out of the way.

I had gone to Washington in person for my passport, so that was in order. My luggage carried nothing that I would have thought was contraband, though I might well have been concerned when I recall the supplies of medication, film,

cameras, an old cylindrical Edison recording apparatus
loaned by Melville Herskovits after long West African service, unworn lace underclothing and party dresses—most of
which went back in the same state—books, camping odds
and ends, Jack Harris' red portable typewriter—for which I
had exchanged my unworkable Remington—enough soap,
sanitary napkins, tooth paste, and hair ointment for the year,
and a briefcase of documents and letters of introduction for
the four islands to be visited, each wrapped separately in
oilskin against climate erosion. My luggage anxieties were
unfounded. At that time immigration and customs were one
and the same to me and had about the same effect on me
as an encounter with a Chicago traffic policeman.

It was only the letters of introduction which the immigrations officer found interesting. By the time he had reached
me, dawn and the magic hour of suspense had long passed. I
was last in line because that seemed safest to my inexperience.
I was justifiably disturbed when I noticed his attitude toward the American ahead of me. My passport would make
me to some degree persona non grata. I counted on color to
offset this, but then there was to offset *that* my sex and class
—the student class, very hard to place. I blushed as he opened
each letter, not only the ones addressed to Haitian dignitaries
like the President and scholars like Dr. Dorsainville, but ones
to the Governor of Trinidad and the Colonel of the Maroons
in Jamaica and Louis Achille, father, in Martinique and Lady
Audrey Jeffries in Trinidad and the Manleys in Jamaica. My
discomfort and indignation seemed only to add fuel to his de-
termination to find some rewarding plot, perhaps one worth
a promotion, at the bottom of the phenomenon of this lone
female loose on shores rightfully only his, and documented
for research in "anthropology and the dance," because that
is the way my calling cards read. I had not been able to
make up my mind to separate the two callings and haven't
yet. My authorizations were also unorthodox: two names not
even sounding American, Herskovits and Rosenwald, and

two universities, when everyone knew not only because of the atrocious behavior of the Americans during the Occupation, but since the showing of a film, *Imitation of Life*, already seen in Port-au-Prince, that blacks, even mulattoes, couldn't attend universities in the United States, much less be sponsored by them. Then obviously just to be confusing he began speaking in French. I hadn't expected to be called on to use French without thinking it over first and was so taken by surprise that I answered in kind, imperfect though it must have been, without thinking. I have some gods who come rushing in at unexpected moments for big things but mostly for niggling little things like this. Everything changed. My interrogator managed a smile, not too wide because of his sores, replaced my letters in their folders, held out his hand in farewell as he rose to leave and pressed mine harder than was necessary. Removing his pince-nez, he looked deeply into my eyes and hoped to see me in town at the immigration office for further "formalities" within a day or two. At the same time, if it were toward evening, he could show me something of the scenery surrounding the capital . . . I made a mental note never to be without hygienic handshaking protection when on foreign territory. In my purse at this moment there is a bottle of slightly scented surgical alcohol for rinsing after long handshaking sessions, which I have become so accustomed to as a precautionary measure that whether in the "brush" of Casamance or Chicago, Brazil or Buenos Aires, it is always with me.

I was free to set foot on my first foreign soil and, though not yet classified, was at least in the active immigration files of Port-au-Prince, Haiti, W. I.

At the Hotel Excelsior my prestige would go from high to low in a matter of moments. Dr. Lhérisson was mulatto, well married, of good background and a top professional. Dr. Price-Mars was intellectual, had been many times close to being elected President of the Republic, and was later to represent Haiti at the United Nations, but he was black.

The position of Price-Mars was quaquaversal and untouchable. but Roger Anselm, mulatto renegade, a really intelligent and sensitive person with whom I used to go riding, refused to enter the Hotel Excelsior when Dr. Price-Mars called—occasions that were rare and extremely important to me. Roger's attitude severed our friendship, after stormy efforts on my part at his conversion to the American way of thinking about classes, not castes.

Another time Téoline or Cécile or Dégrasse might walk or side-saddle in by donkey from Croix-de-Missions or Pont Beudette, pass a whispered word on to one of the hotel maids, or just stand across from the Excelsior in the street waiting until some telepathy drew me to the balcony of my lookout, after which I would descend and meet them at the back garden entrance or a Champs-de-Mars bench, because to have invited them into the Victorian salon of the Excelsior, or even to my studio room, would surely have caused a fainting spell to one or both of the Rouzier sisters. These meetings would, of course, place me at the bottom of the Haitian social ladder: a display of our mutual affection was never hidden, even from the curious street passers-by.

The most difficult problem to face in regard to l'Américaine for all my Haitian-born friends or acquaintances was my close friendship with Fred Alsop. Fred was young and was hard to place socially. He was not self-employed and, though chief mechanic in the only garage in town was automatically considered in the laboring class, not a recommendation that the Haitian élite would have understood. Nor did he evidence potential wealth. In a society as calculating as these ingrown bureaucratic groups of Haiti, he was regarded as an outsider, to be tolerated because he was personable and had not done anything to be held against him, and to be allowed to have among them a few friends, so long as he was not too often an escort to their daughters. Qualities which endeared Fred to me—kindness, wit, intelligence, compatibility, and very good looks—were not sufficient for him to be seriously considered as a number one eligible bachelor. These are my impressions, still vividly retained after so long, and I must have been very aware at the time, suddenly finding myself the object of discrimination inverse from what I had known in America, because of friendship with someone who was non-Haitian, "non" any one of those forty razor-fine black-white mixtures of Moreau de Saint-Méry. In the eyes of the proprietoresses of the Excelsior Hotel, in spending as much time as I did with Fred, I had descended to an ebb as low in its own particular way as slipping out to meet Téoline or Cécile or Dégrasse, or waking at two in the morning, dressing, and with a flashlight and my personal kit setting out to follow the staccato rhythm of a Petro ceremony or the sensuous bass insinuation of the Congo drums accompanying a Congo paillette. For the Rouzier sisters and the Hotel Excelsior my advent and activities were the equivalents of radio, television, and the latest newsreels on world events. None of these distractions was current in Haiti then, and this is a part of why they tolerated me, more, could not let me go, and finally became emotionally entangled in spite of my unpredictability, deliberate clinging to the role of outsider, crashing naïveté, ruthless trampling of customs and often of sensibilities. As the situation presented itself, I seem to have wavered or catapulted from mulatto to black, élite to peasant, intellectual to bohemian, in to out, up to down, and tried hard to keep out of trouble but didn't succeed.

The parade of Senator Zépherin's elegant black Pierce-Arrow cabriolet began with my arrival at the Excelsior Hotel. Late the morning of my arrival in Port-au-Prince, victorious over immigration but piqued over customs delays, I was paid respects by the Senator from his second-floor balcony while I leaned over the protective railing of my tiny one-room perch above, which might have been the gazebo of a roomy French-style villa in times of past splendor. The Senator had a guest with him that morning, but the guest did not look up and we were not introduced. Later I learned from Titine that he was Dumarsais Estimé, President of the Chamber of Deputies.

Dumarsais Estimé must have been about thirty-three, young in those days for a President of the Chamber of Deputies. Senator Zépherin must have been fiftyish, a seasoned old bucktoothed "Lion of the North," black, paunchy, myopic, and, as long as I knew him, hidden behind centimeter-thick smoked glasses. He seemed old to me then and ridiculous in spite of being a Senator, which kind I had never met before. Perhaps I would not think so now. He seemed ridiculous chiefly because he remained in a soiled brocade dressing gown—acquired in Paris no doubt—until he was ready to effect a phenomenal metamorphosis into the striped trousers, top hat, and frock coat of his office. From a fat, lewd voyeur type, he became a statesman—authoritative, fiery, articulate even when bursting into his vulgar-dulcet mother tongue, creole. The fine brocade of his wine-colored dressing gown was spattered with soft-boiled egg, syrupy coffee, and toast crumbs, and, if one wanted to examine closely, there were traces of rice powder, lipstick, straight and wavy hairs, and feminine scent.

Since it was the Senator's habit to receive at his Port-au-Prince pied à terre (he was from Cap-Haïtien) in this dressing gown, and to call on me in it after his morning coffee, just before the exhibition of the Pierce-Arrow, I came to know the shades, nuances, and scents of scraps of food and female cosmetics clinging to it. I could practically tell what heavily veiled mulattress had repented on the dressing gown after sacrificing her honor for a husband's or a fiancé's promotion. I shall tell more about my two friends—rivals—later.

All three of us leaned over the ornate carved wooden railings, they on their balcony, I on mine, and admired the outsize, black carriage that was the pride and joy of the "Lion of the North." A Pierce-Arrow was a mark of status anywhere in the world, and in the setting, this one, polished like marble, nickel-plated mountings bouncing the sun off li doubly impressive.

The driver too was something to be admired. hot countries still resisted cold-country clothir cept on solemn state occasions and at funerals. Diue denim, black poplin, cotton prints, mixed patched colors for the loa were in order for the lower classes; Paris organdies, crepes, Irish linens and voiles, lacework and embroideries made on command at home for ladies of the élite. But almost without exception the dress of the Haitian man of business—and, that went without saying, the élite, because there was practically no middle class then—at home, at informal parties, was the whitest of white suits; either drill or linen. Even at the beginning of the use of nylon for suiting there were some who remained faithful to white. The white starched suit was one of the few things that might be shared in common by men regardless of class or caste. Rare as the white suit has become, in the hills today, as then, one will come across the white starched uniform on some country patriarch, village head man, or bush dignitary. In the capital today a white suit is rare, almost an oddity. One associates it with very old men playing *dames* on the back gallery of a termite-eaten, vine-choked old villa, or meeting on a Champs-de-Mars bench at sundown, not feeling the cold of the cement beneath and around them, drowsing not in the remembrance of things past but still living there, never having moved into the present. Nowadays, in the hottest weather, the younger ones wear Brooks Brothers woolen suits, oxford gray, brown, navy blue, herringbone, all of the cloths and colors made to blend into St.-Germain-des-Prés or Harlem or Fifth Avenue, New York. They have, however, discovered simple hot weather shirts, not as characteristic as the Cuban guyabel, or as elegant as the Philippine barong tagalog, but a cool balance to the rest of the ensemble.

Zépherin's driver was to be admired because he was something right off Place Vendôme—or is it the uniform of the

.otel Crillon doorman which makes me think of the Senator's chauffeur?—complete from visored cap to polished boots and frog-braid jacket. He was a thin little man, very black, and shiny as the vehicle that dominated the Excelsior courtyard. In the center of the courtyard a tangle of frangipani and bougainvillea, together with a coconut palm tree, formed an island which the Spanish call glorieta and for which I can find no word in English as flamboyantly descriptive. A driveway through pillared gates led around this plot to the wide steps of the veranda, then continued around the other side and out the bottleneck drive to the street. I do not know why I think of this as past, because geographically at least nothing has changed (unless hurricane Inez reached farther into town than I know about), not the looped wood-carving decorations from veranda to gazebo, not the gateway or the driveway or the glorieta, though this had run a little to seed when I last saw it.

It was possible, by carefully manipulating the huge machine, to keep driving in an ellipse with only one reversal of direction, which occurred when crossing the entrance of the driveway. At this dramatic point, the visored cap would emerge from the car window, the chauffeur would flash a wide smile in a general upward direction, touch two fingers to his cap in an offhand sergeant-to-captain salute, then begin the maneuver of sliding into rear gear, backing down to the sidewalk without regard for porteresses who might be crossing on foot or on donkeys carrying chickens and turkeys and melons for barter, and of adjusting the gleaming snout back to the veranda stairway. Three turns around the glorieta and the driver would retire to park in the shade of the mango tree, half the branches of which hung over the wrought-iron barrier framing either side of the gateway. During mango season the Rouzier sisters kept a sharp eye for the ripe fruit, which street people felt belonged to them since it was so accessible. Each morning the Senator and I found ourselves simultaneously in Port-au-Prince this ritual took place. I did not ask but presume it not to have been especially for me, but likely to occur for any "personnage," which from my observance of the Senator's habits was by a large percentage confined to ladies eligible for courting.

Once in the shade of the mango tree the driver would remove and fold his frogged jacket, mop his brow and armpits with a piece of toweling kept folded beside him on the front seat, and set to polishing the spotless chassis with a worn chamois skin. The next order of things was for the Senator to focus his thick glasses heavenward from the balcony below mine by craning his tortoiselike neck and straining his heavy waistline. Then he would display a set of teeth going in all directions from a prognathous dental arch in response to my grin of approval. After a two-sentence lesson in creole from him to me, each would retire to his respective "apartment" to finish the tiny cups of burnt coffee that were before-breakfast custom. Then he would face an endless stream of callers; and I, my books, notes, and Jack Harris' typewriter.

On one such morning I looked down into two pairs of dark glasses, but only one smile. The young President of the Chamber of Deputies, Dumarsais Estimé, had timed his visit perfectly, without telegraph drums, without telephones or radar, with porteresses, who more often than not pass each other exchanging the equivalent of a printed page with only a grunt and the exposed white of an eye. I wondered then and still wonder about the system of communication that ties one primitive community to another, announces births, deaths, departures, revolutions, incarcerations, and arrivals with no sign that can clearly be discerned by the less "primitive" eye or ear. Whatever or whoever his informant was, I looked down that morning at the somewhat large, close-cropped head, wide, sensuous mouth, brown wool-suited slender figure of the man who, within a few months of intimacy and a number of years of distant—in the sense of non-intimate—sporadic meetings, so few and far between, would be responsible for most of what I know about Haiti, much of my recognition of the truths and failings among men, and an intellectual awakening in a physical sense—similar experiences previously having been for me confused emotionalism.

Leaning precariously out over the balcony railing, Zépherin was obliged to make the introduction to Dumarsais Estimé, and I was amused at his chagrin. He seemed to have thought of me as his personal find, or that at least this morning ritual would belong to him alone. His hopes beyond displaying the Pierce-Arrow were dim, as I never once, to my memory, rode in the car. Nor was I ever farther inside his room than the doorsill, and he never farther into mine. This was not the first occasion that the young Deputy from St. Marc stuck in the craw of the Senator from the north, and it certainly would not be the last, during the twenty or so years that I kept up with one or both of them, that is, until the death of Dumarsais Estimé, President of the Republic of Haiti *in exsilium*. I refer to their political disagreements during these later years, when each of us was personally engaged otherwise and Estimé and I were only dear friends.

Doc Reeser had been a ship's pharmacist and when the Marines settled in Haiti, supposedly with intentions to bring peace to the troubled island, Doc's genuine interest in things and people indigenous won him a post at Pont Beudette, on whose outskirts there was an asylum for the insane, mostly just a fenced-in pasture with mud huts thrown up here and there. This enclosing of the so-called insane was for the Haitians just another one of the strange ways that Americans have of doing things. Heretofore the mentally deranged roamed roadways and mountains and forests and were aberrations in a scheme of the gods or were hopelessly possessed by them and paying out some time of penance. Now they were little better off, but they were in effect cloistered and in some way cared for, and surely enjoyed some measure of pharmaceutical if not psychiatric care. They also enjoyed the ceremonies and dances and vaudun drums that seemed never to stop from Friday evening to Sunday night, running over even into Monday on the slightest pretext, and these ceremonies may have been their bush psychiatry.

Doc Reeser had set himself up and been accepted far and wide by houngans, the priests of vaudun, the Haitian Arada-Dahomean cult religion sometimes known as voodoo, as a "horse" of Guedé, a human to be mounted or entered into or become embodied in Guedé, sometimes transferring to Baron Samedi, both gods being governors of the dead and of cemeteries. Both Baron Samedi and Papa Guedé are bon viveurs: it was convenient for Doc because he could drink as much clairin—raw white rum—as he wished and indulge in certain extravagances of behavior and obscenities which most of the gods of the pantheon would not tolerate in their mounts.

Outside a sanctuary where only the high-category priests and priestesses sang softly and clapped their hands and intoned litanies among themselves Doc would hold forth, splashing rum in a tin cup with movements less and less co-ordinated, telling tales less and less articulate, forcing a "mama" drum from between the legs of her sweat-dripping rider to demonstrate his own skill at drum beating: snatching a sacred rattle, the ason, from La place, head man after the high priest houngan. Doc could become ridiculous in a need to participate, even to those of us who loved him. All the while he would be working up on a possession. In the years that I knew Doc I was never certain that he had at any time been chosen as a horse. It may have been pure exhibitionism, or the need to belong to something accessible yet always inaccessible, to identify, or simply the quantities of rum consumed before, during, and after each ceremony or dance or pretext of ceremony, that created his seeming state of trance. Or, giving Doc a certain due, and seeing things from a more detached but more mystified point of view, perhaps I should say that Papa Guedé and Baron Samedi had truly decided to bring to this dusty plains community on the outskirts of the Cul-de-Sac some evidence of "desegregation" and nonpreference in evidencing themselves in the white Marine "Doc."

Being seen at ceremonies with Doc created no barrier for my studies. Much of the time it helped, because whether or not he was believed or was accepted into the deepest of the mysteries, being a white American and a Marine at that, whether he was led home flat plastered on clairin by his mistress, Cécile, or whether, on a rampage of possession, he broke up the crossroads rum shop, Doc was loved by everyone, everywhere in Haiti, of all colors, except perhaps Dumarsais Estimé, if he was noticed by him at all. Dumarsais Estimé was, because of several personal experiences, to be related later, very much against the color white, and all the more so since he was courting me at the time of my initiation into the vaudun. As President of the Chamber of Deputies, he was placed in a delicate position because of my association with Doc, with Fred, and with the vaudun.

In those days Doc was a real person, not just the *caractère* he became later. That would have been in the days of his first discovery of Haiti, in those early years before he began to doubt himself and the surrealistic world around him and before alcohol had dulled his histrionic and anecdotal aptitudes and a rather crafty poor white trash quality took over where a good and sensitive soul had started out. Perhaps this later personality took over after he had gone back from Haiti and spent time in Florida. Perhaps Haiti was all just too much for him, or the dipping in magic, as in the case of his predecessor, the one he really hoped to emulate, the creator of the myth of the Magic Island, William Seabrook.

2

When I first went to Haiti there was no way for the owner of an automobile to remain anonymous. Automobiles were few, and the licenses of those were memorized backwards and forwards by all literate citizens. The illiterate made note of the size, shape, and color, sometimes make. Senator Zépherin's Pierce-Arrow needed no tag of identification, nor did Deputy Estimé's tan Oldsmobile. Had Estimé's automobile not been known just because it was new and belonged to him, it would soon have been known for the wide area it covered geographically and socially in my service. I tried without much success bribing the chauffeur into overlooking my vagaries with tips and friendly conversation, but sooner or later my politician friend, now a daily caller at the Hotel Excelsior, would discover that a visit to Dr. Price-Mars might continue farther outside Pétionville and end at the home of Louis Borno, President of Haiti just before Sténio Vincent, or getting a typewriter ribbon might end up at Dégrasse's market corner. Dumarsais Estimé disliked white people, identifying most of them with Marines and functionaries of the Occupation. Another reason for his sentiment occurred much later, after he was President. I shall speak of that elsewhere. At this time, however, he carried as well as his feelings against people of the white race a smoldering resentment against the mulatto élite of Haiti and their multiple ways of preserving within the country a caste system based on color distinctions. He was particularly offended that his car had been seen in the driveway of the Bornos, because for him Louis Borno represented what a freed octoroon collaborator with the French must have represented to the first black leaders of the slave revolt.

Louis Borno, President of Haiti from 1922 until 1930, for a large part of the American Occupation, was mulatto in every sense of the word. His black blood was so attenuated as to be in evidence only to those already aware. He was monied by inheritance, and it may well be that there is no foundation to the claims that he became more so after the Haitian American bank loans maneuvered during his presidency. From 1917 until 1930, the termination of Borno's second term, the legislative bodies of the government, the Senate and Chamber of Deputies, remained in suspension, and absolute power was left in the hands of the President and his Conseil d'État, a body of advisers appointed by the President, with the approval of course of the American High Commissioner or Brigadier General, whichever governed. Melville Herskovits in giving me the name of Louis Borno as reference left to my discretion any contact with him, warning me of possible disagreeable consequences. Feelings were still so high against the former President that being aware of the curiosity of customs officials Herskovits had been reluctant to give me a letter of introduction to him. He regretted this circumstance, having himself a high regard for Borno's intelligence and experience. He commented on his charm, élan, poise, and imperviousness to attack or current feelings, and I found these among other reasons to admire the former President. The Bornos lived well and graciously, and as a visiting young lady anthropologist, friend of Monsieur and Madame Herskovits, I was made to feel immediately at home and, what is more, important. The former President insisted on taking a film of me with his new sixteen-millimeter

Kodak, then had a few feet made by his son, Henri, of the two of us together. This was the first film made of me, to my knowledge.

Haitians of middle and upper class operated at that time on hospitality codes more French than American. At home, wives and daughters were seldom in evidence to visitors, remaining inside, from where they peeked through wooden shutters at husbands and sons entertaining on the veranda. Even years later at lunch or dinner at the houses of close friends my experience has been for the wives to oversee the serving of the table, gravitating between kitchen or serving pantry and dining room, seldom sitting at table with the guests, seldom joining in after-dinner discussions. These had been my experiences when calling on Dantès Bellegarde, Camille Lhérisson, Camille Rousseau, Émile St. Lot, Henri Chauvet, and others. Mrs. Price-Mars was an exception. An ardent feminist, involved in women's suffrage, newspaper publication, and any measures likely to liberate Haitian women from the secondary role they had occupied since colonial times, she frequently came to see me at the Hotel Excelsior and joined in when Price-Mars and I discussed politics, vaudun, methods of research in ethnology, and world politics. She was also at table with us at every occasion for lunch, and represented for me the Haitian woman in full process of evolution. Furthermore, Mrs. Price-Mars was not satisfied with this evolution for herself alone—because as the wife of a man several times ambassador, several times candidate for President, and lecturer at the Sorbonne, she must have had enviable freedoms—but chose as her mission the liberation of all Haitian women of all classes.

Though I now understand Haitian feelings of revulsion toward anyone even faintly suspected of collaboration with the members of the Occupation, having done some research in the control methods used by the Marines and their chiefs, I nevertheless feel that the position of whoever had been President at that time would have been extremely delicate and his behavior not too divergent from that of Borno. The Americans occupied Haiti with very little consideration for the customs, desires, and habits of the people themselves, and with no wish, until the harm was done, to find out what the national character was like. Not until the Forbes Commission of 1930, under President Herbert Hoover, and after much pressure, national and international, to relieve the situation, was any effort made to bridge the void between the Haitians and the occupants. A demonstration on the Champs-de-Mars, before the very same Hotel Excelsior of my Port-au-Prince sojourn, seems to have touched deeply the Commission to whom it had been addressed, particularly the editor-philanthropist William Allen White, who was a member of the investigating commission appointed by the President of the United States. The demonstration, according to Dantès Bellegarde, was on the first day of carnival, but instead of a haphazard popular demonstration it was sponsored and supported by the Church of the Sacred Heart. The following quote is from a report by one William Montavon, present as an observer at the time, and is reproduced in Bellegarde's *Histoire du Peuple Haïtien:*

"The American authorities feared a disorderly mob would emerge from the meeting at the church: there issued from the Sacre Coeur a pious and disciplined crowd, bearing banners of the Sacred Heart of Jesus and the Virgin Mary. The crowd was praying to the Holy Ghost, beseeching it to shine its light on each commissioner so that he might perceive the truth underlying the Haitian situation. It prayed to the Sacred Heart of Jesus, asking that the Commission, President Hoover, the people of the United States be imbued with the charity to find means for restoring those institutions, in defense of which their ancestors had fought until death and which their present-day sons felt impotent to defend by force. The crowd moved toward the monument to Dessalines in the Champs-de-Mars. Recalling the dramatic scene of the proclamation of independence in the 'Place d'Armes de

Gonaïves' on January 1, 1804, the crowd placed its banners at the foot of the statue of the Liberator and made an oath to cooperate with the Forbes Commission and President Hoover in the ridding of evils brought to Haiti by the American Occupation.

"As if by miracle a turning point occurred in the situation. The Commission met on the following day at 9 A.M. There was no longer an air of suspicion. In the interim, the Commission had been authorized to state its objective; that of restoring representative government in Haiti. As with the flick of a magic wand, a feeling of good will, mutual confidence, of reciprocal respect had replaced the heretofore suspicion and hostility."

I refer to these background notes only to emphasize that the President of the republic was truly limited in power at the time. Sudre Dartiguenave, President of Haiti preceding Borno, had tried unsuccessfully to impede the extension of American administration, and the massive bank loans proposed by this administration were considered by him ruinous to the future economy of the country. As Minister of Foreign Affairs, Louis Borno had protested certain Occupation measures; once President the toll to Haitian life and property might have been greater had he resisted the government, unfortunately made up mostly of Marines from the southern United States. Not really belonging to the white resident élite, eyed with suspicion by his own class, and hated by the blacks, Borno must have found his life a busy but lonely one during his mandate. When I saw the man he bore the marks of suffering. But to Dumarsais Estimé and many a Haitian nationalist he was a collaborator, opportunist, and traitor. I could not see these things and protested bitterly when denied the use of the Deputy's car for Pétionville trips, pointing out what I had read and heard of the other side, the little that there was of positive to put in balance against the loss of national autonomy: that out of the Occupation and Borno's presidency came new hospitals, public works, roads, elementary sanitation and the fenced-in farm for the mentally disturbed that Doc Reeser was director of at Pont Beudette.

Dumarsais Estimé's similitude to Toussaint L'Ouverture is marked. Toussaint never forgave betrayal; and Estimé never forgave Borno, feeling that his support of the Americans and his refusal to make an effort to re-establish the constitutional government was the supreme betrayal of his country. It can be believed that color distinctions within the country were tolerated if not condoned by Borno, which attitude would have aroused the same bitter resentment in Toussaint as it did in Estimé. Both men were slight, not totally black in color, not robust in health, not conventionally handsome. Both were self-educated in higher learning, both were philosophers and humanists. Toussaint, though with doubts as to the sincerity of Roman Catholicism, hated the vaudun. He saw in it a threat to his own personal authority. Estimé also hated the vaudun, or I should say held it in ridicule, feeling that the worship of African gods tied the people to ignorance, diverting them from recognition of their immediate and real problems. Soon I was to find my own way without the Deputy's car to the street corners of my vaudun friends, and to the Cul-de-Sac for visits to Cécile and Téoline. But I did not give in easily, and it was only after an experience which even I admitted was more than I would have accepted in like circumstances.

About thirty miles by car north and east from Pont Beudette, about fifty miles from Port-au-Prince, and not far from the Dominican border, is the village of Thomazeau. On the north it is bordered by the mountain ridge of Trou d'Eau, on the south by the Étang Saumâtre. This must have been rich land when irrigated during the French possession of Haiti and for a brief period under the first black rulers. When I knew it, it was a desert of brush, scrub trees, and dust in the dry season, mud and rocky water holes in the rainy season. Today in the plains and valleys near Thomazeau one can see crumbled gateways leading to open fields extending into ruins of aqueducts, and empty canals crossing the earth like tribal markings. In the rainy season water rushes into the canals with the downpours, but the aqueducts are mere shells and the mountain water spreads into the rivulets and streams with little attention for the fields that once produced the world's greatest sugar crop. The day I told Estimé's chauffeur that the Deputy would not need him for the night and had given permission for me to be driven to Thomazeau, I had been to visit Camille Lhérisson, who had just returned from a trip to the Army medical post at Terre Rouge in the vicinity of Thomazeau. There he had learned of the death of one of the last really high-category bocors in Haiti. The bocor was a very old man, wise in the knowledge of feuilles, or herbs, poisons, gris-gris, had taken the prix-de-cloche in the Congo vaudun and was clairvoyant without having taken the prix-des-yeux. He was the most important bocor in the plains and valley region, perhaps in all of Haiti, and he had been dead for three days, lying in state in his own special sanctuary in one of the huts of his compound, surrounded by mourning and party-making acolytes and relatives. I have never known whether or not the people serving bocors are known as hounci—as they would be in the vaudun. Generally a bocor works alone, that is, he is not dependent upon a hierarchy of serviteurs for the execution of his offices. He may, however, have about him a corps of trainees and apprentices of high and low status, and these I have called hounci. The greatest obligation of one of these bush priest custodians of the medicines and magic of Africa is to transmit this knowledge, this ancestral wisdom to the highest in order of his disciples, the most likely in his brotherhood to have those qualities that have distinguished his own career.

My avidity for information and firsthand experience led me to the lie that was almost the end of a friendship turned romance. Estimé's chauffeur, given by me only the general whereabouts of our destination, held out bravely over rough roads with no signposts but plenty of potholes, fissures, and animals half-asleep rising from ditches on one side and plunging into our headlights, almost driving us into the ditch on the other side. Nearing Thomazeau we began to inquire for the compound of the bocor. We were directed wrongly, followed the skeletons of aqueducts nearly to the Dominican border, turned back, and finally at the end of a road of rocks and pebbles heard drumming and singing, which indicated a fête of some sort. I was accustomed to festivities for the dead from experience at like occasions among the Maroon people of Jamaica, but I recognized none of the familiar songs or rhythms of the vaudun and was hesitant to present myself with no introduction at such an occasion. The compound could not be seen from our dead-end road. When the car lights were turned off, as the chauffeur invariably did when the motor was stopped, considering this as an economy for the Deputy, there was absolutely no light, not from stars, moon, sky, or the unseen source of festivity. I sat in the car trying to find courage to descend and make my way up the stony hill in front of us to see what was on the other side of it. The chauffeur had begun to sulk, suspecting my falsehood. I bit my fingernails, fumbled in my travel kit for matches, thought up a few unkind things to say to Camille Lhérisson when I next saw him for not having offered to accompany me, then took the plunge. I got out of the car and asked the driver in what I considered a scathing manner if he would be good enough to turn the headlights on until I had climbed the hill, and to wait for me until I had verified the locale and returned to him with further instructions. The ceiling light went on when I opened the rear door and I saw the driver's face. I knew then that I would have light only as long as it would take him to reverse the car and find the road leading eventually to Port-au-Prince. He was gray with fright, and some of this fear he transmitted to me. I turned in desperation toward the sound of the drums, then back to the car, just about decided to give up this particular expedition and return to Cécile's caille in Pont Beudette where there were always clean sheets and kerosene lamps. It would take some miraculous event to keep me in this godforsaken outpost, and a miracle is what happened. At the top of the hill a light appeared. The driver started the motor of the car and would have taken off then and there had I not had one foot on the runningboard and my hand on his open window frame. The light drew closer and was raised, not to look at us but to show us the face of its carrier.

The man approaching us was perhaps forty years of age, of medium height but strongly built. The face lighted by the lantern was mahogany brown, the color of many Haitians who have lived for generations near the Dominican border. He was dressed in the usual workman's denim trousers but was bare to the waist, though the night was cool and I wore a sweater over my shirt and corduroy skirt. A red handkerchief was tied around his neck, and another around each forearm. He wore sandals and a straw hat. These latter details we saw as he approached the car. He smiled, and I had the impression that it was in amusement at us, that my efforts at insouciance had ended up in the same fright even more apparent now in the chauffeur. I was certain that the driver's apprehension was due to stories of zombies and reincarnated buried-alive slaves especially fond of haunting former plantations. Mine was the nervousness of the unexpected. I was relieved when our apparition laughed and greeted me by name. Then I was astonished. Camille Lhérisson would not have had time to tell anyone of my intention to visit this area. I had not been sure of it myself when I had spoken to him that afternoon.

The man spoke in French. He regretted that I could not go directly to the bocor's house because of special preparations being made there, but offered me the hospitality of his caille for the night if I wished to be near when the spirit of the bocor transferred into the head of the bocor's nephew. This is what I had come for. I looked at the chauffeur, hoping for a sign of encouragement, but he had actually shrunk into his clothing and I knew that no amount of bribery would keep him in this place longer than the time necessary to shift gears and back down the road. I nodded agreement and followed my guide, determined not to ask questions until we had arrived at wherever we were going. At the time it did not seem strange to me or even daring. I had never known physical fear in Haiti and had no occasion to feel distrust. One of the remarkable things about Haiti even today is its low crime rate in a world moving with speed in the opposite direction. Perhaps it is because the gods are always there to punish misdoings; perhaps it is a gentleness of spirit come out of a great deal of suffering with satisfaction in the end, as when the gods of the vaudun brought defeat to the French and freedom from slavery, or when the prayers on the Champs-de-Mars softened the spirit of the American Occupation Commission; or perhaps it is just a respect for others which is one of the qualities of the true Haitian. I am not referring to that new group of hybrid terrorists surrounding the present President. Until the advent of the Ton-ton Macoute I had never been aware of fear in Haiti, that is, fear of other men. There was anger against men during the Marine Occupation, as there must have been in various revolutions. Otherwise, one is afraid of the gods and their doings and creatures of magic and the havoc played by nature and the ancestors if they are not appeased. That is more like being afraid of demons in the dark created by oneself. It leaves room for friendly relations with one's fellow men.

Just over the hill was a caille, its door opening onto a valley opposite the road. There were lanterns inside, and while the occupants could see our approach we could not have seen the light from the road. This still did not explain the mystery of my arrival being anticipated. Also, my name had been used, not just "l'Américaine" as I was known far and wide in Haiti by those not familiar enough to call me by their version of my first name.

I found myself recalling a similar incident once before when Fred Alsop and I were lost at the foot of the mountain, Trou Forban, not far north of Port-au-Prince, trying to find the cave of the "White Witch." We had been told not to worry about how to find our way there, once in the vicinity, and it was true. As soon as we had arrived at the unfriendly little settlement at the foot of the mountain we saw a horseman threading his way down its chalky side. He saluted us, spoke both our names, then, with no explanation, guided us, stumbling on foot, thorn-scratched, sun-scorched, and sweating to the cave just short of the mountain summit where the White Witch, either an albino native or a white man versed in black magic and gone native to practice it, was reported to exact blood bribes and some say human sacrifice in exchange for wealth, success, and political power. Fred and I saw the interior of the chalk cave, with its vévés, elaborate designs of no cult known to me before or since, traced in dark brownish lines that may have been, as claimed, blood. The White Witch stayed in the recesses of his cave the day we were there, and spoke to us as though from an echo chamber. This effect is often produced by charlatan bocors claiming to be returned spirits by speaking in a guttural whisper into a calebasse half-filled with water. But he did answer some questions rather astutely, and I was already thoroughly impressed by the messenger, who knew of our presence in the village and spoke to us by name though we had told no one, not even told Doc, of our plan, Doc recovering, that day, from a possession partly Guedé, partly clairin.

The hut which I entered with my guide was clean, with straw matting on the floor, a Congo altar covered with a red cloth, and on the altar a row of Congo figurines, stylized dolls of blue and red spangled satin. They had fat round bodies, arms like pitcher handles, and tiny feathered heads. On the altar were also hand-decorated canaris—clay water jugs—a pack of worn playing cards, and strings of red and blue beads. A boy of twelve or thirteen sat at a table, reading by lantern light. This confirmed my impression that the owner of the caille was among the rich of the peasantry, that is, with enough money to send a child to school, which all Haitians passionately want to do but can seldom afford. The child rose to greet me and I was about to settle comfortably on the floor mat indicated by my host when I noticed an odor which never fails to set the hairs on the back of my head on end. It was the dry, insidious, insinuating, penetrating odor of Damballa in person, the odor of all serpents, hard to describe but always repugnant to me. This would be from a couleuvre, a Haitian variety of python, nonvenomous, harmless—there are no poisonous snakes in Haiti—but something which I preferred at a distance, not close enough to smell. I froze halfway seated. My host pointed to the rafters, where I had not looked in my inspection of the hut. A couleuvre of approximately eight feet was curled through the thatch and crossbeams above us. A stranger had entered and its head was raised, tongue darting, beady eyes fixed in inspection. The whirring "ric-tic" which set its throat quivering may have been a warning or a greeting. My knees refused to support me and I sank to the mat, wanting to turn to my host in supplication but not daring to look away from the creature above my head. With all the respect I have for Damballa, the gratitude for life guidance even though with constant reprimand, the reverence when in one of his sanctuaries, I have never overcome a fastidiousness since childhood when near serpents. Many Haitians welcome couleuvres in their homes because of their appetite for rodents. It seems to them better to allow a serpent to curl up in the corner of the house or wayside store, or take up residence in the rafters, than have produce and food destroyed by rats. Sometimes saucers of milk are left out, or an egg or dish of flour as a sign of welcome. The eggs and flour are Damballa's vaudun diet, so there may be some confusion in the mind of the casual observer when seeing these offerings on a doorstep. Houngfors frequented by Damballa and Aïda Ouedo encourage the visits of couleuvres and at 'Nan Campêche near Cap-Haïtien they come in answer to the rhythm of Damballa and are a permanent part of ceremonies. At least it was so when I visited 'Nan Campêche.

The snake has no place in the Congo cult as I know it, and the dead bocor's cult was Congo; so I supposed the one lodged above me must have been a simple house pet. Because of it my night was sleepless, and because of it I left early the next morning in a downpour of rain, though I would have liked to stay through the full ceremonies of spirit or soul transfer.

I must have passed the test of inspection. The serpent above me undulated its way back 'to a resting position, head and tail lost in the folds of its plump, indolent body. This variety is sometimes called "couleuvre dormante" in Haiti because, when not eating, its preferred state seems to be sleeping.

My host introduced himself as Antoine, the boy as his son, Calvaire. His wife was at the ceremony, but he had prepared a charcoal fire outside and on it heated a tin pot of sweet burned Haitian coffee. Calvaire served us in thin coffee cups, chipped but elegant, probably from some pre-Revolution plantation cupboard. I tried to forget the serpent and asked about the ceremony. At the bottom of the hill, standing outside the caille, we could see the compound, a spread of huts inside a barrier of chandelle, poisonous cactus plants frequently used for enclosures, called "candle" because of branches resembling candelabra. Outside in the courtyard, light came from a charcoal fire in which an iron rod stuck upright glowed red. This is the sign of the god Petro, whether Petro Simbi or Petro Kita, but it also has some magic significance.

Around the fire were squatted a few people, all with heads turned toward the central hut of the compound—the only one lighted—as though awaiting some sign. A rocky slope of hill and knotted trees kept me from seeing more, but as we drank our coffee, seated on stools beside our fire, Antoine promised to take me close, to one of the windows if not into the room. He was waiting for word as to when and how far I could go, but in the meantime would like to deliver a message the Congo gods had brought to him for me some time ago. He had been waiting for me to come, and the death of the bocor had provided the occasion.

We went back inside the hut and Antoine went to the altar, removed the deck of cards, and waved his son away from the table. Antoine and I sat facing each other. From here I could look across the room at the couleuvre asleep in the rafters over the altar and could hardly smell its obnoxious odor. In Chicago and New York I had indulged in divinations by chiromancy, cartomancy, trance, and spirit recall. I was aware of the practice of divination in Haiti but had spent most of my time until now in research into religious and magic and herb cults. The reading of cards in this remote plains setting came as a surprise, as did the further proof of clairvoyance when Antoine turned the cards to read my life, past, present, and future. Until now I had told no one in Haiti of the supreme tragedy of my life, my brother's illness. Our closeness as children during our early years, my dependence on him during the trying years of my adolescence, the abrupt interruption of his intellectual brilliance as a shining emblem of security for me at a crucial period of my university life, these things were closely guarded by me in my effort to establish a new career of dependency on myself alone, bereft of my brother's criticism and guidance. Antoine told me all about my family, delivered messages from my brother and the dead mother who bore me, predicted my marriage to Damballa and cautioned me about the jealousies that would result from this union, and the jealousies that would pursue my adult life, personally and professionally. At the time I was prepared to continue and take my doctorate in anthropology, and all anthropologists that I had known so far had been surprisingly free from professional jealousies, rather inclined to share findings and theories. So I was somewhat skeptical of this prediction.

As far as my personal life was concerned, I realized that Fred was jealous of Roger Anselm, and Dumarsais Estimé of Fred, and the fiancé I had left behind of a number of people, but I did not see this in its full symbolism. It just seemed to me that people were unreasonable and nonrealistic and overpossessive, and that sooner or later all of this would adjust itself in my life. There I was wrong. The pattern was set and there was no adjustment. As for the advance knowledge that Antoine had of my arrival and my name, this was all explained in revelations from the Congo gods. I am afraid that I felt a little sorry for myself as we delved into past and future, and my eyes were wet when a voice spoke to Antoine from the doorway and he rose to confer with the messenger from the compound of the bocor.

Antoine returned to tell me that the trial had been a hard one, that the old bocor was tired and did not want to return to his body from the shades where he had been hovering near the head of the corpse since his release. Reluctantly, after much pleading, celebrating in his honor, dancing, reciting of magic formulae, and weeping, he had entered his former abode, weakly at first, but at that very moment with enough strength to rise to a sitting position and point a withered finger at his successor. By the time Antoine and I had scrambled down the hill trying to make as little sound as possible, the messenger had disappeared. I would not be able to enter the sanctuary for fear of upsetting the already tenuous, hesitant spirit of the bocor. We pushed through bushes, avoiding the vicious chandelle cactus, and leaned against a window through which only a crack of light showed. I saw the stiff corpse of the bocor sitting upright in the brass bed, one arm rigidly pointing at a younger man kneeling beside the bed. The other windows and door must have been closed because clouds of incense in the room scarcely moved. I could see a few people who came within range of the crack in the window, and by the positions of their bodies judged the room full.

No one seemed to be breathing, and I imagined that at any minute someone would come to the window drawn by the sound of my heart which was beating rapidly and, it seemed to me, loudly. There was no singing and no drumming, just silence. Then from the mouth of the handkerchief-bound head of the grizzled old man there was an unmistakable sigh. The younger man rose, crawled onto the bed without raising his eyes from the hand of the corpse, and placed his forehead against the wrinkled brow. There was a long period without sound or movement. Another sigh, and the body seemed to crumble, sinking onto the pillow behind it as lightly as a feather would fall. The hand fell with the body, and the new bocor seized the hand and pressed it to his lips. People were beginning to crowd around the bed, weeping and moaning, and the whole sound became an anguished chant. I felt guilty at being an eavesdropper to such emotion and was quite ready to respond to Antoine, who touched my shoulder and guided me away from the window and up the hill. Behind us the chant became singing and looking back I could see the light from the open door and shadows of people streaming into the courtyard. They were dancing, singing, rejoicing. The transfer had only begun, Antoine told me when we were back at the caille. Now the spirit would have to be fed, food brought before the bed, and feasts eaten by the acolytes and family. There would be a long recitation of the vitae of the bocor and his most outstanding achievements, then ancestral prayers, and the group would return to the silence of the room to untie the kerchief which bound the jaws of the old man, thus freeing the spirit to speak and give further instructions to the new priest. All of this might take another day and night, but the body must be interred under water before the fifth morning. I felt sorry for the old man, who must have been quite ready for requiescence, now being obliged to work after death. The responsibilities of leadership are indeed heavy. I wondered, too, what balms and ointments would conserve the flesh for more than four days.

Not wishing to offend either my host or Damballa, I accepted a sleeping mat where I had been sitting earlier that night, right under the heavy reptilian knot. The odor stung my nose, and even burying my face in a handkerchief soaked in eau de cologne did not help. Antoine had returned to the ceremony and the boy was sound asleep leaning on the table, his head on his arms. A lantern had been left burning, but whether it was the presence of the serpent, or the scene that I had just glimpsed fragments of, or due to the black Haitian coffee, I could not remain still and twisted from one side to another, moving as far as I could from under the serpent while still remaining on the mat. Finally I sat up. My restlessness alerted the couleuvre dormante and it began a slow series of convolutions that separated head from tail and undid the folds of its shiny gray length. Now I was really in distress. If I moved it might become aware of my fear and decide to fold around me. If I sat still it might descend by the rafter closest to me and slither over me. Either I felt would be fatal. It took awhile for the serpent to undo itself, and while it did I tried concentrating on Antoine. If his Congo gods could tell him so many intimate details of my life they should be able to transmit my predicament to him across the few yards that separated us from the bocor's compound. I had kept my head still but rolled my eyes from altar to doorway and tried to recall the words to one of the two Congo songs that I knew. The song was profane, but that didn't matter in my urgency. I sang, softly. Antoine came to the doorway and I tried to smile but couldn't quite manage it. I went outside and was sick over the side of the hill behind the caille, then I pleaded emotional upset and an early morning appointment in Port-au-Prince and asked how far away the nearest Army post was so that I could telephone a friend to come for me.

The friend was Fred, so many times my rescuer. In those days few phones worked, but one could always count on those of the Army posts, and Fred was on night duty at the all-night garage where he worked so I was likely to find him even if he might be asleep. It was four in the morning and had my host been an ordinary person he would have thought me deranged. I counted on his being extraordinary, which he was. He called a man from the compound below and gave him a lantern. There are times when thanks are inadequate. I pressed Antoine's hand and turned my back on the serpent, which had gone back to its curled-up-asleep position. As far as I was concerned its sleep was only feigned. As I started down the hill with my guide, thunder flashed and rain started. It was the beginning of the rainy season, and was early for such a torrent. But as though Damballa were punishing me, the rain poured in torrents and the road turned to mud and stones. My guide was ahead with the lantern, and I kept my eyes on the ground beneath my feet though it was impossible to see. I held to his shirttail and followed as best I could, thankful that I had worn boots. Then the path was smooth as pavement and I tried conversation with my guide, shouting into the wind and rain. I wanted to know where we were and how much farther we would have to go and if he thought the rain would stop soon. It must have been anything to make conversation, but though my creole was not all bad at that time, there was no answer.

Then the man stopped suddenly and I bumped into him. He caught me in his arms and I flushed, thinking that after all of my kind thoughts about absolute safety when in the Haitian countryside I would have to defend myself at the other end of nowhere and going God knew where. The man looked past me and down, holding the lantern so that I could see our path. I gasped and practically threw myself at him. We had been walking on the edge between two irrigation canals, which could not have been very deep but which seemed bottomless. The path was tricky, because bricks were loose on each side and the rain made the pavement slippery. From now on I would have to walk on the heels of my guide, some of the time with my arms around his waist. I was ashamed of my earlier fears and saw now that nothing was further from his mind than physical violence or violation on this precarious path in a tropical downpour with only a flickering lantern and an occasional flash of lightning to keep us from catapulting into a washed-out colonial canal. In the lightning I could see barren fields and ahead the aqueduct we had passed on the way to the bocor's compound. The canals and aqueduct were short cuts to the Army post. For me the way was long and I was weary, my cotton stockings were in ribbons, scratches on arms and legs and face were beginning to burn, and I was hungry.

Halfway across the aqueduct I sat down. My guide squatted and managed to turn his back to the wind and light a pipe. He sat over the lantern, looking into space, until I had strength to continue. He was about twenty years old, black, friendly looking and by that time, I decided, extremely patient. He had been taken away from an occasion which might not happen again in many years, if at all. Bocors of really high category were dying out and there were few candidates for replacement. The old man who lay dead might have been a relative of his. There was feasting and dancing besides praying and magic seances, and here he sat in the downpour of rain waiting for a foreign young woman to collect herself and find strength to continue the road. Then he would have to return immediately the long way and it would be full morning. To me it didn't make sense. I resolved to find ways of field research that didn't demand such services of others as I had exacted that night.

At the Army post a disgruntled corporal listened to my story that the driver of my taxi who had taken me to Thomazeau to look for a fellow student had misunderstood my directions and returned without me. I had seen my friend but could not find a car to take me back to Port-au-Prince in time for my classes, which I was teaching at a lycée the name of which I made up on the spur of the moment. Fred was asleep, cursed so loudly that I had to hold the phone away from my ear when I told him where I was, then promised to come right away. The guide left me and again I didn't try to find words of thanks for his help. The rain stopped and pale gray streaks were in the sky when I heard the rattle of Fred's faithful old Chevrolet. The corporal eyed Fred as though he were a returned Marine, and didn't acknowledge my efforts to thank him. Fred scolded all the way back to Port-au-Prince. I was thoughtless, obstinate, unkind, inconsiderate, and finally stupid in his estimation to follow continually this obsession to get to the bottom of things. He as well as said that I might as well have fallen into the canal and saved him the trouble of the trip. I of course had no answer, so much of what he said being true. I wondered if my fellow researchers had such troubles, or if they could manage things alone and never involve others or blunder or have food taboos or panic at snakes. I refused to believe that all these invectives were because I was a woman or that my failings were incorrigible. I didn't feel quite up to Doc and the questions of the Pont Beudette community, so I crawled to my rooftop at the Excelsior, treated my scratches, took a potassium permanganate bath, and went to bed as Titine brought early morning coffee. Now I had lost two friends and a great deal of self-confidence. I didn't relish seeing Dumarsais Estimé again soon.

It was a week before Estimé came by the Hotel Excelsior. Most of the week I had spent at Pont Beudette recording songs on my old Edison cylindrical recorder. This gave me a feeling of being useful. I also tried to write up in coherent form the experience of the bocor's spirit transference, but until now it has remained elusive, something which comes back to me over and over but which isn't clear in detail. I have intended many times trying to find Antoine and the compound of the bocor. Perhaps that was the only meeting intended for us.

Estimé took off his jacket and stretched out on my bed as he always did when staying the afternoon. Usually he removed his pistol and holster and put them over the back of the chair with his coat, but this time he left them on and I supposed that meant I was not to stretch out beside him on the bed. I sat at the window and talked of everything I could think of excepting the subject that troubled me. But Estimé was not angry; he was offended and hurt that I had lied and that I had involved an innocent person, the driver, and that I spent so much of my time pursuing the unimportant rather than seeing the important things evolving in the country, and that I made no distinction in my affectional life, as by now there was hardly an interested person in Port-au-Prince who did not know that Fred Alsop and I had arrived at the Hotel Excelsior at seven in the morning, I in a shocking state of disarray, due of course to my night's experience. As he talked I was ashamed and for the first time realized how little I knew about this man who must care for me or wouldn't put up with the way I was, and who had so impressed me when I heard him speak at the opening of the Chamber of Deputies shortly after Zépherin introduced us.

Even in moments of what I would have called tenderness in anyone else, Dumarsais Estimé had seemed hard and aloof. The day he told me about the wickedness of what I had done at Thomazeau I felt closer to him than ever, and after I had tried to explain, and apologized as I could, knowing that he had spared me the most damning accusation, which was disregard for his public office and career, he agreed to remove his pistol and holster, which he never allowed me to touch, and have me lie beside him on the bed and try and make up for the wrong that I had done by being quiet and letting him speak and letting his problems and tension drain into the afternoon sun that flooded the little room. This is the way I remember Estimé, and these were the occasions when he taught me in his oblique way, instructing me in the tools of humanism, awakening a conscience which had been selfish, not social.

I had seen women coming to town from the hills and plains with small children who might not return to the hills and plains with them. There were child servants at the hotel, usually kept in the back quarters, but doing their share of sweeping and cleaning and scrubbing. There were these "'ti moune" in all urban Haitian homes, a regular part of Haitian social structure. But I had not realized or my conscience was not stirred enough to admit that these child servants should be in some institution of learning, have shoes, clothes rather than the rags one usually saw them wear, and their labor have some recompense.

The 'ti moune system was one of the preoccupations of the Estimé whom I knew—and education for the masses, and shoes for everyone, and sanitation in market places, which were the disseminating points of disease, and recognition of Haiti on an equal level in the rest of the world. In broad, less defined terms, Erich Fromm had prepared the way for my receptivity to the thinking of Estimé; I had failed his teaching in my total absorption of self as a means to knowledge. It was now up to me to turn this thirst for knowledge to a way of service, as Estimé's ambition was not for self, but for service. At first I interpreted the rarity of personal approach, the afternoons without handclasp or overture as rejection, and my vanity was hurt, though at the same time I was aware that Estimé was aware that I was not starved for personal attention.

Gradually I began to see the things around me with his eyes, with his evaluations, though never losing the intense preoccupation with what I had come to Haiti for, the vaudun and the complex surrounding it.

3

In Haiti parents of peasant class love their children. They also love the children of everyone else and expect everyone else to love *their* children. There exists a whole naming practice for "adopted" children among the people themselves—Bienaimée, Dieudonné, Bienvenue, others representing affectionate regard. It is also remarkable in Haiti that there are not the roving bands of homeless young that one finds in other islands—Jamaica and Puerto Rico, for instance.

It is this care for the young that prompts parents when they are not able to feed all of the children for whom they are responsible to seek homes for them. It seems best for all concerned to let one or more of the children out in semi-adoption to someone better placed; to one of the élite families of Bois Verna, to the back kitchens of the Hotel Excelsior, to some school teacher or doctor who might provide no more than leavings from the main table, a single outfit of clothing, and a banana leaf sleeping mat. The parent bringing the child to town might be given a few gourdes or a silk kerchief as a token payment, and the parent would return to the country hoping for shoes, sufficient food and clothing, medical care, and eventually schooling for the child. This system was known, when I was in Haiti, as "'ti moune," or the "little ones." I am not at all convinced that it is not in operation on a lesser scale now. The little ones seldom had shoes and seldom went to school until the reforms introduced while Estimé was Minister of Education under President Sténio Vincent and which were put into full operation while Estimé was President of the Republic. This is not to say that others were not interested in these reforms or that others had not brought them to public notice. But social reform where there is no middle class and where there is absentee ownership is hard to bring about. Many of the Senators and Deputies represented land holdings that depended upon a system essentially sharecropping for maintenance and development. With my eyes opened to see these things, I was impressed by the loneliness of Estimé's mission.

Our evenings together were few. All Haitian men lead multiple lives and Dumarsais Estimé was no exception. A few who might not have approved of our relationship referred in my presence to the Oldsmobile as the "tomb of young girls." I doubt the implication, because his political activities would not have left him much more free time than he devoted to me. A good deal of research, planning, and study went into the ten years' political career from the time that I knew him until he became President of Haiti. But even then Estimé was planning the Exposition which brought Haiti to the attention of South America, North America, and Europe as its first positive achievement on an international level in over a century.

Some nights we would leave the Oldsmobile and walk through the slum area facing the sea and within rock-throwing distance of the Palace. We would walk through the narrow passages between huts of cardboard, tin, and burlap, which, thirteen years later, were torn down and their sites reclaimed for the Bicentennial of 1949. The slums were in a grove of royal palms that, as I have said before, still stand intact. In front of the palm grove are now a Swedish-designed fountain, the modern buildings erected by different countries participating in the Exposition, and an open air theater where the Dunham Company performed in 1956. In those days we stepped over mud and filth, and people pulled aside burlap door curtains or rose from squatting positions around charcoal braziers to greet the young Deputy as we passed. He never smiled on these occasions; the misery was too profound and even the beauty of the bay and majesty of the palm grove could not compensate. Estimé seldom smiled. All of life was serious for him, as though he were aware of the dénouement of his own life and saw nothing amusing about it.

I have thought of Estimé when looking at bronzes of Benin, at Bambara and Baule masks: the head large for the body, because there in the head the artists of the ancient kingdoms of Benin placed the spirit and soul and intelligence of a man, which should overshadow his earthly, corporeal self; the full, sculptured Fon kingdom lips; the almond eyes might have been the model for Bambara masks. At times brusqueness, impertinence, aloofness, and rude manners seemed to govern his actions; these were times when an intense timidity, a hypersensitivity were in danger of exposure and would have to be hidden behind the defenses which served him best.

Sometimes we drove on the winding Pétionville road as far up as Kenscoff, élite mountain resort. I listened to plans for the urbanization of another destitute area, Belladère, near the Dominican border which Estimé was later to make into a model city for workmen and their families, and which would serve as model for Paul Magloire's Cité Magloire on the new highway to Pétionville.

Diseases and intestinal parasites and yaws and elephantiasis could be controlled, he felt, by enforcing a law that existed but had been forgotten: all people of all classes should wear shoes at least in the capital, even if they were

sandals of the cheapest manufacture. Other measures would
be to build ditches with running water around market places,
so that the feet of porteresses and traders could be washed,
and shallow canals inside the markets, so that all market
filth could be carried away. The amount of refuse collected
and discarded in any native market can become a health
danger if not disposed of, and disposal was one of the first
sanitation measures undertaken by Estimé after taking
office. Another of Estimé's preoccupations was the educa-
tional system, which he reformed. Haitian teachers gradually
replaced French; the history of Haiti became a curriculum re-
quirement in public schools, because without it the young of
the proletariat would have no reason for pride in themselves,
would be as deracinated as American Negroes, who knew
only the brilliant exploits of people whose skin color automatically made them superior in the social structure. This, I
now realize, was the very beginning of the movement for
black identity, become now a cry for revolution in North
America.

It is only now that I realize that Dumarsais Estimé was,
in his way, courting me. One of my consistent peculiarities
has always been my attitude toward the present moment.
The moment without my feeling it or being aware of it may
be taking some monumental place in some center of con-
sciousness, and the anticipation of it or the memory of it
may be exquisite or painful or both. But like Alice in
Through the Looking-Glass the present diffused in the
roundness of time is the way I see time and events. I took
my guidance in political thinking and intellectual and conscience awakening for granted and did not realize that my
friend was the first in defining the concept of negritude, the
placing of the black race in its proper perspective and accord
with the rest of the world, a prise de conscience. But there
he left it. Negritude, as nationalism, swept Africans in Paris
from the 1940s on and flourishes now as a plea for humanism,

though so easily bordering on nationalism. During the summer of 1965, at the World Festival of Negro Arts in Dakar, I
saw Jean Price-Mars, frail, almost blind, but still the father
of so many of our efforts. I wondered if he thought of Estimé
and the Bicentenary Exposition of December 1949, com-
memorating the 1749 founding of Port-au-Prince by the
French. It seemed hardly the place or time to ask him.

Dumarsais Estimé was born in St. Marc, third largest city
in Haiti, in 1900. His parents were able to afford primary
schooling and he himself continued law training in the
capital. He was brilliant in his studies, practiced law scarcely
at all before he became absorbed in the machinery of
politics as Deputy from St. Marc, then President of the
Chamber, then Minister of Education, then President of the
Republic.

Had I been instructed enough I am sure that Estimé would
have talked of Toussaint L'Ouverture and perhaps given me
firsthand what I now surmise of culture heroes and presidents
or people with power responsibilities or needs. In comparing
Toussaint L'Ouverture and Estimé, I find the ambitions of
the two men are strikingly similar. These ambitions were
personal but selfless, an important factor in judging humanism. In what other way can one have heroes as distinct from
dictators? Both men surrounded themselves with capable
people. Toussaint has been described as "intrepid, ambitious,
and perspicacious." Certainly Estimé was all of these. Toussaint and Estimé both admired knowledge, saw education of the people as important even above cultivation of
the soil. Neither was communicative, neither went back on
orders or decisions. Both were preoccupied with the children
of the country, and both advocated useful vocations as a
supplement to education. Toussaint has been described as
"frugal, sober to excess." Estimé drank no alcohol at all,
avoided social functions as much as possible, and was the
epitome of frugality and sobriety. During his "courtship" I
received from him a single bottle of L'Heure Bleue perfume,

but other material gifts would have seemed out of place. I have already pointed out Estimé's reaction to untruth, and Toussaint is reported to have had a horror of liars. Both were mistrustful, withholding the gift of full friendship and confidence until the last moment.

While disliking white people *per se*, Dumarsais Estimé saw the merits of political and commercial agreements that would be advantageous to the country, turned to the United States for aid in agricultural and cultural development in 1949, and petitioned and was granted a U.N. mission to Haiti for the study of the country from the viewpoint of economics, hygiene, finance, education, and culture. Toussaint in his efforts to break from France proposed commercial agreements with England and the United States. At his highest point of power Toussaint announced his plan for governing Haiti for life with the right to choose his successor. Estimé at the height of his power—some say made more personally ambitious because of the enlarged horizon brought about by the 1949 Exposition—announced changes in constitutional laws that would extend his presidential term. To the French the prospect of Toussaint in increased power represented a threat to be eliminated by fair means or foul. To the Haitians already suspicious of any revision of the Constitution, increasing length of mandate represented a threat to the liberty that had been so hard to obtain and retain. Regardless of the man or what he had done of good, the threat must be removed.

Now come reports of an Estimé foreign to me. The strikes resulting from his announcement of constitutional revision were attributed by his government to communist propaganda. The President ordered the dissolution of the Popular Socialist Party, the Popular Worker's Movement, and the Social Christian Party, closing all organs of publicity of the above. The Senate, with, interestingly enough, Estimé's rival of years before, Zépherin, still in office, voted against the revision. (Zépherin at one time planned to run for President.) The slum dwellers who had come to the doors of their shacks to greet us when the Deputy and I walked through the palm grove joined friends from the outskirts of town, from workers' organizations, the workers who had benefited from improved hygiene and living conditions, education for their children, abolishment of the 'ti moune system, and formed a crowd which sacked the Senate while it was in session. This was not a thinking crowd but a crowd expressing solidarity to a loved leader. Estimé, instead of supporting the Senate, supported the crowd, and in what was, for him, an emotional speech declared the act of vandalism one of "political maturity," and, praised the people for their action: "Your eloquent attitude of this morning, which is without precedent in our history, is a witness of your political maturity and of your direct participation in your affairs . . ." The Senate was dissolved and this was the death knell of Estimé's presidential régime.

Upon taking office in 1946 Estimé had made a brilliant speech to the Army. He congratulated it on its democratic spirit and selflessness in controlling the change of government after the enforced departure of President Élie Lescot, still alive, a man whom at one time I knew very well as Ambassador from Haiti to the United States, a President who had also tried for an extension of term. The results were disastrous.

From Estimé's speech to the Army, August 16, 1946, I quote the following:

"You, who by training and discipline would seem to be born for the exercising of absolute power, have given all of us an example of non-self-interest and democratic spirit which will not be forgotten."

For the Army the dissolution of the Senate was political anarchy and it would have been easy to move into dictatorship. It was the Army, represented by one general and two colonels, one of them Paul Eugène Magloire, which requested that the members of the junta of 1946 accept again the responsibilities of the country, at the same time announcing that "the President Estimé, having resigned, is together with his family under our complete protection."

One would not have thought of Estimé as a protected man, seeing him in Jamaica the summer of 1950. He had fled first to France, then New York, and had gravitated to Jamaica, not because of its proximity in case of a possible political coup or invasion as was .rumored, but because he was a man who loved his country. Of all the spiritual pain I can imagine I can conceive of none more acute than that of forced separation of a statesman from the country which is his own, whether it be his by birth or by adoption. It isn't even necessary to qualify by "statesman," because in Senegal I have seen Guineans who feel unable to return home without a change of government, Haitians trying to make the adjustment to a temperament truly divergent from theirs, American Negroes trying to feel at home, one even giving up his passport and applying for Senegalese citizenship. But there is pain behind all of it, and the laughter of an expatriate always seems false to me.

Fred Alsop married Colleen on one of his trips to Honduras with the naturalist Ivan Sanderson. On the return trip of the Dunham Company to the United States after our first tour of South America we stopped in Jamaica for rest, recuperation, and a three-day theater engagement. There I met Colleen for the first time. Fred was away and we lunched at the Myrtlebank Hotel, eyeing each other with a natural antagonism for a few minutes, then becoming good friends. I had no idea what Fred had told her of our escapades in Haiti, but that seemed centuries ago, though as I write about it, it seems like today. When I saw Fred he told me that the Estimé family was in Jamaica, which was a delightful surprise until I realized under what circumstances. Fred had not seen Estimé and for a moment I thought it had to do with those years of rivalry past. We talked more and the dreadful situation of a refugee chief of state who still carried the affection of the masses of his countrymen became clearer. Estimé was at that time a haunted, hunted man, in spite of promises of the Army. Paul Magloire was now President and undoubtedly already planning an extension of term. It would not be comfortable for his supporters if Estimé were to materialize in Haiti, or if he were to use the populace as a tool against the governing party, use the love and respect which just the mention of his name engenders now.

It was not easy to trace the Estimés. They changed residence frequently, as political refugees must do. In their modest parlor in a suburban district of Kingston I met Madame la Présidente for the first time. I was impressed by her beauty and calm under the circumstances, as I was impressed by the change in the President's appearance. When I had flown from Paris to Haiti in July 1949 to be made a Chevalier in the Haitian Legion of Honor by Estimé, it must have been on the eve of his dissolution of the Senate. At that time it was easy to see that he was troubled, tense, but I thought these things went with being a President. He spoke a few words of praise for the work I had always done to put Haiti in the best light before the rest of the world, kissed me on the cheek, and pinned the decoration above my left breast. Even then he was a different person from the man who had come to take his afternoon siesta in my room at the Hotel Excelsior, or who had talked of social reforms on the Pétionville road. I knew of some of his trials, but not all. I knew that he had gone to Washington for a Pan American Union conference, been refused expected hotel accommodations because of color, stayed in a Negro hotel, I am told, separated from other chiefs of state—those classified as non-Negro—and had left vowing never again to set foot on American soil, though in the end he did.

I had, in the interim, sent small gifts to Haiti—monogrammed handkerchiefs, engraved stationery—and for these he thanked me. I thanked him for the decoration and the honor bestowed on me. He held my hand for a moment in cold fingers, then after an awkward silence we said our good-byes. I did not see him again for the short period that I remained in Haiti, a guest of the government. My guide and driver was Ton-ton Nord, also a close friend and follower of the President, my escort Jean Brierre, poet, friend, and Minister of Tourism and Culture. We combed the country from Port-de-Paix to Léogane and went to parties from political rallies on the beach at Port-de-Paix to a reception given by the President in my honor at Cabanne Choucounne, night club de luxe in Pétionville. Things must have been tense then, because at the last moment Estimé sent his apologies and did not come.

The man in the salon of the bungalow in Jamaica was still another stage removed from the President of the Chamber of Deputies I had known before. There was no sign of diminution of the proud nature, of defeat of the born leader, but there were signs of an illness that gnaws from inside and spreads through heart and head. The President was overly quiet, distracted, and let his wife do most of the talking, frequently looking out of the window as though expecting a caller. Fred Alsop told me later that the house was under surveillance, and that Estimé feared for his life and the safety of his family. I did not see in him alarm or fear, but increased cynicism in a man who had always been a skeptic. The Estimés were pleased when I invited them to our performance, and offered to refuse for my sake. Indignant, I told them that the Alsops would fetch them and bring them to the theater. When I told my plan to Fred it almost caused one of our famous ruptures. He was working in Jamaica, married, and the father of two daughters. There was real physical danger risked in being seen with Dumarsais Estimé in his refuge in Jamaica. Finally friendship and my remarks about people who were afraid of other people or things prevailed. Though the theater stage lights were less than adequate, I was able to see the center fourth row forward during the performance. For the first half of the performance both the Estimés and the Alsops looked uncomfortable. By the end of the performance the pressure had lessened, but the Estimés hurried from the theater without coming backstage.

The following day I was awakened at Mrs. Finzey's residence hotel, where I stayed partly for economy but chiefly because it was outside the center of town and reminded me of the Hotel Excelsior in many ways. Dumarsais Estimé was in the parlor and was troubled. They had had word from the owner of their house that threats had been made of bombing their suburban house if the Estimés remained. They were to be followed and hunted and intimidated until homeless; it was already practically impossible for them to find a landlord who would take them in. I was shaken and felt myself at the beginning of a nightmare that would never end. I knew how Estimé had been loved, was still loved, and the fact that his life would be in danger even outside the country turned all the years that I had known Haiti into a mockery. I had dreamed of, written about, acquired property in, spread the good word far and wide about a country of which I really knew nothing. Here before me the same slight figure with the same dignity of bearing, the same broad, intelligent forehead, the man for one brilliant ascendency President after service of many years was driven by countrymen who had sworn his protection to come to me for aid. I realized the full seriousness of the housing situation when I tried to persuade motherly Mrs. Finzey to rent an apartment of two rooms to the Estimés. Mrs. Finzey immediately abandoned her motherly character, and her refusal was in no uncertain terms. I was glad for the distraction of seeing Agnes De Mille and her husband Walter Prude for drinks in the garden of their hotel the next afternoon. They had no reason either to realize or to try to solve the moral and psychological problems with which I found myself involved. Good friends, I have wondered if they were aware of my misery.

That night at dinner while heatedly going over the situation with Fred and Colleen Alsop, who adamantly remained outside all problems of intrigue or politics, still trying to win my point for a solution, I was stricken with acute appendicitis and was rushed to the Seventh-Day Adventist Hospital, the only one that seemed to be open at that hour of the night for emergency surgery. From then on I have highly recommended Seventh-Day Adventist care when the body is weary and the spirit troubled. The nurses and doctors were kind, and the strict meatless diet agreed with me. Flowers poured in and old friendships were renewed with people such as the Manleys, whom I had not seen since my research days among the Maroons of Accompong in the Blue Mountains of Jamaica. But there was no sign of the Estimé family, or indication of their whereabouts. By now Fred and Colleen were as concerned as I. A friend, Sheila Bryce, with true island hospitality invited me to recover at the lovely plantation Bellevue, high above Kingston. In the quiet rooms that had once housed Admiral Lord Nelson, amid their English paneling and superb eighteenth-century furniture, I thought a great deal about the Estimés. Fred was finally able to locate them and at the end of my ten-day stay I gave a luau luncheon for them in the old-world gardens, inviting only people whom I felt would be sympathetic to the exiled President. Dumarsais seemed more remote than ever, and the illness of the expatriate had increased. I told him of an appointment Sheila had made for me to see the Governor of Jamaica on his behalf. He seemed scarcely to be listening, and did not taste the food which I had prepared myself, but he showed a little of his old public-spirited self when people from the servants' quarters asked to shake his hand. Just before leaving he asked to see me alone. He was embarrassed to make a demand on friendship, but he had no way to contact the notary in charge of his property in Haiti, or his wife's family, and they alone could solve his drastic financial situation. He now saw that his desire to be near to, to return someday to Haiti, to live there as a private citizen, to die there, would never be realized. He had sent his children to France and must now find refuge in either New York or Paris. I was asked to take a letter back to Haiti with me. If it were intercepted the consequences for all of us would be something about which I did not care to speculate.

The next day I left Sheila Bryce and Bellevue, called on the Governor as promised, pleaded the case of my friend, took the plane to Haiti, and wept all the way there, damning Haiti, Haitians, and injustice, flooded with self-pity, diffused pessimism, and acute nostalgia, bearer of a letter which I hope did some good. I continued with my task of making Chez Pauline into Habitation Leclerc—which some say it once was—learned to love Haiti again, rehearsed the company for Las Vegas and Palm Springs, and left Haiti not to return again until after Dumarsais had died, in 1953, while living in the Henry Hudson Hotel in New York. The busy gossips of Haiti had it that he had been poisoned and they pursued all sorts of other speculations as to the cause of his death, all in my opinion rubbish. A man can die of a broken heart, and that is what happened to Dumarsais Estimé. Toussaint is supposed to have died of exposure at Fort Joux in the Jura Mountains near Switzerland, and Napoleon of arsenic poisoning and/or exposure at St. Helena. In these instances it doesn't seem necessary to look for causes of death. Statesmen seem to have a hard time finding reasons to live once separated from the country into which they have poured all of their ambitions, hopes, and life essences. There is a constant to the behavior of men, but something about power, even great responsibility, blinds us to that constant. Toussaint, being led captive into Cap-Haïtien, looked at the crowd hurling insults at him, which only the day before had covered him with honors:

Voici ce que sonts les hommes partout. Je les ai vu à mes genoux, ces hommes qui m'injurient; mais ils ne tarderont pas à me regretter.

"This is what all men are like. I have seen them kneeling before me, these men who insult me; but they will hasten to regret my loss."

Toussaint as soldier and Governor General had begun to fashion the structure for a new Haiti after slavery. Estimé laid the foundations for the structure of a new Haiti after the Occupation, but his time was too limited for its completion. Each had his dream, not for self, but for country.

Concerning Dumarsais Estimé I am left in doubt about many things. At his highest point of power he seems to have changed from his early principles. I have often wondered about his support of mass violence, and whether or not this might have paved the way for the rule by violence by the Tonton Macoute today, whether these pillagers of the Senate were the lumpen proletariat who form the militia of Duvalier. Or did he believe too much in or expect too much too soon from the people to whom he had offered the real benefits of health, education, freedom from serfdom? Perhaps he saw in this act of destruction an opportunity of a people for "self-expression" and "political maturity," and could not foresee the outcome. Perhaps his program of freedom by enlightenment was misconstrued, misused, and was unworkable. Whatever the answer, I doubt that the exile of any president has been as much regretted or death as much mourned by an entire population as Dumarsais Estimé's.

In these many years since, I have not revisited the Hotel Excelsior. Perhaps I have been afraid I might hear the sound of my own castanets when I went through the hallway and past the shuttered salon; perhaps afraid that I would not recognize the maid Titine, or Zépherin, were he still alive, or some pensioner who stayed these thirty years staring at the

Champs-de-Mars from the bougainvillea-covered veranda, moving inside only in the event that the sound of political conflict might approach the iron-grilled gates, when the evenings became chill, or when the ship's dinner gong acquired by the Rouzier sisters during the Occupation announced mealtimes.

Perhaps I would be tempted to climb to the turret where I had sat on a chair at a window sorting notes or typing or reading and lie on the brass bed, where I had often lain staring at the ceiling in the day or listening to drums at night or dreaming of my work and play. Perhaps the real nostalgia would be in recalling the familiar measured steps of Dumarsais Estimé, whom I might have been waiting for for hours.

4

Doc Reeser told Fred Alsop and Fred then told me that a lavé-tête, the first stage of the vaudun (voodoo) initiation, was being planned at Madame Henri's near Croix-de-Missions. But the news was all wrong and it turned out to be a canzo, which is trial by fire, second stage in the initiation, and for that I wasn't ready. When we found out the lavé-tête was at Téoline's houngfor, Fred tried to discourage me from entertaining the idea of becoming a hounci, and, by consequence, I grew more determined than ever. I had to move very carefully, however, among the followers of Cécile's compound, because, while all of them were close friends to me, and we danced for hours under the same tonnelle, and ate from the same cook pot much of the time, and exchanged face powder and toilet water, still I continued to observe the strict regulation of vaudun, that it does not proselytize, and, by the same token, does not accept petitions for entry. As a matter of fact, there is no such thing as strictly "belonging" to the vaudun. One is or one isn't; one practices or believes or one just stands on the fringes and watches and interprets as one chooses. It is the god and some indefinable combination of circumstances or need or propitiousness which brings about the "marriage." The houngan, mambo, and hounci intervene—a word here, a personal service or gesture there. Glances that were at one time passing, or of no consequence, or indifferent suddenly became full of meaning. Little attentions are paid at ceremonies. A seat is set aside at dances, not for l'Américaine, but for one about to belong. Then there would be unsolicited explanations of ritual detail, La place or the mambo or houngan staying near with the ason, watching for signs, eyes following when a bosalle, an uninitiated, is pitched violently to the ground by a loa issuing a warning or punishment. Then one night Agwe or Damballa or Asaka or Petro Simbi approaches the potential initiate and manifests in greetings his presence, at the same time delivering messages from 'Nan Guinée, from the dead, giving instructions, making demands.

These demands may be for an offering to appease some unquiet ancestor, of a promise to perform the simplest of ceremonies in preparation for a later fulfillment, or, if the time seems right, to fix a date for an initiation ceremony or *service* itself. All this circumactivity may take days or months or years. I have never heard of anyone, however, accepted into the true vaudun upon brief notice, and surely not, as many tourists now claim, overnight and for a fee. It is conceivable that some Prête savant directly from 'Nan Guinée, still damp with sacrificial blood from his own temples and scarred with tribal markings and jangling gris-gris from neck to ankle, as is the custom in Africa, could so impart his "belongingness" that taboos would fall, the way would be immediately opened, and centuries and oceans bridged in moments. But this would be a special and very rare case, and the stranger would have to evidence in some way his intention and willingness to submit to the protocol of the local vaudun, for the Haitians are very proud of what they have conserved of the power of 'Nan Guinée from preslavery times, and rightly so.

The weeks or months or years that it takes to be sufficiently acceptable to such a community to be taken into its inner cult life depends equally upon the community and the would-be initiate, perhaps more so on the latter. It is assumed that anyone issuing from anyone remotely joined in kinship with 'Nan Guinée, from Africa, is potentially "vaudun." If they do not practice it, it is because of ignorance, and those of us black people carried from Africa to other parts of the world, especially to the United States, are known to be in total ignorance of many truths, including what we are really like, what we have been made into by slavery and/or colonialism, and above all, how to care for our lares and penates, our household gods. But some communities are more closed than others, even within small geographic boundaries.

For months preparations had been made for my lavé-tête. I imagine preparations for the others who were to be baptized with me might have been made for days or weeks, these hurried preparations usually being emergency measures; before birth precautions, extreme illness, family crises, or such as mine, ritual governed by time. Others might be the result of penny-by-penny saving for years. All of us had new baptismal clothes, white from inside out. These were to be "couche'd" in or to be "put down on the floor" in. For the arising after three days "floored" there were white veils and for those who could afford it a marriage ring. There were also all sorts of special lotions and Florida water and liqueurs, mostly non-alcoholic, and foods for sacrifice, and cornmeal and oil and seasonings. There were also clothes and rum for the drums being baptized for me to carry back to the University of Chicago, drums at that time isolated in the sanctuary next to where we nine candidates lay.

We were lying on a dirt floor spoon fashion, well fitted into each other, nine of us, ranging in age from seven to seventy, both sexes, all of us candidates for initiation into the cult of Rada-Dahomey. All of us were waiting for some manifestation of the presence of some one of the roster of gods serving the most powerful order of the Haitian system of vaudun, the serpent cult. This was the second of three days' isolation on the floor of Téoline's houngfor, temple of the vaudun gods on the plains of the Cul-de-Sac, set apart as the period of head cleansing or lavé-tête. All that was of the past and shouldn't be, was washed out or exorcised, and into the purified temple the god would enter and from it he would speak, or by some other sign show his relationship with his hounci, or devotee.

My particular god, I had been told by the woman Dégrasse, was Damballa, the serpent, the rainbow; his wife is Aïda Ouedo, the virgin mother; his mistress, Erzulie. Together they inhabit the sky and do more to determine the destiny of man, particularly Dahomean, Aradan, and Haitian, than any of the many other gods of this possessed and obsessed island. Erzulie likes perfume and orgeat, a syrupy almond drink, and elegant clothes of filmy pale blue and silver and white. She walks in beauty and her very nature is coquettish, so that she attracts all men, and when she enters into a woman this woman in turn attracts all men and is at the same time wife, mistress, and mother. Not mother as Aïda Ouedo is—holding up one end of a rainbow that people say is the tail of the giant serpent Damballa which supports the world, or rather the universe, as there is no geographic limit in Haitian thinking—but mother in the all-encompassing way that I have just said. Once married to Erzulie there is no mystery of life or love left unknown and man, woman, or child may be chosen by the goddess of love. But in all this protocol selection there is a trap, often not so tender. Of his many hounci Damballa chooses some whom he places in protocol order equal to his Erzulie: he "marries them," and of these he is remarkably jealous, as any other husband or lover, and as avenging, pursuing the unfaithful through time and geographical barriers, as I myself can testify.

The woman fitted into the curve of my lap began to tremble. Softly at first, so that it might have been a chill from the damp earth, then violently, so that all of us were jarred by her cataclysmic tremors and knew that her god had entered. To me it was a great relief because it meant that I could move, even stretch without attracting attention, without breaking that somber expectancy that we had lived in for twenty-four hours. This was an Arada-Dahomey initiation, and, by all the rules, other gods would be reluctant to enter. There were enough vaudun, enough of the hierarchy of Arada-Dahomey: the husband and wife at the top of the pantheon branched off into lesser and minor gods; Legba, Shango, Aguasu, Sobo, Erzulie, Agwe, all of the Oguns, Asakas, Guedés, and Sokos and a host of others who have grown and multiplied steadily since the landing from 'Nan Guinée, which has come to mean all Africa.

The slaves may have come from Abomey, Boké, Loanda, Uganda, Cabinda, Somaliland, or the Isle of Gorée, near Senegal, but for the Haitians the exodus was encompassed in Guinée, or 'Nan Guinée. The names of kingdoms, royal families, ceremonies, celebrations, historical events, and gods are sometimes confused in the litanies which precede most vaudun ceremonies, whose intonation is copied from the Roman Catholic Church, complete to the interspersed ringing of the bell, action de grâce, and incense-filled censers.

I did not know all the signs, the nuances that led a priest to declare with no hesitation, on the first movements, sometimes on the changes of facial expression, or something more intangible, that a loa, a god or envoy of the god, had entered an acolyte. I had known until now only what took place under the palm- or banana-thatched roof of the outside tonnelle, the clearing where sacred and profane met around a central post called *poteau mitan* in sacrifices and ceremonies that frequently ended more profane than sacred.

As the tremors increased the woman began to speak in "langage," older than creole, the real language of Africa. There was unrest among the other closely huddled initiates and Léonce, the seven-year-old, began to whimper. The stir among us must have reached the sanctuary, the divided-off room of the mud hut where only those of high category could enter. The white curtain dividing us was thrown aside by the priestess Téoline. Ason in hand, she stood majestically in the doorway. "Hounci lavé-tête," she said, "rise up and turn." We sat and turned to the other side, as we had done every few hours since our confinement. As we settled on the other side Téoline moved toward us, her bulk blotting out the light from the kerosene lamps in the next room. She shook her rattle to the four corners of the room, bending her knees in the slightest obeisance, inclining her body backward. Then she passed over each one of us, touching our bound heads with the ason, searching for a certain disclosure, further demonstration of the presence of some loa. She passed over Léonce and the woman from Mirebelais, and Vierge, her huge body making no sound, her small feet somehow finding place between our tightly pressed bodies. Then she was at the head of the woman in my lap, who was not from our compound or houngfor, our peristyle or place of worship. "Alliance," she said, "open up and let Papa Guedé in. Come, my child, you are now one of us. Let Guedé talk to us." Téoline began to breathe heavily, and squatted down above me. I could smell her starched skirts and talcum powder and the perspiration from between her thighs. I had seen gods only when already in possession of their "horses," not in that in-between limbo stage, which in the uncertain lamplight gave me the feeling that the god would emerge from between the priestess' wide-open legs and trickle into the ritually matted head of Alliance. Then I too jerked convulsively and must have turned red in the darkness, not because of a visitation, but in simple surprise, then in a quick succession of anger, frustration, and annoyance. In releasing her mait' tête, whatever substance she might have inherited in a "genii" of control or character, or in the purging of bosalle, unclean qualities, which must be done in order to open up and receive her god, Alliance had lost control of her bladder and the hot stream of urine spread over my new baptismal nightrobe from crotch to knee. Then it turned tepid and, when Alliance answered the summons of the ason and rose trembling from the floor, the cold night air sent me into chills and I tried to turn away from the sharp odor. Téoline was watching and no extra movements were allowed. Her hard knuckles pressed my shoulders back into position against the damp floor. I held my breath and concentrated on following the entrance of Guedé into Alliance.

It was night when Papa Guedé came to make his declaration to Alliance. Heretofore during our initiation I had thought of her as unassuming of nature, rather plain, not at all aggressive. I had seen Papa Guedé before, in his black top hat, tail coat, with his cane, strutting through cemeteries smoking a pipe or cigar, or, not as fully dressed, when entering a ceremony or mounting a "horse" in some simple setting. Now seen from the floor after a day and night of ritual fasting, orchestras of drums, unknown tongues in the next room, occasional possessions, there was a quality not quite belonging to the community which I had known so well. Téoline brought the top hat and cane and black coat from the inner room, and someone lit a cigar. All of us sat up under our sheets and watched the first possession of our initiation. Papa Guedé had established himself in Alliance with a few nasal greetings and an obscenity or two that brought titters from some of my companions, a reaction not at all approved of by Mambo Téoline. His "horse" led him into the circle of hounci in the sanctuary, where he behaved in such a fashion that we were unable to restrain laughter, some of it, mine at least, of embarrassment. There were rude remarks from the inner room, and the odor of clairin and pipe smoke, which Papa Guedé always demands. In the dim reflection of candlelight from inside, against light from charcoal fires from outside filtering through the cracks in the single door, figures moved in obscene postures which might have been amusing or exciting under other conditions. But I was hungry and thirsty and thought only of how I would be able to swallow the sacrificial food to be brought around later in the morning and how I would avoid tasting whatever would be passed out again before the ordeal was over. Then to pass time I tried to figure out just how I happened to be here in the plains of the Cul-de-Sac not far from the capital of the island of Haiti at four in the morning wearing a nightgown wet by someone else's urine, chilled, disconsolate, feeling none of the promised ecstasy, and no signs of it, alien to gods, people, and land.

I started with Dr. Redfield. Had he gone about Mexican village findings this way? Perhaps not, but Fay-Cooper Cole's field instructions on how to go about camouflaging disgust at a dog-eating ceremony in Borneo, or how to react to the first vilely seductive taste of durian fruit at a feast of maharajahs in Kuala Lumpur could stand me in good stead; and Melville Herskovits was a fantastic guide for getting people to the bottom of things, the heart of the matter. So often I have regretted not staying closer, not remaining faithful to the path that Herskovits had chosen for me, but he was single-minded about an object, a thing, not the person and what the person was made up of and how much the person could take of one thing, no matter what great vistas would be opened. Herskovits' one *thing* was Africa in terms of the New World—a fascinating, complex, never-ending study. My librarian background as well as my serious interest in social anthropology led me to respect the detail of cataloguing hand movements, voice tones, food seasonings, storefront churches, political trends, and palaverings all as relating to both areas.

I was greatly impressed by the prestige of the University of Chicago, which in those days—I do not know whether it is still true—was, with the University of Berlin and the Sorbonne, the Phi Beta Kappa of intellectualism, as opposed to Northwestern University, which had an air of suburban gentility, bourgeois beyond belief. The personal appeal and dry wit of Robert Redfield, the crashing daring of a man like Robert Warner, dapper, far-traveled Fay-Cooper Cole, droppers-in like Margaret Mead who exposed sexual habits in the Pacific, Malinowski who exposed sex habits wherever he happened to be stationed, monocled Radcliffe-Brown, an Australian being Oxford, a gaunt old yellow-toothed lion given to floating around the lecture hall dropping verbal bombs on tender blossoms—I being one of them—then retreating and grinning at the wreckage.

The last handshake was with the father of them all, Franz Boas, just before I left New York for the Caribbean. I was still unnerved after my first air flight from Chicago in a two-motor plane, and still wondering how I had gotten through my first night alone in my life, in a Harlem hotel recommended by a taxi driver because Mary Hunter and Jack Sullivan—where I was supposed to stay—hadn't received my wire.

I am thinking now of when I went back to the University, after the Great Experience of which the dirt floor was only a small part. At times I wonder if I have ever again felt such shame, such helpless embarrassment as when I phoned Herskovits from a booth in Ida Noyes Hall on campus. I had just left Redfield. It had to be decided. Even without the formalities of degree examinations the material collected on this Caribbean voyage had already been approved by the department for a Master's thesis. But in spite of having sat in on practically every course offered in the department, examinations had to be gotten over, then all the things hardest for me, which I had started and dropped out of, or skimmed through by sheer luck and doggedness—linguistics, archeology, German, the Northwest Coast Indian, advanced psychology—before the Master's degree. There was no witchcraft in this, just despair, hard study, and sometimes going hungry. Melville Herskovits saw one side of me which even I did not know at the time—the eternal chercheur, the eternal commentator on the flux of people in life. What he did not see was the step beyond the chercheur; another person known perhaps to my brother and to Robert Redfield. Because the latter advised me to decide immediately where my scholastic loyalties lay, I stammered and stuttered into the phone on an icy day a few weeks after my return from Haiti, spoke to Herskovits there in his office on the campus of Northwestern and told him of my decision, then repeated my message at the end of a long silence. And that was that. So many had been responsible for the making of me up until then. I won't name them, because they will come into this story as they are called. But had Charles Johnson and Erich Fromm not combined one evening at a Rosenwald "salon" where some tatty African group held forth, the painful decision of where to study after eighteen months in the Caribbean wouldn't have had to be cast over the wires from Ida Noyes Hall to the Department of Anthropology at Northwestern University.

The decision was much easier about whether to be a dancer or an anthropologist by profession. Robert Redfield simply came straight to the point, on one of my many visits to his office. He had seen a sort of amateurish affair at Lincoln Center on Chicago's South Side, where I did a Brazilian dance mime, and there had been choreography for the Century of Progress Exposition, and several other small efforts. That day he didn't wait for me but just said, "What's wrong with being a dancer?" I suppose my mouth dropped open because I thought of what I considered the fortune the Rosenwald and Guggenheim Foundations had spent on me, of the first lady anthropologist to camp out with the Maroon people of Jamaica, of my baptisms into the mysteries of the Haitian loa, of Erich Fromm, of Brown's Chapel Methodist Church, of the Dunham family . . . It must not have taken long for my mouth to close, because soon I was in New York, not long after on Broadway, then Hollywood, then Europe and a large part of the rest of the world, with not only the cult of Arada-Dahomey to serve, but the gods of Cuba, Brazil, and Africa to remind me that they had started it all.

Lying on the damp floor of the houngfor in a cold chill, probably because I had forgotten a supply of quinine, aching from head to foot, I condemned all mysticism, all research, all curiosity in the ways or whys of other peoples, all "calls," all causes.

I longed to stretch out on the deck of a patched-together fishing boat with sun and clean, fresh air playing on the hand-sewn sails and two or three men of the village guiding us out of the bay at Vauclin in Martinique and into the Atlantic. I wished I were again driving on the road to Cap-Haïtien with Fred with the moonlight so bright that, in a bad humor, I had been able to read a book part of the way. What I didn't know lying on the floor of the houngfor was that arthritis added to the agonies of my cramped knees; since then it has been too evident as a part of my life, but interesting, as a constant companion, after all. With aching knees tucked under the buttocks of the woman in front of me I even wished I were back in Chicago or in Joliet, which indicated a state of total eclipse. Then I continued sorting out my situation, because, after all, I was there for the purpose of learning and experiencing the unusual, and my Fellowships were a trust more sacred than any vows yet taken.

Dawn was on its way, and in spite of crowing cocks there was an intense stillness that I did not know then is so characteristic of tropical predawn. The dead calm of night prepares to slip away, then turns back for a suspended second as though looking over the scene giving way to day. Those who are up and about stretch and yawn and stand still at this point, holding the stretch at its maximum. The most activity otherwise they will indulge in will be scratching or expectorating. It is also a good moment for men to release the night's kidney collection of water and stand, hypnotized, watching it soak into the earth. Chickens and turkeys expand their plumage to double, geese extend their rubbery necks and close their angry beaks for once without sound. A donkey rolls over on its back then rises and stands motionless, head down as though waiting to be beaten for the frivolity. A dog walks nowhere stiff-legged, cats arch their backs and stay for a long moment slit-eyed, exposing pink gums, paws pressed into the earth, claws distended. Babies fight their way through the reality of dreams into the unreality of waking and keep their eyes shut as long as possible, protesting while doing so. Then with a burst of red gelatin stage lighting all action breaks loose.

So many things were happening in the outside world; for instance, the decision of the United States to enter World War II was near, and this would eventually change the thinking of the student body of my Alma Mater, in my time dedicated to the nonviolence program of its president, Robert Hutchins. It would undoubtedly cause disruption between humanists and conservatives at that great university and eventually activate the resignation of the man responsible for abolishing the age limit up and down on learning. The man who, new, dynamic, daring, cultured, in the sense of "*of*" culture, the first of those very young which have made themselves recognized in many ways, indirectly in his capacity as President, was responsible for my being on the dirt floor just then. Here I lay aching and feeling a sore throat coming on, all in the cause of curiosity or science, I, as Iphigenia tied to the mast, as Erich Fromm had pointed out in friendly conversation, and all the while the black race broiling on hot coals below.

One of Téoline's assistants came to the doorway and clapped her hands three times. We all turned over, trying not to break our pattern, and settled again facing the side wall of the hut. This was the second morning after the first night of lying down: I counted on my fingers to be sure. Time heretofore seemed to have had no value other than the intervals between turning over onto the other side. It turned out to be Saturday, the last of the three days of confinement that should make the nine of us secluded in the small space of about twelve feet square into full-fledged hounci, first-degree servitors of the pantheon of vaudun gods brought by our ancestors from Africa.

No money is exchanged in the induction into the vaudun, but much is spent. Theoretically one spends what one can, but it is not so simple as that. Leaving out the possibility of a charlatan houngan or mambo, the gods themselves are whimsical in their demands. There is a standard minimum for a hounci lavé-tête in the Arada-Dahomey cult—a new white cambric sleeping garment, a new attire in the colors of the promised god. There are always a few extras and accessories kept in the sanctuary of any well-organized houngfor to personify or at least pay deference to an unexpected loa. Also on demand is the continuous sacred cuisine, including one or more of the animals habitually the diet of the divinity. In my case, on this occasion, a pair of white roosters was the pièce de résistance. The ointments, beads, liqueurs, holy pictures, perfumes, and so forth for the nine of us now being initiated would have stacked a country store for months of ordinary buying. None of these is exorbitant as a single item. The humblest of everything is acceptable except in the case of live sacrifices. These are supposed to be of the best quality, which is saying little. No one questions a bottle of the cheapest perfume or liquor, but there would be great disapproval and ridicule were Petro offered a scrawny pig, or Damballa a thin hen, at an important ritual. But just as one poor soul may have saved for months to put aside just the right quantity of cornmeal, dried beans, bottles of sweet syrup, demijohns of peanut oil (imported, unfortunately), thread and cloth and a pair of new sandals and one dollar for a brace of Guinea fowl or two dollars for a goat, the loa speaking through his

representative may at the last moment ask for an extra portion of something or a special offering at some habitation or
dwelling place of his. This habitation may be a waterfall or
one of the many springs, such as those issuing from Source
Leclerc or at the base of the giant mapou where the mountain
and town roads meet at the fringes of Habitation Leclerc.
The roots and trunks of the mapou tree have grown together in such a way as to form multiple mysterious cavelike
recesses, in which are wax drippings of all colors, and feather
and fur and blood traces. Some say these date from over a
hundred years past, which I doubt because a good part were
fresh when I first saw the mapou eighteen years ago, many I
have seen added, some I have added. Wood rats eat what is
left of the sacrificial food after the loa have finished, and in
time of famine fall upon the candle wax as well. There is
probably no trace of candle wax more than a day old now,
after hurricane Inez of 1966.

Fortunately promises, practically promissory notes, can be
made for excess demands which the unprepared hounci cannot raise at the moment. Some Haitians, rich and poor, élite
and peasant, live a lifetime never fulfilling these promises,
making other promises and a small offering each year or when
pressed to make up for the unfulfilled ones, going to their
graves believing that the poverty, disease, premature death,
hunger, loss of property, lack of success in love, drought or
flood on their own small plot of ground, was caused by de-
fault of a *promesse*. I wonder what they feel now, with hurri-
canes battering this portion of the island more than the
Santo Domingo side, and treating Haiti more severely than
any of the sister islands in the Caribbean or Florida mainland. They are too poor now, I am told, to make the sacrifices,
so they probably just go on making promises, calling on the
ancestors and gods of 'Nan Guinée.

'Nan Guinée is not doing so well herself these days, it
seems to me. Man using magic as a control over nature
weakens what he has to develop within himself. Man ap-

proaching nature through himself alone strengthens himself, and makes peace with the unknown and would-be unfathomable. Also, this law works out daily in Africa, and if I were to look at the rest of the world, it would be there, symbolically perhaps, but there. It is the key to the symbology that we lack, because blood sacrifice isn't just the slitting of a cock's throat or winding warm entrails of a beef around one's loins before going into the sea. We do these things, in Haiti and Africa and Brazil and among close-knit ethnic groups in New York because we don't know what else to do, and when the law of averages brings us a return, we hasten to repeat our propitiatory act and double if necessary to be doubly safe with the gods; or, if an act of vengeance or violence, double it also to be doubly safe from our own fear.

According to Edgar Cayce, the American clairvoyant healer, the main seat of Atlantis should have been inundated somewhere between Bimini Bay and Port-au-Prince. Perhaps this is why there is such radiation from some of the springs that even Seventh-Day Adventists and Pentecostals have been overcome by "the spirit" when in proximity to the springs of Habitation Leclerc, for example, not to mention what happens to those touched by the loa. Perhaps this is what has given Haitians the magic with which to retain and serve the gods of Africa intact, even reinforced, for so long through so much strife.

The Haitian peasant must be feeling that Kebiosu or Sobo or Agwe Woyo or Ogun d'l'Eau or la Sirène or Nana of the bottom of the sea haven't had their due.

My requirements, Damballa's demands, were surprisingly modest considering my being an American. Being an American meant to the Haitian peasant a whole complex of things at one end of the balance, just as being a "member," a term not used in those days, one of the "race," a "sister," tipped the scales into balance at the other. The Marine Occupation was not long over and I am afraid that some of the atrocities committed against the Haitian peasant were not simply fireside stories. No matter how idealistic and far-seeing Presidents of the United States are from time to time, and certainly the one who sent the Marines to Haiti, Woodrow Wilson, is known popularly as a sensitive intellectual, often this idealism carries vision beyond realism. The State Department, never having been accused of this sensitivity and intellectualism, sent raw Southerners in as Marines to put peace into the troubled little black island, going through one of its characteristic blood baths, and made hell out of purgatory. Haiti was good practice ground for what goes on now between black and white in the United States of America, excepting that the Southern Marines were not accustomed to retaliation, nor were they accustomed to differentiating between degrees of blackness. The peasants who could, fled to the hills with their "voodoo" drums as they had during the slave uprisings. The élite froze into stony uncooperation behind their festooned villas, and bands of peasants returned like for like in encounters with Marines, until a more realistic President of the United States put a stop to it all and restored the republic to its independent status. Americans have remained a confusion in the Haitian mind ever since, and there seems little to do about it. Some kinds are to be feared, some to be ridiculed, some to be tolerated as one tolerates rich retarded children, some are to be exploited, some to be loved. A few fade into the Haitian landscape as fixtures or frameworks or a color tone when the landscape becomes too monotonous. I suppose myself to be among this last category, because I feel myself to be so and the evidences have been many. For the rest, it doesn't matter too much that I am always surprised at negative vibrations rising from the pavements of New York or Paris or Rome or elsewhere. I am beginning to feel that it is the wise man who carries all that he has within himself, and is grateful for the occasional warmth from a charcoal fire if it is cold outside.

Being a member of the race was a distinct advantage. Skin color, hair texture, facial measurements, yes, these are the external part of "race"; but, as Fay-Cooper Cole so often pointed out, race is psychology. I don't know how much time my husband, John Pratt, has spent in our turbulent twenty-five years of marriage thinking over my "blackness," and I know that the pace of keeping up with life and the Dunham drives and Dunham Company and Dunham multiple personality, as John Martin once described me, has taken too much interest and effort for me to think of skin colors or of his "whiteness." I am, however, sensitive to "kind," to blackness in the sense of spirit, a charismatic intangible, and this is what the Haitians and Brazilians and Malaysians and Chinese and those Africans with whom I have had time really to discuss things must have felt, must feel. I am inclined to think that the real creative work of mankind is the discovery and good treatment and nourishment of these things, with no guiding handbooks that teach in the intellectual sense, just as I feel that there is no way to teach choreography. This "kind" that I speak of is of the human race, and for my part I feel it rarer and rarer, like the duck-billed platypus, so that soon we will have to go to zoos to see a single specimen. If all goes well, if I work at it, and I last long enough I may end up being able to offer myself in exhibition. Fortunately I am near to some such other specimens.

Not to be too discouraging to noncandidates for hounci-hood, however, it was perseverance, many common interests apart from common ancestry, love for babies and old people, enough medical background to see my way through diagnosis and prognosis of minor cuts and burns and snake-bite and intestinal parasites and first-stage venereal disease, preferably guided, but working on my own if necessary, and intuition, and the flawless training in social anthropology field technique begun by my professors at the University of Chicago and polished off by Melville Herskovits, that tipped the scales in my favor.

So here I was, a wanderer returned about a year and a half after the first drive into the dusty plains with Price-Mars to pay homage to ancestors I didn't know, the day before the last night of three days and nights of secret rites and purifications. Damballa had his bride for the price of new nightclothes (his bride who wore no nightclothes even in Chicago winters), the new ceremonial dress, the necklace of blue and white trade beads with snake vertebrae interspersed for the ason garniture, the cocks, Florida water, Havana influence, no doubt, barley water, strawberry soda and sugar cookies and eggs and herbs and roots and powders that I didn't recognize, for the bathing before and after the ritual lying down. There was also a picture of Saint Patrick driving the snakes from Ireland, which, for Haitians, is Damballa, though they do not necessarily explain this to the local Catholic priest, and a portrait of the Virgin Mary, who is, of course, Erzulie. Erzulie must witness my ordeal and marriage to Damballa, and, thereafter, I wouldn't have to worry about her jealousy, only his. The gold ring, with a band of intertwined tiny rubies and diamonds about a fourth of the way around, old English or French, undoubtedly went through purification and would be replaced on my finger when I arose and would belong to me, but with a new significance. It had taken many days shopping with Cécile and Dégrasse and Téoline to gather these things, with the exception of the ring, which was given to me by Fred Alsop. The initiation paraphernalia don't just happen, and it was as though one piece of cambric were not like another, or the same with one bottle of barley water or Florida water. I began to feel in the personal care and effort in the choosing of each object its inherent "mana," its mystic power, as different from the object next to it—similar in appearance but utterly profane and unmystic. I had watched the cocks fatten and was a little reluctant to feel under their feathers and squeeze their breasts in appraisal, because they were too familiar, having been picked out by us, bought off the camion from the Pine Forest a few weeks back and kept shut off in a corner of Doc's chicken run to be ritually fed since then. They were practically of the family by now.

The camion which came down from the Pine Forest was one of those wild little cross-country trucks with benches glued in for passengers to cling to. They all bore names, probably as fetishes, or magical protection, or for the same reason that Haitian élite installed inside their new villas modern equipped kitchens those days for prestige, while actually using only the outside charcoal ones. This rattletrap was named Jésus Dieu Sauv'teur, very simple and direct in its printing, compared to some of the bright flower-decorated lettering above the driver's window of other camions.

With all of my close friendship in this plains community outside Port-au-Prince, where I spent most of my time, in addition to the ever-closer intellectual and emotional ties in Port-au-Prince, I was, in all honesty, aware that my relationship to my offerings was not as personal as though I were one of the people. In that instance, one item might have come from my own plot of land or that of a relative, so that I might have walked from Port-au-Prince to the high mountains of frosty foggy Furcy where strawberries grow if I had a cousin once removed who had hens, then down to Léogane for a few ears of corn. I might have set aside the barley water and perfume for many months in a corner of the shelf at the village shop, unknotting a damp handkerchief tucked away in my sweating bosom to pay for them piecemeal in grubby centimes. On the other hand, had I belonged nationally and not only *nation*, I would have gone to the same couturière as I did go for fittings, because no one in our region had a sewing machine excepting the niece of Madame Henri. This had always been a little delicate for two reasons: Cécile, Doc's housekeeper and favorite "wife," Haitian standing, because Doc was married and father of two beautiful children whom he adored, and who, until his death, as far as I know, returned this sentiment to him, was pestering Doc for a sewing machine. This, truthfully, went with her status as "mariée avec un blan'," Haitian accouplement with a white person, meaning American because Syrians didn't count colorwise, and because the possession of a sewing machine in the compound of a rival houngfor produced natural competitive jealousies. The niece of Madame Henri made all our baptismal and marriage robes and was well paid for them; but, it was Cécile, eventually, who managed to have two gold teeth, not part but all-of-the-way gold, and a sewing machine and the white Marine, then considered a little "fou" but loved nevertheless, as husband as legitimately as was then permissible on both sides in social stratum in Haiti.

5

A mambo came to the door and rang a bell. It was time for our morning ablutions. One by one we were beckoned to our feet and motioned to a corner. Guedé Nimbo should have waited before mounting the woman in my lap. He had been too eager and had ridden her too hard for one not yet through the mystic preparation. She had slept heavily since inserting herself again between us, angled backward into my lap, scarcely waking when we turned. She breathed open-mouthed, and even with her back turned I could smell Guedé's alcohol and pipe tobacco. Everyone else seemed keyed up and expectant. Perhaps it was the physical need for some change, if only to turn over on the dirt floor and bring momentary relief from the cramp of our awkward positions. Perhaps the fasting, the incessant subdued drumming, the intermittent ringing of the bell and the rattle of the ason, the smell of burning charcoal, fresh and dried blood and incense, the intoned instructions to our departing "selves" and entering "loa" were gradually effecting hounci out of bosalle.

Squatting over the calebasse, the gourd shell cut in half which served as a chamber pot for each of us in turn, was an ordeal for me. There was barely a chance to stretch my throbbing knees before two hounci with no-nonsense hospital manners held a sheet across the corner where I had been led, thrust a calebasse between my ankles and pressed me down to squat over it. It was half full of water, but in my case as with the others this did little to alleviate the odors of evacuation already heavily mingling with sweat, bad breath that accompanies the first stages of fasting, damp earth, burnt kerosene oil, and cheap perfume. We washed, still singly behind the sheet, using our own soap and fresh towels, then dusted in talcum and went back to the floor. I felt greatly refreshed. We were not required to resume our spoon formation until the last initiate had been washed. This gave me an opportunity to look over my companions and reflect on what they were like as far as I knew them, and how they came to be here, this brotherhood that was bringing us closer to an unknown quantity.

I was beginning to feel at home with them, to sense the tie of kinship that must hold together secret societies the world over. We were associated in things not common to all men, and still, this should be a reason why I would have no place here other than scientific investigation, and I was not at all certain that this was true. In all my adult school years, I had rigidly avoided sororities and club memberships of all sorts, secret or otherwise—all forms of belonging that required an etiquette or process to achieve a belonging. I had always prided myself on thinking only of "man" in the broadest, most inclusive usage of the term. Here, three thousand miles from my center of learning, either for my own awakened and undefined needs, or under pretext of fulfilling a mission, or a mixture of both, I was deep in the most banal and, at the same time, most esoteric of secret society inductions, that into ceremony, ritual, secret pact, blood sacrifice, into the vaudun or voodoo of Haiti. There we lay, scarcely breathing, waiting, listening, senses alert, packed like sardines much as the slaves who crossed the Atlantic, motionless as though chained, some of us afraid.

The eldest among us was Madame Éliane Soulouque. She lived north from Pont Beudette on the Cap-Haïtien road at a crossroads called Cabaret. She was owner of a plot of land of about an hectare, about two and a half acres planted in *figue* bananas. Madame Éliane claimed descent from the last Emperor of the island and, though married to someone of another name, had never called herself other than Soulouque out of deference to her royal ancestor. Madame Soulouque spent much of her day on her vine-covered front porch rocking in a cane and bentwood chair that would have brought a small fortune on Second Avenue in New York. Seeing her staring out through the great flat green leaves of the banana trees that pushed against the steps of her two-room brick house—some say the overseer's house of the big plantation demolished in one of the many slave uprisings pre-Leclerc—I would have imagined her to be trying to reconstruct in her mind's eye the Palace balls as they are reported, even documented, to have been in the time of the Empire. We of the houngfor, however, knew that she had been concerned over her many unfulfilled promises to her god Lenguesou, that she could easily afford the costs of lavé-tête and should have paid them long ago; but she was too miserly to give up the necessary money, and so spent her nights worrying about the consequences and her days rocking in the daudine, thinking about the same thing.

A decision was made brusquely for Madame Éliane one night at Madame Henri's temple at Croix-de-Missions. Lenguesou entered, pointed her out, and punished her severely. He stripped off her prim black poplin dress and white petticoats, exposing soiled underpants and a money belt full of gourdes and worn twenty-dollar bills. Then as final warning for so many unfulfilled promises Lenguesou snatched the descendant of the Emperor and placed her astride a bullock waiting to be slaughtered for Ogun. The animal pulled up its stakes and charged through the tonnelle scattering drummers, dancers, hounci, and high priests in all directions, then tore down the road and came to an abrupt halt at the life-size crucifix erected at the crossroads at Croix-de-Missions. The hounci canzo on hand—this was too important for mere lavé-tête—gathered up Madame Soulouque's belongings and carried them to her to spare her a return to the congregation. She dressed under the crucifix and the hounci hailed a taxi on its way to the capital from Cabaret and for the first time in years Madame Éliane was obliged to delve into her money belt. Ashen—the story is told—and with trembling fingers, she sorted out a five-gourde note and the driver turned to retrace the road to Cabaret. A bosalle punished this way publicly, she must have been too embarrassed to face Madame Henri again, because a few days later Téoline added her to our list of initiates. This could be called an emergency case, though after her disgrace there were weeks ahead of us before the bedding down.

Soulouque's blood, which by report was that of a pure black, must have crossed later several times with foreign strains. Madame Éliane was reddish with frizzy hair that may once have been reddish but which was now white where black dye did not cover it. Lying there examining the back of her head, from which her kerchief had come loose, I wondered if it would be all white by the time the sacrificial bits were allowed to be washed out of our hair. We were not supposed to unbind or wash our heads for some time after the "arising." Mine felt uncomfortable, and I wanted badly to scratch some of the cornmeal, feathers, orgeat, blood, herbs, and raw eggs favored by Damballa, out of it. Sometimes some of the cooked sacrificial food was added to the mess under the kerchiefs, and toward this by the third day I felt an intense repugnance.

Madame Éliane must have been about seventy but looked younger before her experience with Lenguesou's messenger and much older afterward. Perhaps the "lying down," the cloistered initiation, would revive her. With Haitians it is sometimes hard to tell age and much of the time they are unable to help. Small children simply stare if asked their age, as though it would be something belonging to someone else. If they think it over they might say, if no older than seven, twenty-nine or sixty-one or whatever comes into their heads

that they may have heard as a number, no matter in reference
to what. Between adolescence and thirty, people often just
shrug their shoulders or laugh self-consciously when pressed
by a curious tourist or doctor filling in papers. After thirty
they begin counting by Presidents. Ton-ton Joseph at Leclerc,
who came into my life years after the baptism of which we
have been speaking, insisted that he was fourteen but agreed
that he was born under Alexis Nord, who was President of
Haiti from 1902 to 1908. That would have made him past
eighty. Since the presidential term is one of six years—barring
revolution, accident, exile, or self-reappointment—this system
sets an approximate age and is a useful one in a country as
largely illiterate as Haiti. When the mellowness of age sets in,
six or more years one way or the other mean little, especially
after many seasons have passed in descending the same
mountain path at dawn and mounting it at dusk, digging in
the same little plot, passing the same porteresses en route to
market, or their daughters or their granddaughters, watching
as many babies die as survive, watching the seasons change
from rain to dry on schedule. The dreamlike pattern of peasant life is interrupted only by a change of President, often
discovered after another has taken his office, if one lives far
enough back in the hills. One remembers a hurricane by the
damage done; there was a war like the first one against the
French; much later, a caco or ambush war against men in
khaki uniforms who treated peasants in a way Haitian
peasants don't like to be treated. Where there once was a
marimboula played by an itinerant musician on Saturday
night at the general store, there is a machine that plays music
and delivers speeches in creole when knobs are turned. Americans come less by boat and more by the silver machines in
the sky which still make noise even when out of sight in
the clouds over the mountains. A foreign girl evidently a part
of the lost 'Nan Guinée family lives in the community and
gradually melts into the daily life, even to being made a
hounci lavé-tête, then hounci canzo. This is the way time is
reckoned for those over thirty, so that being born under a

President a few terms sooner or later is of no consequence at all.

By her looks Madame Ezméry Dessalines must have been born under a President two terms after that chronicling the birth of Madame Soulouque, but she was among those who had come by their baptismal clothes the hardest way. Of her five children only two had the same father. There is a nonpartisan attitude toward parents among Haitians of the peasant class, but usually the father is pleased and proud to recognize his offspring and if he is not affluent enough to have his several wives in one compound he will visit them regularly, bearing gifts of food and clothing, sometimes assuming schooling, often petitioning the mother to turn the child over to his main household presided over by his more fixed or placée wife. There are variations, but this may be said to be the general pattern of Haitian accouplement and family life whether the sociological group be traceably Arada-Dahomey, Congo, Ibo, Yoruba, Malinké, or other. There has been a fusion of the forms of polygamy which flourish in variety in Africa, to produce the Haitian system. In Africa custom is clearly marked off by tribal, clan, and national grouping. As opposed to the New World most of the acculturation is surface, as this continent is finding out, the hardest way.

At times the strongest impression I have of myself in Africa is that of a fly on the edge of a vortex, sensing danger but held by a magnetism issuing from the axis of the vortex, the fly detachedly fascinated. (I have been unable to feel emotional in Africa, but of that I hope to say much in some other place.) Sufficient here that as this fly within the narrow confines of one country, Senegal, I see the tribes of Ouoloff and Lebou draw their boubous aside so to speak as a Toucouleur passes, and hear sly remarks by Serére about Diola, Mindingue, about Malinké. In the midst of this nationalism, of all the ethnic groups of Senegal the Diola interest me most. Although it would take more than a lifetime to know even one of these groups, there is no harm in a special interest, and mine so far is these Diola, habitants of Casamance, district south of Gambia, tiny English-speaking republic stuck into Senegal from the west coast like a pencil line. The Diola interest me because of their stubborn retention of animism as a religion, not just as fetishism, in spite of being constantly besieged by proselytizers of Mahomet and Christ. Some of the eagerness to convert the Diola is surely because of rumors of anthropophagy as a practice, which may actually be necrophagy and which is a curiosity when found in original, primitive form, not symbolic form, these days and times. The Diola also interest me because of their extreme individualism, which by the law of averages should one day crash under the inevitable standardization that goes with bureaucracy, the autonomous form of governing which may be necessary for these African states if they are to survive in "civilization." Of all of the tribal, clan, and nation groups here, the Diola have been known historically and until now for an equalitarian social structure. Stratification may be by age group, sex, or community leadership, but it is never caste.

The Diola came to mind in thinking of Madame Ezméry Dessalines' family situation. Madame Ezméry was a woman of total family responsibility. Among the Diola the mother, while having her field work set out for her by marriage contract, has remarkable freedom from the responsibility of her children. Women have absolutely no rights of inheritance, but excepting for the fact that they cannot leave home between sowing and harvesting, and their menial position as laborers in the tedious part of rice tending, they are at set periods free to leave the children in the husband's care and gather together for palm-wine drinking among themselves, or to return to the parental barrack and there receive as many lovers as they wish. Meanwhile the father is obliged to take care of his children. These represent a considerable investment and insurance against old age, which is not peculiar as a concept of reproduction to the Diola or to Africa. After one of her "walkouts" the wife may decide never to return to the house in which her married life began. The husband continues his care of the children, aided by another wife if she accepts. If she doesn't, the responsibility is his.

Madame Ezméry Dessalines was pursued by bad luck with "husbands." The answer probably lay in an initial mistake. Her first two children, twins, or "marassa," sacred in Haiti and the vaudun pantheon, were testimony to fraternizing of a kind not so common as one would have imagined during the Occupation. Haitians, though poor, are proud. These boys, fair-haired, light-eyed, about ten years of age, had been sired by some Marine long since forgotten. They tended bullocks at the cane cutting and hauling season of HASCO, the Haitian-American Sugar Company's plantation. This work meant all day in hot sun or rain-swamped fields yanking and pulling and pounding the stubborn beasts. Haitians are not kind to animals under the best of circumstances. Animals simply do not count, on the scale of emotions, and are to be eaten, or sacrificed to the loa, or are used to fulfill beastly services of burden. Otherwise they are taking food in some form or another from those who have every right to it and who have too little of it most of the time.

After the twins, three successive "husbands" left Madame Ezméry, each while she was her biggest with child. When she tossed on the floor of her mud hut neighbors came in to console her, bury the afterbirth, and burn the soiled rags. When she had a roadside delivery, she had never been fortunate enough to deliver in coincidence with a passerby who could help her remount her donkey or hold the child for the first few miles until she got used to the empty feeling.

She made her way regularly to market with mangoes in mango season, cane at cane-cutting time, oranges in orange season, and each time stalks from the dozen or so plantain that thrived miraculously in the rocky soil of her front yard. The other market produce she traded for on the edges of the plantations or filched if she felt she could get away with it. At the Iron Market in the capital she haggled back and forth and came out enough ahead to return to Pont Beudette with candles, matches, bits of cloth for headkerchiefs, dried fish and kerosene, which she might sell out on the way home. She preferred it this way because then she didn't have to under-sell Frémance at the Pont Beudette crossroads to be rid of her goods. A great deal of scrounging and deprivation had gone on to provide the inferior-quality nightdress and skimped rations for the goddess Erzulie's meal. Madame Ezméry's stomach hung down with a swelling that wasn't a pregnancy and her tired smile never reached her eyes.

Erzulie had come to Madame Ezméry many years ago when she kept house for her first placé, the Marine, sire of the twins who tended the bullocks of HASCO. Erzulie was not at all happy with the union and had demanded many things, among them a blue satin dress and white canvas slippers. When the Marine set sail with the others of his kind evacuating Haiti, no means were left behind for either the care of his offspring or the appeasing of his indigenous mate's gods. Never able to arrive at the means of satisfying the exorbitant demands of Maîtresse Erzulie, Ezméry had finally, after several visitations, consulted Téoline, and a more modest wardrobe was settled on—sky-blue cotton with the cheapest nailed-together Iron Market sandals, but new.

By craning my neck and rolling my eyes upward on the pretext of yawning I could see the next in line on the floor of the houngfor. It was still dark inside, but the sun outside was high and hot, and we were all perspiring heavily, wet, sticky with sacrifices and our own sweat. A pleasant odor drifted across Madame Ezméry Dessalines and Madame ' Soulouque. It was from the fine black skin of Vierge, who slept peacefully as she had every moment since the beginning of the initiation when we were not under shifting orders. Vierge was about twenty-eight and the mother of children by Alexis, who worked at the government farm, Damien, cleaning the stables of the Guernsey cows. Alexis had three wives placée, but he wanted a legal marriage with Vierge. His court-ship gifts were gunny sacks half full of the droppings of the prize cows imported from the United States during one of the bursts of paternalism which gave the Occupation a raison d'être. The quality of the fertilizer must have been superb because Vierge's garden was the finest this side of Kenscoff, mountain resort where the best of everything grows, fertilizer or not. Aïda Ouedo had been manifest in Vierge as far back as she could remember. At twenty-eight she looked eighteen. Her smooth marabou complexion, velvet black, her curly, not kinky hair, her fine features and complacent innocence recalled to me the black Virgins of the Cubans—the Virgin of the Cobre or the Regla or the Caridad. Vierge had no problems in supplying a luxurious feast for Aïda Ouedo, and was bedded down in nightgown and kerchiefs of the finest batiste . . .

Marie Claudine was a quiet child of nine or ten related in some way to Téoline. She was a born serviteur of the loa, and when she wasn't carrying a jug of water on her head from spring to caille or tonnelle, she was squatted near the spring beating clothes, usually clothes of the hounci or loa, on the boulders of the rivulet and spreading them to dry on the poinsettia bushes. At night she fetched and carried for Téoline and visiting mambos and houngan, joined the answering choruses in a shrill, clear voice, fanned flies from the altar, and danced gracefully to her mistress. She was pledged to Maîtresse Erzulie. Her baptismal nightdress was machine-stitched, but she had embroidered it herself with pale blue flowers, as she had the ruffle around the mosquito-netting bridal veil and percale bridal dress. Had she found a needle strong enough to pierce her white canvas slippers I am sure they too would have fallen into flower patterns under her rapid little black fingers. Marie Claudine awaited the coming of Maîtresse Erzulie and the wearing of the bridal robes as in my illusioned childhood I had awaited Santa Claus at Christmas, and a new dress at Easter.

Marie Claudine was destined to wear the dress on only one other occasion, the following year, when Téoline and a group of wet-eyed hounci and mambos and relatives followed the small coffin put together by Boss Meus down the dusty road to the cemetery just before Cabaret. Marie Claudine had succumbed to a bout of malaria, but I was told that she complained not at all, and was smiling when Maîtresse Erzulie appeared at her cot in the crowded public hospital to lead her to the skies, perhaps to 'Nan Guinée. I was also told that Papa Guedé and Baron Samedi, even on Toussaint and All Saints' days or when they are carrying on at their most outrageous in cemeteries, religiously leave the small grave enclosed in a white wooden fence intact. More than this, on two early-morning occasions porteresses from Cabaret have reported seeing a shower of small blue flowers drift down on the grave of Marie Claudine, though there are no trees near the Cabaret cemetery, only stones, dust, and the stone houses of the dead. The story is supposed to have been supported by the driver of a camionnette, the Glorie' Excelsie', loaded with passengers from St. Marc. All this took place during one of my several protracted absences from the island. I am told that passengers were all asleep and the driver nearly ran off the road at the sight of the miracle.

Behind me, when lying on my left side, was Georgina. Georgina was a girl of the village often ridden by Papa Guedé or his associate, Baron Samedi. She was a bosalle, was rough and loudspoken in everyday life and the essence of vulgarity when being made sport of by the loa. She bragged of male propensities and tendencies, and it was rumored that she had proven these aptitudes to several young girls of the neighborhood. No loa could be expected to appreciate a bosalle who makes sport of being one. There is an early limit to patience among the gods, and an unlimited capacity for vengeance. In the case of Georgina, Papa Guedé made his final demonstration of authority and issued his final warning by sending her one Saturday night naked from Descayettes above Source Leclerc all the way down the road to the general store at Carrefours. Red-eyed and breathing fire, smoke, and white rum he entered the store and demanded red pepper. The startled shopkeeper produced some dried pods from the bin under the counter without touching the coins which Georgina (Guedé) spat rudely out of her mouth and threw at him. Guedé then rubbed the peppers into Georgina's eyes, stuffed them down her throat, and when she ran screaming back up the road and across the cane fields and shrub cactus and up the mountainside to the houngfor, Guedé was there with his top hat and cane to whip her over the floor and up into a sablier tree. Climbing a sablier tree without serious injury is a feat when fully clothed. Vicious spines stick out of the trunk and branches in all directions, lethal if one runs into a hedge or fence of them by accident, as has been known to happen at night. Fences of sablier are now forbidden by law in Haiti, and the row which separated the forest and residence of Leclerc from the hills on the other side and which served to keep out half-wild pigs and troublesome marauders has been uprooted.

Georgina was soon badly lacerated by the thorns and bleeding from hands, thighs, and stomach. Houngan Julien, his La place, mambos, and hounci pleaded with Guedé, honoring him with song after song and dance after dance. Some of them fell into possession. The entire pantheon of Guedés strutted about and told vulgar jokes and seized each other or bystanders in grinding, sex-inspired buttock and pelvic movements. Through the hills of Descayettes came Guedés bearing candles, wearing top hats and black coats, swinging canes, smoking pipes and cigars; eyes red, nostrils flaring, staggering from tobacco smoke, clairin, anger, and ecstasy. The vainglorious bosalle was being brought down to size. At one point the priest Julien and his mambo caille—his housekeeping mambo—feared for the life of Georgina and now began the task of persuading Guedé to leave.

Julien tried signaling the drummers to play the maison rhythm that normally by its grouillère or rotating pelvic movement distracts or gratifies the loa who has overstayed his time and sends him on his way contented. The psychological explanation of refocusing attention is a simple one. But it was hard in this case because Guedé was already focused on the same interests and locale as the maison engenders, and the split difference between sacred and secular sex didn't get across to him. Besides, he had not finished with Georgina. She had hardly been helped down from the sablier tree by La place and the mambo caille when Guedé commanded her to purify her genitals, of which she had boasted so many times, with a good application of piment rouge, this time powdered red pepper. When Guedé finally conceded and left for other parts, it was noon of Sunday and the girl was more dead than alive. Drums went on playing, passing from soaking wet drummers to replacements. People still came during the night and early morning for miles around, bringing their own cane chairs and water jugs. This was not to be missed. Other loa entered. Hounci circled and dipped and bowed and fell into the churned dust of the tonnelle floor or ran down the mountain as far as Source Leclerc if Agwe, god of water, entered, or farther up the hills into terraced fields if it were Asaka, god of cultivation, who takes on a country bumpkin air, greeting everyone as "couzin," acting witless and out of place in a crowd but bringing important messages from the earth gods. Georgina's eyes were cleansed with lime juice and bound with slices of lime applied to them, her burning middle portion was cleansed as well as possible, a midwife being called in to complete the job, and when Doc and Fred and I arrived, late because we had been to the Pine Forest, Doc took over salving and binding the scratches from the sablier tree.

Georgina's experience sent her straightway to the Iron Market for lavé-tête shopping as soon as she was out of her poultices. As an occupation she sat on the curbstone outside a Syrian shop in town and sold limes and other citrus fruits chiefly to Bois Verna and Pétionville élite who came to buy imported foodstuffs at the Syrian-owned Bazaar Izméry. They seemed to understand and appreciate her rough and direct manner, her brusquerie. Also, she was very shrewd at selecting the best of citrus fruit at the market before it opened to the

public, and several of the young mountain porteresses were
said to be in her "stable." Georgina's gruesome experience as
abosalle had chastened her somewhat, but I never felt quite
at ease with her, though I did at times dance the grouillère
with her since she was better at it than anyone in the community.

Desmène liked to drum. His uncle excelled on the asotor,
the eight-foot drum carved from a single tree trunk. Desmène
played the kata, the smallest of the three vaudun drums, but
his ambition was to work through the boula to the maman,
then to the asotor. Asaka talked to him frequently, interrupt-
ing his drumming with his country-cousin manners, and as
Desmène was still a novice he felt this a great hindrance. His
reasons for becoming lavé-tête were purely practical. Without
status he could never rise to the position of head drummer
that he coveted. He would lavé-tête, then canzo, then take
the prix of the ason. To be a first-rate drummer he need
go no further. Most drummers seldom went beyond lavé-
tête. Desmène was fifteen, muscular, and a great fisherman,
swimmer, and lover of the sea. His people came from La
Gonâve, the brooding little island dominating the bay of
Port-au-Prince. Desmène sometimes wandered the docks of
Port-au-Prince begging for passage to La Gonâve. He would
work his way on sails and oars if necessary, but sometimes it
was enough for him to sing and drum and the fishing boat
passage was his. He always returned to the houngfor in the
Cul-de-Sac in time for ceremonies without having word sent
that anyone knew of. Agwe was his patron and Agwe surrounded La Gonâve and must have carried the message. Still,
his lavé-tête was for Asaka. Undoubtedly some day later he
would take his canzo or ason for Agwe, who was a family protector, and frequently entered the head of his mother and
grandmother but had never manifested himself directly to
Desmène as had Asaka. I often think of Desmène, these years
later when there is a storm over La Gonâve, which I can see

from my balcony at Leclerc and wonder if Agwe came to him, and under what circumstances.

Sitting in my lap was Alliance, in her early thirties, scrawny, big-boned, frenetic, jerking, and receiving her loa. I have already stated why I felt fastidious toward my floor mate, but as I thought things over after the second turning Saturday afternoon I remembered that I had always had the same feeling about Alliance, avoiding her limp handclasp when she stopped by Cécile's on her way to consult Dégrasse, and how irritated I was at Téoline for putting me to the test of having this woman in my lap or placing me in hers as the direction might be. A further revelation in my thinking was a realization of how simple it was to associate a given personality with the behavior patterns, diet, colors, mannerisms, characteristics, potentials, predictabilities of the loa whose alter ego, identity personification, they were to become. It worked out something like an IBM machine, or vote-predicting poll, both of which were unknown to the general public in those days. It was as though an electrodynamic pattern were at work, loa choosing abode because of qualities of himself already latent in the abode, or abode gravitating to loa and discovering itself on some polar current. When a loa becomes dominant enough to indicate to a houngan or mambo the timing of an initiation or disclosure it was about like a psychoanalyst discovering a dominant personality hidden under the social layers of his patient. There are often several loas served by one person, and frequently they are at war, especially if they are high-echelon ones or powerful or jealous ones as mine, Damballa. This causes discomfort in the ill-at-ease serviteur just as the multiple-personalitied patient must strain and make all sorts of "sacrifices," symbolically or otherwise, to appease these multiple selves, keep order at home, and avoid the splitting off of any precious part, especially in anger or dissatisfaction.

As far as Georgina's experience with Guedé is concerned, I have never been able to tolerate close proximity with these consorters with the dead and do not find the antics of "Papa" Guedé amusing or exciting or profound. Rather, repulsive and at best pathetic—which makes me think again of necrophagy and how I upset a chercheur (French for ethnologist researcher) here in Senegal by pointing out a drummer at a healing ceremony as anthrophagynous.

"How do you come to that ridiculous conclusion?" he asked, sword hand on hilt prepared to draw, as all French ethnologists seem to be when in the presence of American ones, and all male ones of all nationalities are, to begin with, in the presence of female ones, and I suspect all scientists are when in the presence of theatrical entertainers claiming to have a scientific background.

"I don't know, I just know." What could I say about the inner ear and inner eye and inner nose?

"Mais c'est fou, cette idée! Ridiculous! In the Congo, perhaps, or Guinée [relationships with Guinée were very shaky and soon snapped under the pressure], or Gambia . . . but not in Senegal for, oh, since long before the French."

"Yes, but— Oh, never mind, let it go. Look at that woman digging in the ground. What is she being? What is her genie?" There are rab or possessing spirits and genii or egos or selves in Islam-animist Senegal, but no gods or loa.

Defining the indefinable is a precious waste of time, I have learned, if nothing else, during my years of performing the exotic on stage and following the curious. The people of the dead, Guedé's people, abound, but all aren't as clearly in evidence as Guedé Nimbo, Nansou, Vi, Zeclai, Zile, or Gran' Guedé Zombie in Haiti. Neither are they as uninhibited as a small underground sect of the Diola in Casamance in Senegal are said to be. I do not know if the drummer referred to by me at the healing ceremony was necrophage or not, but he surely had a seasoned air.

I preferred to be behind Alliance than in front of her. Even over my shoulder her breath smelled fetid and dead. I wondered why she had come to our tonnelle. She was a frequent passenger from Mirabelais to Port-au-Prince, which meant that she frequently passed Pont Beudette. She had known Dégrasse from somewhere and felt this to be her place of worship. She also knew Doc because she had been "confined" to the compound of the asylum as an incurable for a brief period during the Occupation.

'Ti Joseph was from Cécile's compound and was accepted as one of the "adopted" children. Where he came from or who his real parents were I never knew. Lys had taken him over for basic needs of his initiation, and, as preparations for the lavé-tête were underway, came to be known as mother, for reasons as important to herself as to 'ti Joseph, or more so. Soliciting for his paraphernalia, explaining our instructions, keeping an eye out for signs from the loa compensated for her own deeply deprived existence. 'Ti Joseph was not out of my life or preoccupations with the ceremony of lavé-tête, nor has he been even with a number of departures and returns to Haiti. He was ugly as sin even as a small child, horse-faced with square teeth set far apart. His head was classic dolicho-cephalic then and has grown more so since: that is, commonly, long-headed or bullet-shaped.

Children in the generic sense are much loved in Haiti. They drift from caille to caille (wattle and lime paste huts called *case* in Senegal, with mostly trade tin roofs now, palm-leaf-thatched then), usually attaching themselves permanently to one compound around the age of puberty. Cécile's house, where I lived when not at the Hotel Excelsior or off on some trip of investigation, was the head one of her compound and better than most because Doc had built it for her. I have said before that Doc was married to someone else at the time that he met Cécile and for many of the years that he knew her. He loved his first wife dearly, though she could put up with just so much of the Haitian system of polygyny and returned permanently to Miami with their two children. But Doc also loved Cécile, and more than loving her he was tied to her as he was to the vaudun and to the soil of Haiti, where, after thirty years of knowing it as inevitable, he found his way back to die, like old elephants are supposed to do in Africa. All kinds of people—Marine friends, friends of the family, his wife's relatives, her relatives' friends, tourists, good white Americans, perhaps even his children, though somehow I doubt this—had tried to pry Doc loose from Cécile, then from Haiti. But it couldn't be done. He stayed on at a meager salary or none much of the time and fulfilled his duties as chief of the asylum until replaced years after our present story. Sometimes Cécile served table for guests at Doc's screened residence in the middle of the asylum compound, which he kept proper "white place" fashion, separate from Cécile's house in our compound, a half kilometer away. Sometimes she hovered in the background as most Haitian wives still do, supervising the cook and the 'ti moune, the children doing odd chores for keep. After dinner, when it was served at his place, Doc would call Cécile to the screened-in veranda for coffee and liqueurs if the guests were in high spirits and protocol permitted. Then Doc would sing songs of Erzulie and Ogun and Congo Moundong. If the party continued gay enough, Doc, with a twinkle in his turquoise-blue eyes, would begin to brag about Cécile's English acquired during the Occupation. This is the sort of intro-duction I had to the household, through a letter from Mel-ville Herskovits which I often regret not having read. With a wide smile, gold tooth gleaming, Cécile would begin with "Come here, you f——g black bitch!" and gaily recite the list of endearing obscenities which constituted her English in-structions from the Marines who had solicited her favors a few years earlier. Sometimes Doc would go through this act in broad daylight, at lunch instead of after dinner, if he wanted to be rid of or get even with some bigoted tourist or other.

'Ti Joseph wandered naked from hut to hut sleeping where it was warm at night, eating from any pot where he could put his grubby grasping fingers. He stayed in a state of no clothing until discovered one day at about the age of seven trying to penetrate Madame François' niece with his first erection. There was a great marveling at Joseph's precocity, once he was shooed off the niece, and he was teased much of his life for this one malfeasance. He was also made to wear a shirt, which at first served to cover his sex, but after a few washings and his rapid growth it resembled a waistcoat. There being no replacement in sight for the shirt, 'ti Joseph went around our compound in a constant state of uncon- cealed erection and, as though to accompany this, developed a bass voice way out of proportion to his size and presumed years. Embarrassed and inhibited, 'ti Joseph began to show signs of attention from the vaudun. He was thrown into the sea from a fishing boat by Agwe. He leaped into a Petro fire but was spared contact with the red-hot iron bar in the center of it. He crawled across country in the form of Damballa, the serpent, at the wrong time of the year, Rara, or La Loi Dit (Lalawdi), between Christmas and Easter when the loa are supposed to be taking time off, and climbed trees to preach sermons to farmers when Asaka took over. Téoline watched all this, became alarmed at the diversity of manifestation, and decided on a lavé-tête for 'ti Joseph's protection. We of the compound nagged by Lys contributed the necessary objects and clothing. About 'ti Joseph's adult life I shall find some- thing to say when discussing Habitation Leclerc.

These eight were in effect my blood brothers, Madame Soulouque, Madame Dessalines, Vierge, Marie Claudine, Georgina, Desmène, Alliance, and 'ti Joseph.

6

Something should be said about the two women who were in charge of guiding the transfiguration of our nine either chosen or bosalle initiates—leaving the rest of the vaudun hierarchy to be spoken of later. Dégrasse was slender, about sixty, neat, nut brown in color, with eyes that changed from gray to hazel, gray in the sunlight, hazel with red glints when passing the fires of the tonnelle or dancing in ecstasy to her loa. She earned her living selling lace and tooth paste and thread and findings and Florida water from a tray or her lap at the corner of the Iron Market in Port-au-Prince, and if business was not good on one corner she might try the docks or Champs-de-Mars or even make her way to the Pétionville road. Dégrasse reminded me of a will-o'-the-wisp. When I had just about given up finding her, she would be there, a smile of pleasure at seeing me lighting the fine lines of her face, a pleasant odor drifting from her talcumed neck and shoulders. I would offer to squat beside her, but the stool always ended up mine with Dégrasse squatting beside me unrolling and rearranging bits of lace and ribbon, sorting, putting things in order as I have seen her do so many times at the altar which she shared with Téoline in the plains. Then we would gossip and make plans. As my initiation approached, the car and chauffeur of Dumarsais Estimé might be waiting a few squares away where I had, out of deference for the position of the Deputy, stationed it and continued on foot.

Dégrasse frequently disappeared for days on end and rumor had it that she had gone north to fulfill her duties as prix-des-yeux—prize, or sometimes explained as "price," of eyes—or clairvoyant, highest stage of induction into the vaudun in Haiti. I have known only two prix-des-yeux in my many years of interest in vaudun in Haiti, though I have known a number of people with "second sight" who had not passed the successive stages leading to the three to nine months of isolation, fasting, prayer, instruction, and considerable financial investment before the final award. What interested me on hearing this rumor about Dégrasse was how easily she adjusted to a position of inferior status with Téoline, actual mambo at our plains houngfor, creating no situations of jealousy, exercising no protocol over a lesser mambo. When at ceremonies, Dégrasse invariably took the position of prix de la cloche, or bell, a step below Téoline, and not once admitted that she might be of higher degree. Dégrasse officiated at plains ceremonies not because of local ties, position, vocation, or profession or calling, but just because and only when she felt like it. She could not be possessed either by us or by the loa, and thus gave the impression of having arrived at a true state of what Eastern religions call nirvana.

Téoline, on the other hand, was fat, with buttocks, breasts, and stomach always bursting out of her white mambo uniforms. She was black, with shiny skin that reflected light night and day, typical Haitian eyes which I have since heard described as "muddy" but which type in Africa I have called opaque. There is just no reading behind them any more than there is reading the slits-for-eyes of a Bambara mask. In spite of her eyes Téoline was warm, solid, outgoing. Most of her time was spent controlling bosalle, divining, taking care of services for ancestors and family and individual crises, receiving her husband Agwe, her other spouse Damballa, his wife Aïda Ouedo, and with occasional visits from Asaka and Guedé or Baron Samedi. Once in a long while a Petro or

Congo god would join the Arada-Dahomey ceremonies, and these occasions I loved for a change of pace. I particularly loved to dance the various congos. But it was while dipping and swaying, knees close-pressed, bent back undulating in the yonvalou as seen in Dahomey today, in obeisance to Damballa, the serpent, that Téoline had decided on my loa.

Téoline was mother to us all as well as mambo. In my many months as guest at her houngfor and at the clean-swept little patio before her snow-white caille where we sat for hours under the almond trees exchanging stories, I had only once seen her in bad humor. On second thought it wasn't even Téoline, because Guedé was in her head and Guedé and I had never gotten on well together. After the usual obscenities and vulgar hip-grinding movements Guedé had grabbed my navy-blue corduroy skirt, which with a white cotton T shirt, cotton stockings, and moccasins or boots, depending on the weather, was my uniform for night excursions into the bush. Guedé had spat at me and, speaking in the characteristic nasal tone, asked that I remove the skirt and give it to him. Why should I have something better than the others? If I thought myself a blanc I shouldn't be here. Téoline's (or Guedé's) eyes were red and her nostrils flared. She smoked a cigar and rudely blew billows of smoke into my face. I was in the early stages of this sort of thing and felt myself humiliated and betrayed until Doc assured me that Téoline had no control whatsoever over her actions and wouldn't remember in a few hours what had happened. In the back of my mind, however, was a cobweb of doubt which refused to be swept aside. Now I remembered Téoline fingering my skirt, asking about the material and if such a thing could be found in Haiti. Had she not been twice my size I might have given it to her.

In the dim, cold dawn of the last morning of waiting, Erzulie settled on the child, Marie Claudine. It was Erzulie Freda, the Virgin Mary, identified in every houngfor by an oleograph bought in markets or stores of Catholic votary supplies. At that time a song now become banal through

numerous popular recordings was still purely devotional—
the song to Erzulie Freda, melodically a fusion of Africa
and the Roman Catholic Church, the text indicating a plaint
and appeal from "Yagaza," which place, being somewhere on
the "other side," might be Africa or the world after death. In
the sanctuary the drums played softly as Marie Claudine
began to tremble, then rose to meet Erzulie Freda in her
stately glory . . .

> *Erzulie Freda,* (the song goes,) *Grandmother, the dew
> dances the banda* (dance of carnival sometimes associated also
> with Guedé) *but all the time the sun does not rise! It is I,
> Yagaza, calling to you from the other side, from Yagaza!
> Where are you? I am on Yagaza side!*

I have heard this song so often since then, on many
theater stages of the world, in many ceremonies, but never
with the same mystery, the same poignant fusion of Catholic
and vaudun ritual and belief. Téoline emerged from the
vestuary, a small room off the sanctuary where some of the
robes of the gods were hung. She was dressed in the robes of
Erzulie and approached the child, a fixed smile on her face,
the smile of the plaster figures of the Virgin. Perhaps it was
this other nature of Téoline that drew me to her, a purity
which balanced her earthiness, warmth, authority of Damballa, and abandon of Guedé. She had chosen for her first appearance of Erzulie a spangled net gown over a heavily
embroidered white satin slip. She wore jewels, a crown of
paste diamonds, many real gold rings. Mambo Dégrasse
emerged from the shadows, clapped her hands three times,
and all of us sat up, all of us wide-eyed because the sight was
really one of splendor. Marie Claudine, tears streaming down
her cheeks, rose, still trembling, scarcely able to stand but refusing help. She held her hands outstretched to Erzulie, who
led her to the center of the room. Candles were still burning,
down to their last wax, some to small floatings of brown lint
in oil colored from herbs and incense. The drummers entered
slowly from the adjoining room, playing softly, answering

Erzulie's song, which, when developed, becomes a choral litany. Téoline held her bell and ason in her right hand, held her other bejeweled hand out to Marie Claudine. Dégrasse remained near, watching Téoline's possession for any sign of loss of control, watching Marie Claudine for signs of her possession, which surely was imminent. Marie Claudine fell at the feet of Erzulie, embraced her flowing robes, buried her head in her knees, then permitted herself to rise and salute her mistress. The formal salute of the loa, the testing of formalized directions and positions and attitudes began, and Marie Claudine proved herself a true adept of Erzulie. The tears dried and the same smile that Téoline carried illumined her face. Her mouth was slightly open and her small white even teeth showed, giving her the coquettish look that many Virgins, especially Italian, have always had for me, and the look that is characteristic of Erzulie.

Téoline clasped Marie Claudine's two small hands, crossed arms in a deep knee bend of salutation, turned her to left and to right in an under-arm London Bridge movement, released her hands, indicated a turn and salutation to the four corners of the compass, kissed each cheek, then twirled the child and sent her off staggering into the arms of Dégrasse. Madame Ezméry, property of Erzulie by now, tried to rise from the floor but fell flat on her face at the splendid apparition of her goddess. She stayed there, jerking in spasms of ecstasy, until long after Erzulie had left us. Vierge, serving Aïda Ouedo, rose and accepted the salute of Erzulie, the two being closely associated as wife and mistress, respectively, of Damballa. Vierge and Marie Claudine and Mambo Téoline, now become Erzulie, danced the stately dance of the goddess, and the houngfor, as dawn light entered, seemed to be flooded with pure white and pale blue rays, some few pink lights streaking the filmy robe of the Maîtresse. Erzulie's dance has always intrigued me; still, it is something that is hard to define choreographically. It is more an attitude, an atmosphere than a dance. They moved, these three, with feminine grace, gliding, eyes downcast, in a world of their own. In Africa, aside from the Blue Women of Morocco, only among the royal dancers of Dahomey have I seen, and that recently, the flowing arm movements, the extreme femininity of wrist and hand, the sinuous movement emanating from the vertebral column and sending its flow into the far corners of the room. The salutations were repeated frequently, Téoline always imperious, head slightly inclined, the true Virgin Mother with a secret all her own.

Erzulie had scarcely departed when Cicéron, the drummer, began the ric-a-tic sound of Damballa, the serpent, fell flat on his belly and circled the room, finally approaching me. I was relieved to be closely wedged between my companions, as possession was far from my mind at that time. Noting choreographic patterns and songs difficult to decipher, this and the surrounding complex of the ceremony had kept me on a profane level. Téoline brought an egg and flour from my store of sacrificial food and Cicéron, undulating, writhing, hands clasped behind his back, tongue darting, advanced to the egg which was placed in a mound of flour in a saucer, crushed the shell, sucked the contents, then backed his way through the door of the houngfor and into the tonnelle. I knew from previous experiences with Damballa that had we been in the open a whole ceremony of hiding the act with sheets would have been performed. But we were in the sacrosanct. Cicéron was black and the white rim of flour around his mouth would have made a minstrel comic cartoon had the circumstances been different. At that time, and in that lighting, it was grotesque. I felt ill and squeamish about the diet of my mystère and shivered under the shower of cologne water generously sprayed over us by our high priestesses in honor of Damballa's visitation.

The following morning, toilets completed, our heads bound with new kerchiefs, we dressed from inside out in our new clothes. As the drummers walked out of the sanctuary into the burst of morning sun we could hear the murmur of children sweeping the peristyle, the braying of donkeys, early morning greetings from visiting houngans and their houngenicon, the assistants. Suddenly we seemed to be late. Hounci scurried to empty our calebasse chamber pots; other hounci buttoned us into our bridal or initiation dresses. If one were completing a marriage along with lavé-tête, as I was, and as was Marie Claudine, the ceremony must be performed by a houngan, with mambos assisting. The bosalle, Georgina, and the regular initiates would have to wait for us and escort us outside to the tonnelle. But before this there would be final instructions for all of us.

My greatest relief was to be able to walk around, stretching my stiff knees, and after that to be able to use toothbrush and toothpaste, both forbidden during the fasting. I had to be reminded that "brides" should show no sign of discomfort after confinement and that it was ungracious for me to linger over tooth brushing or leg stretches or knee bends. Waiting for us were people who had come from all over the plains and as far away as Descayettes and Léogane. In the tonnelle, wooden benches were filling, demijohns of clairin were being passed around and outside all was festivity, with sounds of laughter and joking reaching us in the houngfor. The hounci maison had been busy since the early hours of morning pounding millet and grating manioc for the sundown meal, goats and pigs had been butchered the day before and were now roasting on grills set over charcoal fires in pits dug in the ground. We could smell grillot—fried pork bits dipped in 'ti malice, Haitian hot sauce—and I am certain that the rest of the mouths watered along with mine after our meager, unsalted, unsavory sacrificial repasts. Behind the houngfor a few latecomers had deposited live chickens, and we could hear the chickens' frantic protests as hounci and neighbors twisted their necks with no ceremony before plucking them, marinating them in lime juice and simmering them, disjointed, in peanut oil, garlic, bay leaves, basil and peppercorns. Outside all was Sunday best and one would never know that half the congregation had danced most of the night under the tonnelle.

Most of the previous night I had thought about myself, about this country and what I was doing there. I thought a great deal about Fred and Doc and Dumarsais Estimé and resolved to try and unravel at least some of the complexities of human relations once over this first stage of acceptance into the folkways of the country. The drumming, possessions, and celebrations outside seemed banal. Just after midnight I had slept, with no feelings at all of gratitude for the demonstration, which, after all, was for us, the hounci lavé-tête. The beat of the asotor upset my stomach during the early hours; then it seemed to enter the houngfor and penetrate my body and eyes and head, finally lulling me into a sleep that was disturbed only by the tinkling of a bell and the handclapping for our readjustment on the floor.

Inside the houngfor, with the sun high and hot, we began to perspire in our new clothes, and talcum powder caked on our noses and underarms. I could feel a sticky trickle working its way from the matted top of my head down to my temples, where it was absorbed by my headkerchief. I hoped fervently that it was orgeat and not decongealed sacrificial blood.

We were seated where we had lain before, facing the wall of the houngfor and facing our pots têtes, our head pots. These were white china cylindrical pots, often seen in old-style pharmacies, with close-fitting lids, and in each were relics of each stage of our initiation. I cannot name the exact contents of mine because once the pot tête is closed it is almost never reopened. It is to be kept as a sacred object, to be talked to in times of stress, decorated with strands of trade beads or snakes' vertebrae and to have the food of the god who resides in essence inside placed before it for consumption, whether on a family altar in the plains of the Cul-de-Sac or some remote hotel room in Hamburg, West Germany. In my case my sacred head pot may very well be in Joliet, Illinois, because unless this particular pot tête is among reliquia on deposit at Southern Illinois University, in the United States, among my archives, still being collected by that institute, it may very well be buried and forgotten in some warehouse in Joliet, Illinois, or long ago destroyed. Woe to the keeper if he dares lift the top! Pot tête should always be kept from profane eyes, as should certain kinds of fetishes in Africa. There are some fetishes which, tightly and ritually bound in fine leather and stitched by a holy man, may be worn in view of others, and a certain prestige is derived from the size, form, shape, and quantity of these when worn in full view. Others are private, and as sacred objects are kept in some secret, sacred place, out of the sight of profane eyes, cared for and cherished as one should the repository of the anima or effluvia of oneself or one's god.

I sat cross-legged facing my spirit pot, between Alliance and Georgina as when couchée, lying on the floor. Téoline and Dégrasse stood, walking between us and around us. Joseph began to cry. He had not used the calebasse and was afraid to ask for it now. Téoline took him into the sanctuary, and he returned smiling. Then with the noise from outside suddenly become like some sound a long distance away, the two mambos lifted ason and rattle, and started the ritual of forcing into us the meaning of the vaudun.

It is hard to describe to an uninitiated the process of becoming initiated. Harder still when one remains for years on a fringe border of belief and nonbelief, because the two are so close. A thing happens, you experience it often without seeing it, and it is true. From then on the bitter battle with society begins, whether the thing that happened was acceptable in the society judging it. There must have been, I have since reflected with my jaded observer's mind, drugs of some mild kind administered, incense and herbs burnt that added to the trance feeling that made me see with startling clarity the meaning of this marriage to Damballa, to someone outside the sphere of human acquaintance, the total acceptance without loss of self. Then the sensation would leave me, and instead of feeling the god in possession of me, the calculating scientist would take over, and I would be making mental notes on clothing, social organization, speech habits, associated traits, and so forth. This split in attitude I have always found difficult to reconcile in any sort of research into private habits, whether of cult, religious practices, marriage customs, or otherwise. It is the feeling of being outsider within, or vice versa, as the occasion dictates. And when people ask me, as they do now, what of those mystic or occult experiences I believe in, or why I spend so much time in their search and research, I find myself answering as I did even as far back as those houngfor days, that I honestly do not know. I am there to believe or not believe, but willing to understand and to believe in the sincerity of other people in their beliefs, willing to be shown, to participate, and where the participant begins and the scientist ends, I surely could not say.

Facing our head pots, we were given the meaning of what was in them; why a sacrificed animal was considered fortunate to be allowed to take messages to the god to whom this animal represented an approach; how the prayers that were said to this fowl or goat or pig or beef and the prayers for its safe conduct to the god made it indeed superior and privileged beside others of its kind who were butchered without care or rite. How the offerings of foods which had come from Africa could carry a certain part of our spirit back to Africa, which country understandably enough is the Mecca of the Haitian peasant cult worshipper. These messengers could save a trip in person, which, to 'Nan Guinée, was outside the imagination of even the most imaginative of peasants. The race had been severed from its motherland, excepting through these mystic ties. There was a certain special attention to me which I had experienced at my first ancestral service with Dr. Price-Mars. I was unfortunate, I was told, in having been separated from those of my race who remembered the customs of 'Nan Guinée, but fortunate in seeking to re-establish the tie-corroborating stories told them by old houngans and bocors, the bush priests who occupy themselves more with magic and divining than with contact with ancestors and loa. That I would come into their midst, able to worship these gods in dance, and knowing, if fragmentarily, the essences of the religion which had meant for them spiritual and, in periods of their history, physical survival, confirming to them that segments of family, relatives known to have been separated from them and carried to some land vaguely north, others vaguely south, seemed to be of utmost importance to the cult itself—as it was important that I carry the meaning of the true vaudun to my people in that other country. I made no effort to disillusion these well-meaning informants about what might be expected of the children of Guinée dispersed to the north, but listened, repeating as I could the songs and litanies and instructions. The language barrier, my rudimentary creole, was not as important as one would have thought, there having always been a language barrier between the widely conglomerate tribal groups of slaves.

We were permitted to speak to our pots têtes through a small crack as the mambos held the covers lifted before the final sealing. All of our hopes, aspirations, troubles were confided in whispers to them; to the bits of feathers, blood, cooked and uncooked food, liqueurs, perfumes, clippings of hair from the center of our heads, incenses, and I know not what else. The head pots were passed around our heads three times, then emphatically closed by the mambo, with orders from her to each of the pots, which orders were, I presume, to grant us what we had requested, carry out our wishes, and act as intermediary between hounci lavé-tête and our gods. Then we chanted in unison and sang in unison, ason and bell the only accompaniment. In the most sacred of inner houngfor services the drum is rarely used.

The songs were for the most part in "langage," a mixture of pure African languages and dialects of the surviving tribal groupings represented in Haiti. The three major sources of slave origin in Africa terminating in Haiti were Dahomey, the Congo, and Nigeria. There were others, but most of the "langage" contains words traceable to these three areas. And there were and still are numerous linguistic and tribal variations within each area. Enough to say that I have never been able to capture the secret of "langage," and that learning creole has had to suffice me for living and research in Haiti. But on this occasion, whether due to the strenuous period of commensuration with my brother and sister hounci, to the solemnity of the cult atmosphere maintained for these days and nights, to fasting, or to incense, now permeating the houngfor, thrown by the handful as soon as it diminished onto the charcoal braziers, I had the impression of following the songs and ritual in creole and "langage" like a real trooper. The mambos must have had the same conviction, because I could sense no such doubt or embarrassment as I remember when simulating possession at the houngfor of the priest Julien at Descayettes, some time later. For those interested in becoming initiates of the vaudun the text of these exercises went somewhat as follows:

_____ Hounci (by name, name of birth and name conferred by initiation), you have gone through these days and nights close to the vaudun, most powerful in thinking of gods or ancestors. You have been commanded in marriage or by cleansing your body to receive the benefits of this god. This god is _____ (the name of the god; then the characteristics of the loa, in my case jealousy being foremost, and to the jealousy of Damballa I can surely attest! Then followed a long list of what the god likes to eat, drink, do, how and why; his favorite places to frequent and be found in and inhabit. Next was a list of countries in Africa from which our ancestors had come, and I must say that they were surprisingly accurate; the conduct in presence of these loa, clothing to be worn and artifacts to be carried upon their appearance, and the salutations to them were demonstrated.)

We rose from our squatting positions and I restrained myself from rubbing my knees only because Dégrasse was watching me hawk-eyed and severe, unusual for her. She seemed determined that I would pass my examinations with flying colors. We began the ritual of the crossed and recrossed handclasp, the bow with knees flexed, turn under-arm, hounci of highest protocol guiding the other. Then the turn to all four directions of the compass, hand gripped tightly in hand, with sacred words spoken in each direction, the approach to the altar, the recognition of each grade of protocol by obeisance and word. I was not required to prostrate myself before the mambos as is the practice, flat on the ground, face down, bracing oneself by toes and hands, body rigid, touching each cheek to the ground, swaying side to side. It was up to my instructors to decide what to do, and I followed them, asking no questions. Each point of the compass has its own explanation and these inner sanctum asides I do not feel important for the uninitiated. I feel also that some part of the belief of real believers should be left in reserve. I have no feeling of guilt or punishment or mystic retribution should I disclose these secrets. If any one of my readers could receive satisfaction or find the end of a quest in what I have experienced I would be more than happy at some time to make these revelations. But if a curiosity is for neither scientific records nor self-examination these things are best left within their sacred environment where for those who experience them they represent truth.

We danced, not as people dance in the houngfor, with the stress of possession or the escapism of hypnosis or for catharsis, but as I imagine dance must have been executed when body and being were more united, when form and flow and personal ecstasy became an exaltation of a superior state of things, not necessarily a ritual to any one superior being.

There is something in the dance of religious ecstasy that has always made me feel that through this exercise man might come into his own, be freed of inferiority and guilt in face of whatever might be his divinity. Outside the houngfor of the Cul-de-Sac I have not had the good fortune during any ceremonial dance to reaffirm this certainty except in one situation; that was during visits in New York, on Long Island, to the temple of Her Majesty, Mysikiitta Fa Sennta, Imperial Ruler of the Gheez temple (Ghiza, Egypt; before that, Gheez, Ethiopia). About Her Majesty and her temple I hope to write more some day, but she exists and the temple exists, and around her a group of right-living persons such as

I have not known outside a true folk or primitive setting; and in the Gheez temple on Long Island Her Majesty, an imposing person of statuesque proportions, leads her temple followers, young and old in dances of religious ecstasy which are not the uncontrolled, spasmodic reflexes of some of the storefront churches of America, but of expertise, dignity, and choreographic development hard to imagine outside a performing training center. The male members of the temple are karate experts and I have seen some of them excel in a defiance of gravity, while praising the divinity, that would astonish a Bolshoi Ballet lead dancer.

This day in the houngfor, just risen from our isolation of initiation, we dipped and swayed, drew close to each other, separated, went to our knees before the altar, lifted our head pots, balanced them on our bound heads and promenaded with them. They seemed to stay in place of their own accord. There were no possessions as such, no loa asserted his presence, but my feeling was closer to belonging to something all encompassing than I have known since. And I say in all honesty that my knees, which ordinarily were not supple, permitted postures and extravagances that I would not have dared attempt under other circumstances.

Clean in body and spirit, purified of whatever bosalle or tormenting spirit had prevented us from meeting our loa on peaceful terms, we prepared for our exit from the houngfor. The bosalle and those others fulfilling the *service* of initiation were released at last from formalities and stood to one side examining the artifacts of the altar and eyeing each other as though some major outward change would have taken place since the Thursday before. They also looked at us, the brides, somewhat enviously as we entered the sanctuary for the completion of our "marriages." Somewhat dubious at the time, I have since had every reason to feel that the burden of being "married" to a loa is best avoided. The demands are rigorous, the jealousy constant, the punishment for mishaps severe, and there is no divorce, which is one of the many compatibilities between the Roman Catholic religion and the vaudun.

The whole experience of my initiation was, I believe, easier for me than for some outsider belonging to an orthodox religion, Albert and Annette Dunham never having insisted on christening for their children.

At the time of my wedding to Damballa I was already married, though hardly mature enough of spirit to realize it, to someone who would perhaps rather remain anonymous; I felt myself in love with a dear friend who might also rather remain anonymous; I was smitten with one or more college professors, fascinated by Dumarsais Estimé, and engaged in more ways than one to Fred Alsop. Seen now after time and distance, I realize that this might be considered peculiar, but then, one condition seemed to have nothing to do with the others, and marrying Damballa was an added experience to a life that I have always hoped returned a good part of the richness it received. But I could not take fully into account the significance of this pact believed by some to be more magic than religious. In none of my affections have I been so punished for infidelity as by my Haitian serpent god, the rainbow holding his tail in his mouth and supporting the sky to keep it from falling on the earth. I have not considered it of my doing if other gods such as Agwe of Haiti or Yemanja of Brazil or Ogun and Oxun and Santa Barbara of Cuba or these impatient genii of Senegal make demands through emissaries. They appear without my solicitation and keep appearing. Of course, I could turn away from these overtures, but there is always curiosity, and the element of chance. These are the driving forces of the will to seek one day after the next, why we go on when at times it seems unreasonable.

If it is possible to imagine standing before the altar of decision with circumspection and belief each as strong as the other; with revulsion such as I felt because I was hungry and a little faint and because I don't like the company of snakes; but with practically assurances of success in whatever I wanted, protection from ill-wishers, good health, salvation from loneliness, and a clear path of fulfilled ambitions; with some hope that by this deed my brother would be released from the torment that had confined him to St. Elizabeth's Hospital in Washington; but at the same time to imagine being an observer with the skepticism of youth bound by intellectual obligations and trying to live up to a higher education of cold science; and more important than any of these, as Iphigenia ready for the supreme sacrifice, then this is just about the way to imagine my feelings at this marriage ceremony to Damballa. The chanting of pledges, citing of responsibilities, the avowals, the contracts read to us from worn, scratched-on, flower-bordered scrolls by a houngan and a bocor whose names I have forgotten, with Dégrasse and Téoline standing by as matrons of honor, were more solemn than the marriage to my present earthly husband, which has lasted for twenty-five years. I signed a contract written by some local scribe in flourishing letters with, it appeared, a quill pen:

> Moi, (baptismal name), en mariage accepte le main de Damballa Ouedo en mariage sanctifie messieurs et dames temeigne. Recevez salutations, Damballa Ouedo, Arc-en-Ciel. Signe ce jour par
>
> (Baptismal name of bride)   ———
> (Houngan temeigne)   ———
> (Bocor temeigne)   ———
> Majesté, Damballa Ouedo, Arc-en-Ciel
>   Date: ———
>   Lieu: ———

The ring of tiny diamonds and rubies which Fred had given me was placed on my finger in marriage to Damballa and I promised not to remove it.

Once a Cuban santera, or priestess in New York, Rosita, sent an urgent message to me by my dear friend Julio Méndez. Ogun Hierro of Cuba was making demands on me, along with minor demands for Oxun and Elegua. I had not, that I could remember, made any promises to Ogun Hierro, though I had been present in Cuba and elsewhere when he had visited at ceremonies in his honor. I went to see Rosita and learned in a letter from her which she wrote under Ogun Hierro's guidance that aside from mixing the gods of too many countries, thus causing intense jealousies among them, I had also misplaced or put aside a piece of jewelry not of great value but of great importance; this piece of jewelry must be found and cared for. Searching through my memorabilia I found Damballa's wedding ring missing. Somewhere in changing habits and tastes from costume jewelry to collectors' items of value, this, which should have come before everything else, had been lost, had strayed, been stolen, or was simply missing. Ogun's demands were fulfilled chiefly because it seemed easier than protesting, but all the while I thought of Damballa and would right now give a great deal to know where and when during these crowded years Damballa's (by way of Fred) ring went out of sight, and how. Anyone wearing it must be having as sleepless nights as I have had without it.

As we made our preparations to leave the houngfor, I had the feeling that I had experienced in leaving Joliet, Illinois, for larger ports of the world, combined with an experience more recent and one to be repeated too many times in my life, the leaving behind of close, unclassified ties with no explanation for their substance and intensity; a part of oneself walking through the exit, another part staying behind for eternity. A year before my initiation I had left the isolated Maroon people of Jamaica, where I had been the first outsider to live intimately and for a time with them. I felt the separation as an end of some part of me, as I would experience when leaving Haiti, when saying farewell to the Dunham Company in Tokyo or Vienna and realizing that the separation might be for a year or forever; the sadness of always leaving a part of myself behind, still knowing that moving on is inevitable.

I touched my pot tête and the necklace of snakes' vertebrae that encircled it. The necklace of blue and white trade beads crossed my neck and passed under one arm, a way of wearing it which signified "marriage" to a loa, or canzo status or higher in the vaudun priesthood hierarchy. Before the altar of the houngfor we all bent down to dip our fingers in the many-times-consecrated water of the altar pool. Some of the hounci became enthusiastic and drank of it from their cupped hands. Seeing the scum of algae and droppings on the surface of the water and at the bottom of the pool, I made a great display of touching my forehead with the water, then scooping enough in my two hands to offer three splashes from left to right before the altar, as one should with all libations in the presence of or in habitations of the gods. Because I was under surveillance I touched my lips with the sacred water, making note not to forget my quinine tablets once I was back at the Hotel Excelsior.

The altars of houngfors vary in embellishment, subject to the fantasy and tastes of governing houngan or mambo, artifacts available, and financial status of the community supporting the houngfor. According to Harold Courlander, the dean of authorities on Haitian music and its surrounding complex, wood carvings and forged-iron altar objects can still be found in Haiti, chiefly in the south. My experiences with forged-iron sacred objects in Haiti has been limited to small stands for holding candles or ceremonial offerings, the iron twisted into simple, nonrepresentational patterns, sometimes adorned with crosses or tritons. At Nan Campêche, near the Citadel of Christophe, a dinner plate from the table service of Napoleon I, Sèvres blue and crested with golden bees, was a prize altar piece. Christophe was supposed to have eaten sacrificial food from this plate, and rumor has it that at Nan Campêche his suicide was predicted. (At Nan Campêche the couleuvres, or local variety of boa serpents, are fed by the mambo maison and when I was there they glided into the peristyle when the rhythm of Damballa called them.)

Téoline's houngfor altar was a cement cube with a square recess in the façade which likened it to the masonry ovens still to be found intact in the subterranean kitchens of the Citadel. The recess was filled with plates of offerings, and every centimeter of the altar was taken up with head pots set on china plates. In saucers or forged-iron candelabra, handmade candles, brown with herbs and incense, burned or floated in their own residue. There were also saucers of flour, eggs, bottles of clairin, Rum Barbancourt, liqueurs, toilet waters, scented soap, fading crepe-paper flowers, bead and snake-vertebrae necklaces, pieces of costume jewelry, a dust-covered bottle of champagne, oleographs of saints and over that of the Virgin Mary a bridal veil hung on a nail, probably held over from one of Téoline's "marriages." In the sunlight that now streamed into the houngfor, shattering all sense of mystery, the altar objects seemed poor beside those I had seen at Léogane, south of the capital, or at Nan Campêche in the north. I was ashamed of my reflection and was gratified to glance into the inner sanctuary and see the richness of the designs and colors that covered the four walls of the small room, the elegance of the carved wooden table probably dating from colonial times, and the snow-white embroidered and crocheted linen cloth that covered it. The walls were true "primitives," the kind that, put on canvas, would delight a dealer in rare paintings. Agwe, Erzulie, Damballa, and Lenguesou were there in vivid colors. Soon we would see them in powdered cornmeal drawn on the dirt floor to make vévé designs that serve to attract those gods anticipated. On the altar were a straw knapsack for Asaka, two satin and spangled flags wrapped around their poles, a small figurine dressed in the top hat and tail coat of Baron Samedi. There was also a pot tête, which I have since tried without success to locate for the colonial collection of Habitation Leclerc. It must have dated from the period before General Leclerc and was draped with a necklace of highly patinated snakes' vertebrae heavily interspersed with cowrie shells. Cowrie shells are rare in Haiti, as any ones still to be found must have come from 'Nan Guinée with the slaves or their traders. The necklace blended into the designs encrusted in gold, sky blue, and white which decorated the pot.

I wondered if it could belong to Dégrasse. It seemed too delicate to be a part of Téoline.

Both altars contained oleographs of Saint Patrick driving the snakes out of Ireland, which would be Damballa, of Neptune with his long beard and triton, which would be Agwe, ruler of the seas, of the Virgin Mary, identified with Erzulie Freda, of Legba, opener of the gates, who was Saint Peter with the keys to heaven, of Saint George, worshipped as Lenguesou, on his white horse, killing the dragon. Both altars contained the ason and ogan, iron bell, of one or more mambos and houngans, and thunder stones were there, as on every altar in Haiti. Ethnologists have discovered that many of these magic stones are stone-age arrowheads which must have been brought as sacred objects from 'Nan Guinée.

As we passed the altar we curtsied and placed our pots têtes before the deity of our initiation. They would be given to us again after sundown, when we would be free to return to our respective homes, leaving the visitors to continue the festivities. Then we left the earth dampness and incense and food and body and sticky sweetness odors of the houngfor behind us and filed out into the tonnelle.

7

Nietzsche, in *Thus Spake Zarathustra*, says:

"I could only believe in a god who would know how to dance; now I am without weight, now I am flying; now I see myself raised above myself, now a god dances in me."

Outside the houngfor the gods were dancing, and we were soon to join them. They had danced all night, impregnating their strength into our heads as we lay cloistered inside. The morning air was brilliantly clear after the blackness inside and we stood blinking and trying to gain our bearings. The tonnelle floor was swept clean, and Durcel, guest houngan for our initiation invited by Téoline and Dégrasse, was, assisted by his La place drawing the vévé in honor of the gods who should by all laws of expectation appear. Durcel was known all over the plains area for the beauty of his floor designs, traced by passing a thin stream of fine ground meal between his fingers and "painting" the design in dimensional form. I have heard that mambos also trace vévés, but I am inclined to believe it is an art traditionally restricted to men. For what it is worth, I have never seen a vévé traced except by the officiating houngan or his La place, and this from a bent-over position, moving from place to place under the tonnelle, never rising, knees straight, feet slightly apart, trunk parallel to knees and head at a right angle to the ground. This

creates a really striking effect, and is a position which never
fails to charm me here in Africa, where most household and
courtyard sweeping is done by women domestics bent as
though folded over in this position, with reed hand brooms
resembling the royal buffalo tail switches used by kings to
chase flies. One can see the same exaggeratedly bent-over position in rice-planting time in Casamance and in the gathering
of cut sheaves of millet in all parts of Senegal at harvesting
time. This is one of the classic postures depicted in West
Coast bronze figurines.

It seems that the houngan never tires, though the complicated vévé sometimes takes hours to accomplish. It may
be purely decorative, a valentine lace heart or circle around
cabalistic designs serving no purpose other than gratification
of the artist's creative urge. When traced by a dedicated
houngan such as Durcel, this fantasy urge is channeled and
no matter how elaborate the design each convolution has
its own representative or symbolic meaning. This Sunday
morning Erzulie was prominent—a heart pierced by two
swords, two lines ending in crosses passing through the center
of the heart. Stylized flowers, dots, spirals within loops
formed hoops around the heart. Erzulie's vévé was there for
us to walk across, exiting from the houngfor. Damballa and
Aïda Ouedo circled the post in the center of the peristyle.
This post, the poteau mitan, should attract the gods in the
same way that a lightning rod draws electricity to itself,
deflecting it from where it might cause destruction. By this
post the expected gods enter; others, guest loa or interlopers,
may come from the houngfor, peristyle, or surroundings outside. Damballa was also at the four corners of the peristyle,
holding his tail in his mouth, Dahomean symbol of continuity,
the roundness of time, of indestructibility by time. Agwe's
vévé could have been the German training ship *Elsen*, anchored in the bay of Port-au-Prince since the week before,
escorted in the same way on the houngfor dirt floor as in the
bay by a fleet of one-mast fishing boats and small, oar-
propelled skiffs.

Around the base of the center post was a cement altar decorated with worn paintings of the Haitian flag, a black goat, a serpent, crosses, phallic symbols, and the like. On it were candles in iron holders, and facing the houngfor, which also meant facing us as we exited, was Papa Guedé, a stuffed burlap figure such as is carried by lalwadi (la loi dit) dancing bands after carnival and burned on Good Friday, representing the traitor Judas. The notion of the traitor is extremely important to the Haitian peasant, no matter who the traitor or what the circumstances, as testified in so many and continuous revolutions. The figure was dressed in the black frock coat worn by Georgina when Papa Guedé had visited her the night before last, the same top hat and white spectacles with no lenses. One half of his face was white, one half smudged with black soot, half to represent the living, half the dead, and a white clay pipe was stuffed into the hole that made his mouth. Papa Guedé slouched against the center post as vulgarly as when "mounting" a "horse." A cane was clutched in his straw fist.

There were other vévés and objects representative of other loa that we could see as we came out of the darkness into the bright sunlight. Asaka was designed as a straw knapsack on the ground, the cork-topped bottles sticking out from under the tasseled flap surprisingly realistic. Lenguesou was a series of arches which may have represented a rainbow surrounded by lacework patterns. I have had only one experience with Lenguesou. At our initiation festivity, Lenguesou, never aggressive, remained in the background.

Legba must always be given recognition, whether in Africa or the New World, though Legba is not recognized as a loa in the strict sense of the word. In Ibadan, Nigeria, in Cuba, in Brazil, and in Haiti I have called upon Legba to open gates for me, to open the barrier between my petitions and the supreme:

> "Papa Legba, ouvrié barrié pou moi, la vie nou mandé, nou mandé bien!"

"Papa Legba, open the barrier for me, life sends good things for me." Or it could be that life demands good things, depending on how the creole is translated.

I like the first translation. Legba is polynational, serving, among others, Yorubas, Arada-Dahomeans, Ibos, Nagos, Congos, as gatekeeper or spirit intermediary between humans and true gods. He seems to be as strict as Saint Peter in judging entry into the promised land, but, by reputation, he is easily bribed or cajoled. At our ceremony a small clay mound represented Legba. This conical mound may have been a token phallus, as I have heard that Legba is noted for a remarkably outstanding generative organ. In the Haitian hills, offerings to Legba are in close competition in popularity with those to Guedé: canaris—earthenware jugs of water—or food under a doorpost, or two forked posts with a cross-bar.

The sun was high and there seemed to be no breath of air across the scorched plains when we moved out of the houngfor, passing inspection before our audience, singing, swaying, following Dégrasse and Téoline in a circle counterclockwise around the center post. Doc was with Cécile in the front row of spectators, smiling and nodding, and already aware of the proximity of Guedé, and Fred was in the crowd standing under the tonnelle. I kept my eyes down and knew that it would be wrong to give any greeting, any sign that the mystery of the inner sanctum and houngfor might be dissipated by the outdoors and proximity to the profane. The two mambos were in starched white dresses beneath which embroidered petticoats showed. They wore white cotton stockings and new market sandals, white kerchiefs and necklaces of beads and snakes' vertebrae. Dégrasse's ason was threaded with cowrie shells and vertebrae, her bell, a small one, of pure silver. Both bell and ason must have been very old. Téoline's ason was meshed with multicolored beads and vertebrae, and her bell was one of those found in the shops of Port-au-Prince that sell Catholic altar objects. In front of the two officiating priestesses and at a distance, La place, flanked by two flag bearers and brandishing the sword I had seen in the sanctuary, made his obeisances to the poteau mitan, to the audience and participants who were crowded into the three sides of the tonnelle and extended outside the peristyle. Seated on benches, cane-bottomed stools, packing cases, and chairs, or standing, the guests joined in the singing, keeping rhythm with our motion by clapping and swaying from side to side. The song was to Aïda Ouedo, and we made the tour of the peristyle taking care not to destroy the vévé or to disturb Durcel, who was still bent over, drawing. The whole community rejoiced as we filed past, veiled, powdered, perfumed, and in our Sunday best, because it was Sunday as well as the day of our rising. Marie Claudine's mother began the trembling that announces the presence of a loa, fell over on her neighbor with slight jerking movements, then collected herself and continued singing and clapping in rhythm. Handclapping during ceremonies is not a common practice in Haiti, as it is among the Shepherd groups of Jamaica or Sanctified Churches in America where exaltation is expressed in violent concentrated loud handclapping motor activity. In Haiti, La place may pass before the spectators from time to time or stop to give a cheer-leader exhibition to hounci to heighten their fervor, and this is emphasized by handclapping; but it is for the most part at the beginning of a ceremony or at points of high tension that the audience joins in clapping. I have noticed this when observing the boumrab, the Senegalese equivalent of hounci, at healing ceremonies. This substantiates a theory which I find enlarged by Agnes De Mille in her comprehensive *Book of the Dance* that handclapping is essentially, and more than likely was originally, a ritual means of clearing the air of evil spirits or unfriendly elements, not a sign of joy or approbation as we see these things in our Western culture. Small children clap their hands for joy, but that may be a conditioned reflex, or borrowed from adults. Among folk and primitive people I have noticed the distinction of "clapping in" and "clapping out." In the former the palms are struck in a pacific manner, and with a fluid movement are drawn toward the body before separating the hands; in the latter they are moved sharply outward from the body after the concussion of the palms.

We made our circle clapping toward our bodies, petitioning our deific benefactors to enter, and all the while Téoline and Dégrasse turned and curtsied in the graceful movements of Erzulie. The reason for the decision of an homage to a particular loa at the opening of a ceremony is one of those incomprehensible things that does not support investigation. I have tried to find out, with no real success, what decides the order of rhythms, how a mambo or houngan decides which loa is dominant at a given ceremony, why some are allowed to stay for the evening or until the next day, while others are sent away—if possible—shortly after their arrival. The answer must lie in a maze of extrasensory perception, personal taste, custom, and the multi-theistic mysticism that makes the vaudun what it is.

Our Erzulie circle led us back to the houngfor entrance. On each side were benches. The drummers who had been to one side now walked, straddling their drums, into the space before the doorway, trodding barefooted over the vévé to Erzulie Freda. Ciseaux at the mama, the largest pegged, hollowed-out cylinder, Marius at the seconde, next largest, and a boy of fourteen or fifteen who was the son of the houngan Durcel at the smallest drum, the kata. These are the official Arada-Dahomey drums, scarcely changed in form since they were brought to the New World by the first slaves, and, like some of the songs and ritual practices, show less sign of acculturation changes than their counterparts found in urban centers of Africa today. As we sat, the drummers stopped playing long enough to tune their instruments by pounding with a wooden mallet on the pegs set around the heads of the drums, and the crowd took this opportunity to shift places, laugh and joke one with the other, exchange greetings, wander over to the porteresses under the figuier to buy hot morsels of grillot or bottles of warm kola—Haitian fruit drink—or a swallow of clairin.

Téoline and Dégrasse re-entered the houngfor on some business of their own, La place cleared his throat, spat into the dust outside, drank kola brought to him in a tin cup by a hounci, and made a few overhead feints with his saber, which he had removed from its case. We full-fledged hounci lavé-tête removed our shoes and stockings and veils and handed them to hounci canzo, who were our handmaidens for this one occasion. Hereafter, we of a category below them should render small services to them when called upon at important occasions. Our feet on the hard-packed, hot earth, we were ready to venerate our loa in dance, nervous at the anticipation of a "possession" but confident that we would not be mistreated or embarrassed because of our new, hard-won status.

Seated between Georgina and Marie Claudine, I tried to absorb all there was to see of people, place, and objects. At that time, painting of drums was rare, and I was extremely annoyed to see my baptismal drums to Damballa, which I was to take back to the University of Chicago as the most important of my artifacts, freshly painted in sky blue and white. Then I considered that they were new, and it would have taken years for the wood to patinate, to arrive at the same maturity as the set of natural wood drums I had acquired, by one means or another, from somewhere near Ville Bonheur. These drums of Ville Bonheur, village of the Black Virgin of Haiti, had been hidden behind a waterfall during one of the Occupation "purges" of vaudun temples and, traditionally unpainted and unstained, glowed with the usage of time like old museum pieces.

I used those drums of Ville Bonheur for some time while touring with the Dunham Company. In a period of great financial stress, as arrives now and then to any group of itinerant performers such as we were, a boxcar in which the drums were stored, along with costumes and decor, took fire on a railroad siding in New Jersey and burned to the ground. This was just after the Broadway production of *Carib Song*, and while the loss of the sets, some of them designed by Jo Mielziner, the rest by John Pratt, was covered by the insurance company of our producers, the sacred drums of Damballa were indisputably mine. The insurance company was taxed for many times the price I had paid for them, which is understandable in view of the care, feeding, ritual bathing and anointing, customs duties, and preservation which all my sacred percussion instruments have cost over the years. Papa Augustin, Haitian bocor living in New York, friend, guide, and counselor to me, faithful drummer and consultant on Haitian folklore at the Dunham School and with the Dunham Company, interpreted the loss of the drums as Damballa's jealousy. Profane hands had touched them since I had acquired them, and I had admitted Cuban and Brazilian drummers into the close-knit group controlled by Papa. I, on the other hand, true to my nature of diffused optimism, had interpreted the insurance payment at that moment of need as a sign of Damballa's protective surveillance. And since I might not at that time have had the perspicacity to turn the drums over to a museum, I could think of no better finish for them than in a blazing fire on the siding of a New Jersey railway, enveloped in clouds of smoke from the clothing and stage decors of the mistress who had transported them so many miles and for so long.

Overhead in the peristyle, suspended from the crossbeams of the tonnelle, was a wooden ship in full sail—Agwe as protector. There was also suspended from the ceiling the finest set of Arada-Dahomey drums I have seen outside the pre-Occupation ones of mine which were reputed to date from President Boyer, 1822–1844. That would have made them over a hundred years old. During my initiation they were confided to the care of Doc, who played them from time to time to keep them in tune or, as he said, to keep them "happy." The houngfor drums were, like mine, carved at the base with three indented bands. This seems to be a classic design, though small doorways, spirals, animal representations, and alligator teeth carvings are common. I wondered if these were the drums that had played in the sanctuary while we lay cloistered. Once seen, they dominated the tonnelle, half in sunshine, half in leafy shadow, still, somber, like gods hanging in the rafters.

My baptismal drums leaned against cane chairs beside the poteau mitan and were freshly dressed in white embroidered petticoats and pale blue cotton handkerchiefs. I was pleased to see La place make the libation from left to right in front of them with his kola, and at one point Doc poured a drop of clairin in front of each. One or three drops of any liquid about to be drunk should always be poured in front of an altar, baptized drums, important or highly accomplished drummers, at times at the doorstep of a house when visiting. I have not seen this act done before houngan or mambo, but these days, much later, when I return after a long trip to Habitation Leclerc the first rum is often dropped in front of me in welcome.

One of the village boys stood fingering the ogan, the iron bell, which must have been handmade, and very old, from slavery times. He struck it from time to time with a long iron nail tied to his wrist. Often I wonder by what means the slaves carried these sacred objects from 'Nan Guinée. Certainly lithographs of slave ships show there would not have been room between one body and another to hide an ogan, a calebasse, or a zin—the iron pots used in canzo initiation ceremonies, the oldest of which are supposed to have come from Africa. Perhaps their sorcerers had ways, or perhaps among the callous traders there were some with more humanity than we know about, who, taking pity on one family sold by its own or another, felt that at least the simple things of the household gods should travel with them to the unknown. There are supposed to be iron figurines in Haiti brought by the slaves, but I have not seen them. Iron is important in all of West Africa, a sign of prestige, at one time equal with gold and silver. Its religious significance carried over and still persists into those areas of the Caribbean and South America practicing ancestral cults. I have not noticed iron as important in Congo ceremonies, but in Cuba the ogan is played for Congo popular dances. In the Petro cult, iron is not used as a percussion instrument but is present in the form of an iron rod planted upright in a charcoal fire, where it remains red hot, even if the ceremony takes days.

Outside, near the figuier tree, Fred was eating grillot and drinking kola, and from my seat near the houngfor door I could see Doc, who had joined him, adding clairin to a bottle of kola, gnawing at roast goat bones, a smile of cherubic contentment on his oily mouth. I swallowed my saliva and concentrated on La place preparing for the actions de grâce, the intoning of the Catholic liturgy. We wouldn't be allowed to eat until we had danced, until the loa who had chosen us entered into our heads, or spoke to us through an emissary. I looked around nervously for an emissary of Damballa but saw only Doc, already singing and showing signs of welcoming Guedé, the signs being unmistakably clairin-induced on that occasion. The rest of the congregation sat or lounged at ease, pleasantly expectant.

From inside the houngfor came the sound of the ason and bell. All of us turned to the doorway. Téoline appeared, barefooted as we were, carrying a cloud of incense with her. She stayed there shaking the ason and bell in steady rhythm while La place herded the hounci of higher category to kneeling positions around the poteau mitan. He began the liturgy in the same high, piercing voice as the grand Marabout muezzin who awakens me in Dakar at five minutes after five if the breeze is in the direction coming from the grand mosque in the medina. In our houngfor it was Islam and Catholicism and vaudun at one and the same time, but the drums began their rhythm and submerged everything but the vaudun. La place dipped and turned, stopping to light the candles on the four sides of the center-post altar, ringing the bell he had taken from the inner altar objects, placing candles lighted from those already burning in the centers of the vévé, touching a hounci from time to time on her bowed head, and stopping in dramatic postures to exaggerate the effect on us of a high nasal tone. With the answering chorus the hounci fell flat on their faces.

"Marie, pleine de grâce, le Seigneur est avec vous . . ."

The hounci were demonstrating what we had been taught in the houngfor.

La place was black, wide-faced, with staring eyes that sought me out more often than was comfortable. I thought of the imminent entrance of the gods, wondered what sort of spectacle I would make of myself if by chance possessed, what would be thought of me if I weren't. Then I decided to let happen what would, not to fear my divinity but not to seek him falsely. Each hypocritical move or act is not only immediately discerned but severely frowned on by the priests of the vaudun. La place's seeking me out as he performed the actes de grâce brought to my mind some thoughts that had troubled me during my long days and often sleepless nights of initiation.

Now I was hungry, not very comfortable, tired, beginning to be sweaty, seemingly untouched by the ecstasies, even the graces from which the others benefited. Just what was I doing there, and what was my capacity in that friendly, sincere community? How much of what I was doing was in the interest of science, how much succumbing to the neurosis of the country, how much just a seeking for knowledge, for a key to an unknown from which body and soul would benefit and with which doubt and fear would be dispelled? What did these people really think of me, one who could scarcely speak their tongue, who was completely lost in the secret "langage," who turned—and still often does—to left instead of right in the salutes between houngan and hounci, or two hounci, who during the process of initiation ate only token portions of sacrificial food, who was put off by the sight of killings and of blood, demanded special concern even when in the inner sanctum of the gods . . .

The ring of Téoline's bell and the subdued clatter of her ason were in my ear. It was as though she had sensed my self-doubt and, probing beyond the houngfor and the initiation, regarded my entrance into the vaudun as a personal need and quest, and wanted to assure me that all that I had seen and experienced would take its place to be interpreted in its symbology through the years. I remember thinking, when man is looking desperately for salvation he shouldn't turn his back on doorways. That is not to say that he should follow each "call" or every soothsayer, who sensing his need, approaches his horizon, but with discrimination should keep seeking, and should not find one structure of beliefs serving well another human being to be outside the scope of his own credibility. I felt that Téoline in some way understood my thirst for knowledge and scientific documentation and would be willing to help me to the full extent of her vast matriarchal intelligence.

At that moment more than any other before or afterward I appreciated the large, earth-mother benevolence of the authentic African woman, undefiled by colonialism, untouched by the inroads of Western civilization in her own country, and enriched by the experience of slavery in the New World. In the New World, however, this earth mother, instead of remaining in the background, has been given her just due, perhaps because she fought for it, perhaps because there was so often opportunity for her to prove a selflessness and courage that is not typical of the Africa that I know. Téoline restored my confidence in what I was doing and why. The cause became worthy of the deed.

The litany over, the hounci dispersed and eyed Téoline, who held her ason poised, dramatically surveying congregation, drummers, and us, the new hounci. Ciseaux held high the curved stick with which the mama drum is struck and continued massaging the cowhide head with his other hand. He shifted from one foot to the other and caressed the body of the drum with his flexed knees. The drummer of the seconde played with a straight stick, the drummer of the kata

with two lighter-weight straight sticks. Each drummer had
replacement sticks in his pants belt in case some were broken
or if hounci were possessed to the point of falling into the
drums and scattering the playing sticks. At any cost, the
rhythm must not stop. Téoline pointed the ason at La place
and started the song. He was to answer. Her contralto voice
was pitched so low that La place and hounci sang their
responses an octave higher. With only the bell and ason she
began the petition to Papa Legba:

> "Legba! soleil te lève, Legba,
> Ouvri barrié pou mon, Legba,
> Ouvri barrié pou toute moune yo
> Mait' passé toute moune moin Bon Dieu . . ."

She was asking that Legba should open the gate for her,
for everyone; to let the good god enter. We answered:

> "Oui, Papa Legba, écoute gros mambo
> Écoute houngan lui pou pauv' neg's 'Nan Guinée
> Ouvri barrié pou entré, prie la vie nou donné
> Fini soucis nou."

Our answer was to say yes, and to ask Papa Legba to listen
to what the great mambo said, what the houngan was petitioning for all the poor ones from 'Nan Guinée, to open the
gates so that we could enter and pray, so that life could send
us an end to our troubles . . .

The kata began the sharp staccato rhythm of the 'zepaules,
classic introduction to the pure dance part of the Arada-
Dahomey ceremony which serves to purify the air and prepare the body for the reception of the loa. One of my
absorbing interests has been the interrelation of form and
function, doubtless sharpened by my Haitian experiences. If
the execution of our doings and the form which this execution takes could be related to a known, conscious function,
then we would be far ahead, it seems to me, in the examination and understanding of human behavior, and closer to the
ability to discriminate in our actions in order to have some

guide as to whether or not what we are doing is for the reason
that we believe it to be. My first preoccupation then being
dance, I was struck by the direct relation between the form
which the movement or floor pattern took and the function
it served in the community or to whatever or whomever the
subject. On the relation between form and function I have
since written elsewhere.

At a given moment Téoline set the rhythm for the
'zepaules. La place catapulted into the air, landed on his
knees, circled the altar kissing the emblems painted on it,
then whirled, bent at right angles, the circumference of the
room, miraculously avoiding vévés and drummers. At each
vévé he lifted arms and legs high in a whiplash movement so
convulsive that we wondered how his head remained attached to his body. He cross-stepped and turned around
himself, flailing the air with arms and legs. These "breaks" or
feints are common at the high point of all ceremonial dances
in Haiti, serving both to release the tension of the dancer and
to clear the air of unwanted spirits. The drummers take complete control of these feints once the dancer has indicated,
consciously or not, that he is ready for them, breaking the
rhythm, sucking air in and hissing it out, ejaculating glottal
sounds which are supposed to beat the "broken" or out-of-
rhythm dancer or group of dancers back in line and to show
that it is they, the drummers, who dominate the rhythms. I
regard the feints as release periods for both drummers and
dancers, and have seen signals calling for the broken beat
pass between the two when one or the other is overtaxed.

Téoline continued singing, emphasizing the rhythm with
her ason. She had handed the bell to a hounci canzo to guard
until needed. Without breaking rhythm she changed from
Erzulie to an Ibo song to the river Artibonite to Aïda
Ouedo in tempting some loa to enter. She pushed her solid
body past us and started to dance. "Ah, Bobo!" we all cried
as La place fell flat and kissed the floor at Téoline's feet. The
houngan Durcel, showing signs of trance, turned slowly then
curtsied, knees together, in a slight dip before Ciseaux. One

by one the attending hounci did the same, and we followed behind. Some hounci were overcome and fell prone before Ciseaux, as La place had before Téoline. Others knelt and placed their wet foreheads on the drumhead, risking injury as Ciseaux, nostrils flaring, muscles distended, beat the gods into the drum with his gnarled stick and with his left hand, the fingers of which were curved as the stick and rough as tree bark. "Ah, Bobo! Ah, Bobo!" we cried in ecstasy perhaps to honor the Bobo-Oulé, oldest tribe of the Upper Volta, formerly a part of Western Sudan. Some of the old ones who spoke "langage," even when not delivering messages from the gods, repeated over and over "Kébiosilie!" similar to a word used in Dahomey and Yoruba ceremonies in Cuba which might be associated with greeting the loa Kehiousu or might be an acknowledgment of royalty, I have never known which. All present, whether sitting, standing, or squatting, began a spasmodic hunching forward and releasing of shoulders, which, when continued for some time, particularly when driven by the piercing beat of the kata, enriched by the broken rhythms of the seconde, and eroticized by the deep, insistent tones of the mama drums, produces a state of mixed lightheadedness and well-being. The forced regular breathing would be autohypnotic under any circumstance, and the uninterrupted monotonous shoulder movement engenders an awareness of self, and acts as a catharsis, along with a sensation of equilibrium between head and chest and, eventually, in a Haitian houngfor, unless restrained by one convention or another, possession. All of us who could crowd into the peristyle—now packed like sardines—shuffled in the warm earth, effacing vévés, raising dust, rocking from side to side as we progressed, knees relaxed, turning now and then with the concentrated shuffling, shoulders moving like pistons of a high-powered locomotive.

The joy of dancing overwhelmed me and I found myself sometimes in front of Doc, at other times in front of Téoline or La place or Georgina in the ruptured movements of the feints, then gasping, stumbling, teetering on the verge of

rhythm- and fasting-induced hypnosis, returning to the sheer
joy of motion in concert, of harmony with self and others and
the houngfor and Damballa and with all friends and enemies
past, present, and future, with the wonders of the Haitian
countryside and with whatever god whose name we were
venerating, because by then a number had been honored and
I had lost track. It was so good in every sense of the word to
dance to the drums of the gods that Sunday in the Cul-de-
Sac, and this feeling of the rightness of these cult dances has
never left me. Now I knew the meaning of the words of
Nietzsche that Erich Fromm had pointed out to me, but the
full meaning of which I wasn't prepared to grasp. Now I was
"out and above and beyond myself," dancing.

Téoline rang the bell and we fell into our seats in front of
the houngfor, sweat pouring from under our headkerchiefs,
face powder streaked or washed away, feet powdered with
dust to our knees, but spirits heightened by the fraternity
of joy that permeated the peristyle. The sharp odor of body
perspiration was exciting rather than disagreeable, as were the
other odors—piment with incense, dust, kola, and grilled
meat. Doc walked unsteadily toward us, speaking in the nasal
voice of Guedé, but somehow we knew that Damballa was
waiting and ignored him. How we knew this I couldn't tell.
Dégrasse came to the doorway of the hut, slender, proud, the
bell and ason in her right hand quivering to announce the
entrance of a loa, an important one. La place mopped his
brow while one of the hounci dried the streaming faces and
throats of the drummers. At the end of the 'zepaules the
tonnelle had been a ferment of heavy breathing, subdued
laughter, uncertain steps until earth was regained after the
off-ground state. When Dégrasse appeared we were immediately silent, tense, expectant.

She spoke a few words in "langage," which sent several of
the hounci whirling like dervishes, then pointed the ason at
Durcel, who, during the 'zepaules, had been to one side leading the answering choruses, sometimes shuffling toward La

place then back beside the drummers. As though hit by lightning, Durcel convulsed, contorted, found his way to Dégrasse and saluted her, grasping her hands, his nails digging into her palms, twisting under her arms while she remained stationary—proof of her control and protocol status. Though we on our benches were not fully conversant with the varied behavior patterns of the gods toward mortals, we sensed immediately that Durcel was about to receive some message of extreme importance, more than likely unpleasant. It is not often that a houngan of high category is thrown about like a simple bosalle, especially in front of an important gathering. I was embarrassed for Durcel and turned my attention to Dégrasse.

Damballa had entered Dégrasse, but he had not possessed her. Among the most authoritative of houngans and mambos, the god is there, speaking through the person but not attempting to take over the person in terms of unlimited control. It is hard to describe the difference between this and the personification possession, but in this detached relationship the devotee becomes the abstracted nonrealistic embodiment of the divinity. I could never, for instance, have imagined Dégrasse slithering over the floor of the peristyle to a saucer of flour with an egg perched on it. And yet in that given moment she was as Damballa, as one could feel or sense Damballa to be, barring imagery. This fine point, I have learned, is the secret of the symbology of Africa, of the black peoples of the world.

Dégrasse raised Durcel from his inclined position and began to speak. The phrases were in rhythm, the bell and ason continued to quiver, Ciseaux began a gentle, broken roll on the mama drum, and the rest of us sat immobile, some understanding, some hoping to understand. I was of the impression that the messages had something to do with La place, with Durcel's relationship to him, and this Doc verified later. Durcel listened, his eyes rolling slowly back until they were nothing but whites, turned ice cold, because somehow one can sense measurable temperature and circulation changes in possession, and sank gently to the ground in either a dead faint or a trance, I wouldn't know which to call it. He was carried inside the houngfor and stayed there until the end of the ceremony. After that, when we saw him at Téoline's or Madame Henri's, he was without La place.

Damballa was there in his majesty in Dégrasse, but he had come to exhibit his virtuosity in the boy playing the kata drum. Durcel was scarcely stretched out and covered with sheets in the houngfor when the youngster threw his sticks in the air, which were caught by a man standing near him in time to continue the accompaniment with the loss of no more than a measure. The boy stood, waved his arms across each other before his face in counter rhythm to that begun by Ciseaux, and slowly sank to the ground in the sinuous serpent movements of the snake god. I felt real panic as he started in our direction, but his attention was on Dégrasse. Head sliding from side to side, tongue darting, he writhed his way past the other drummers toward the priestess. Ciseaux was disgruntled at having his orchestra interfered with, even if by the loa. We all felt that something had to happen that would involve all of us and restore the atmosphere of group worship. Dégrasse never sang on these occasions. Téoline, at the far end of the houngfor, began a song to Aïda Ouedo, Damballa's wife, and the waiting drummers plunged into the rhythm. It was my favorite dance, the yonvalou, dance of humility, assurance, worship, the movements pacific as opposed to the 'zepaules and other more frenetic dances of adoration. I forgot the kata drummer, who had slid past Dégrasse and out of the peristyle. Dégrasse and Téoline were to dance together and honor the loa with their hounci before seeing after the boy who was already lavé-tête and seemed to be in no difficulty. We moved aside, dancing, making way for the two priestesses.

"Damballa . . ."

Téoline's throat swelled as she sang, head and back parallel to the ground, crouching, knees together, hands clutching her dress over each knee. The movement of the yonvalou is slow beside the 'zepaules, Petro, or Ibo dances. It is fluid, issuing from the base of the spinal column, mounting the spinal column to the base of the skull, at the same time penetrating and involving the solar plexus, the plexus sacré, the pelvic girdle, and when this circuit is finished, mounting to the chest and head, drawing the attention of these in an unbroken circuit back to the plexus sacré.

Melville Herskovits has called this the "begging" movement in petition to the gods of Dahomey, and reports the same movement in dance and ceremony there. I have always known it as serpent mimicry. Not long ago I experienced a high point in my career as an anthropologist-researcher when one of the kings of Dahomey brought his wives to Dakar in a dance theater performance, and, among other movements and patterns, I recognized the yonvalou, performed by the massive, steatopygic wives of the king. For anyone interested in the vaudun, the yonvalou becomes its signature. The movement is prayer in its deepest sense. The rhythm is three-four or six-eight. I once wrote of the yonvalou: "There is no tension, not the least rigidity of muscles, but a constant circulatory flux which acts as a psycho-narcotic and catharsis of the nervous system. The dancer is left in a state of complete submission and receptivity."

During the yonvalou we gravitated to partners, outdoing ourselves in undulating to low squatting positions, knees pressed against the knees of someone else without even realizing the closeness, each in his own transported world. I would feint and realize that I had danced with 'ti Joseph as I saw his bullet head turning away, or with Desmène or Georgina. I would salute the drums, then begin again the serpent movement that had brought under its hypnosis all whom the peristyle would hold, as well as bystanders outside. Fred had in all probability gone off to wait and sulk at Doc's compound at Pont Beudette, but in the thick of the crowd Doc and Cécile were squatted facing each other, edging forward by centimeters, foreheads touching. Téoline and Dégrasse, dancing the yonvalou, were respectively like an ocean wave moving to a beach, Téoline overpowering, Dégrasse receiving, yet secure. The kata player was forgotten as others fell to the earth, and the *ki-ki-ki, ric-tic-tic,* and tongue-whirr of the serpent god cut through the drumming, singing, and heavy breathing and cries of "Ah, Bobo" and "Kébiosilie" which filled the peristyle. Téoline and Dégrasse came toward me and we crouched together, touching. Our hot breath, the moist odors of our bodies mingled with perfume and talcum powder were overwhelming; I felt weightless, like Nietzsche's dancer, but unlike that dancer, weighted; transparent but solid, belonging to myself but a part of everyone else. This must have been the "ecstatic union of one mind" of Indian philosophy, but with the fixed solidarity to the earth that all African dancing returns to, whether in assault upon the forces of nature or submission to the gods. I felt sublimely free because I was experiencing the ecstasy without being taken over, "mounted," or possessed. For the Indian guru, sexuality is identified with the "serpent power." I have not been able to ascertain whether or not the symbology of the serpent is consciously sexual to the African, but by its use in decorative or representative art it is surely highly considered. As for Haiti, Damballa has an undisputed position of sexual authority.

Someone discovered the boy who had been playing the kata high in the figuier tree and the dance ended. The two mambos and La place led the way to the tree, cautioning us not to approach too abruptly or to make any efforts at rescue. It took a moment for some of us to compose ourselves, but Dégrasse and Téoline immediately became the efficient, commanding high priestesses they had been for three days and nights in the houngfor. They approached the boy speaking in "langage," while La place turned slowly around the tree, fell flat on his face to kiss the earth at its base, then led the drummers to our houngfor group, which had been called with the other hounci to form a circle around the tree, pressed forward by bystanders. Women selling candies and food placed their wares on their heads and, moving forward, joined in; some people carried chairs from the houngfor and some stood on benches to see over the crowd. All faces were turned upward to Damballa, who had "mounted" the drummer. Téoline and Dégrasse spoke to the boy, shaking their rattles and asons with vigor and authority. There were calls from the assembly, petitions for Damballa to speak, to deliver some special message to some individual or to the group. I was afraid for the boy, and felt the concern of the mambos and La place. A song began and others possessed fell to the ground in possession, writhing through chairs and dust and bare feet to the base of the tree. The boy remained on his precarious perch, legs wound around the figuier branch, waving his arms and again shaking his head in negation in face of the overwhelming homage to Damballa. One wondered what other evidence, what excess the god expected, what it took to appease him and send him away to relieve the boy. We danced the 'zepaules again, then again the yonvalou. The boy, his eyes rolled to the top of his head and froth showing at the corners of his mouth, started to dissolve into the fluidity of the serpent, and began to descend the tree, winding around it head first. It was a formidable feat of acrobatism, and at each pause the crowd beneath broke into cries of delirium, "Ah, Bobo," "Kébiosilie," and "Ki-ki-ki." At each progress of the boy they gasped and moaned and petitioned Damballa for the safety of his "horse." From above, the earth must have seemed like some heaving, primordial monster activated into all of this motion, this heaving and churning, by a blind confusion and intermingling of agony and ecstasy.

The air was heavy with odors, sounds, and the unmistakable presence of an acrid, introverted sexuality aroused by symbolism and gratified in the motor activity of the dance. Ciseaux drove his mallet through the head of his drum in an attack commanding a feint. The sacred drum hanging from the roof of the tonnelle replaced it, and this seemed the signal for an extra burst of frenzy. Skirts whirled in the laillé —the swirling movement of exorcism—bodies pivoting with arms extended and body inclined toward the ground. Head-kerchiefs flew off in all directions or were taken off the heads of bosalle by La place and the mambos to let the loa enter. I stood to one side, exhausted, and watched the base of the tree fill with "horses" of Damballa struggling to climb the trunk. I wondered whether their effort was to reach the boy or to climb to the top branches as Damballa had conducted him. Halfway down the trunk of the tree, which by its forma-tion seemed like a number of trees gracefully grown into one, the boy stopped, gripping the trunk with his thighs, and, arch-ing his body, raised his head and began to speak. I made my way to where Doc was, for translation. Doc knew little "langage" and pieced the message together with the aid of a vendeuse. Damballa wanted to remind everyone there that he was a jealous god, and a powerful one. True, they had danced to him earlier, but the ceremony had opened with another god and the big mambos and powerful priests and priestesses who were assembled there should have known that this day was his and given him first recognition. Aside from that, there were several people assembled there who had been remiss in sacrifices and *service*. Someone must fetch a white chicken immediately or he could not guarantee the safety of the houngfor or its followers. It was all right to take in the foreign girl because her family was from 'Nan Guinée, but she must remember that Damballa stood for no nonsense and expected to be rewarded for his gifts and to be offered at regular intervals the foods and drinks of his taste no matter where in the world she might be. The message to me was delivered in such an emphatic way that I felt the skin on my back tingle and wished that the marriage part had been left unexplored in my research. Then there was a message from an ancestor of Téoline's and a demand for a yam service—the feeding of yams to the ancestors—at the appropriate time.

Someone had scurried off to find the white chicken. Damballa stopped talking, the crowd had become subdued, and I was embarrassed at the scrutiny given me after the message. I tried to become inconspicuous and in the effort found myself near the white cock which La place was talking to and swinging to the four corners of the compass with messages for Damballa. The singing started again and I tried to move out of the crowd, which had gravitated to where the mambos and La place were passing the chicken over people to whom Damballa had delivered special words. I was included, and the chicken, already showing signs of dizziness, had scarcely passed over my body and three times around my head when the kata player slithered from the tree to the ground and in my direction. I was brushing feathers from my eyes and mouth, trying to back away and not caring much whether it looked like retreat, when Dégrasse held the chicken to the boy's mouth. More quickly than I could turn away, he had seized its throat in his teeth, torn feathers and flesh away, and was avidly sucking as much blood as wasn't spurting in all directions. He rose with the chicken still in his mouth, and hounci gathered around to thank Damballa for accepting their offering.

In the tumult of drumming, singing, and exulting I found a way to push through the crowd to Doc and Cécile. I have never fainted in my entire life, that I know of, but I have no memory of leaving the houngfor, of kneeling before my baptized drums, of saluting my co-initiates and the two mambos and La place, then being violently sick to my stomach at Cécile's place before going to bed between her cool, white, pink-embroidered hope-chest sheets. This is the way Doc tells it, or told it to me the next day. In the middle of the night I was awakened by Fred, who had been to Chez Kahl in Pétionville for dinner, no doubt to be as far as possible from the crescendo of the houngfor. He brought with him a ham sandwich on a long piece of French bread, buttered, and I secretly blessed him for this reminder of a world outside the vaudun. Doc told me that before the ceremony ended at sundown all the sacrificial food had been eaten, the mahis, nago, and banda had been danced, Petro Simbi had tried to enter and been sent away, Asaka had come in from the hills with his pipe and knapsack, 'ti Joseph had received

Agwe, Vierge had worn the clothes of Aïda Ouedo, and Georgina had seized the trappings of Papa Guedé and entertained for a half hour before trying to climb on top of Vierge, who was lying on the houngfor floor recovering from her possession by Aïda Ouedo. Téoline had had to intercede and direct the drummers to play the rhythm of the maison to persuade Guedé to leave. He left, promising, to the distress of some, to make the houngfor his pied-à-terre in the Cul-de-Sac. For my part, I could find little difference in Georgina's social behavior after a three-day trial of initiation excepting that what she chose to do was no longer attributed to her, but to her gods, and that she had bestowed upon her a kind of heaven and local sanction for her eccentricities.

Book II

8

For one week after our arising we wore the feathers, sacrificial food, liqueur, orgeat, blood, and other items of our initiation in our hair. Our heads remained bound with our baptismal kerchiefs. Since I wanted no questions asked at the Hotel Excelsior or by friends more curious than sympathetic, I covered the baptismal evidence with a blue headkerchief and sometimes wore a straw hat on top of all this. Titine, chambermaid at the Excelsior, was aware, of course, and wore a wide smile when she saw me unpack my ceremonial clothes. When the week was over, I returned to the Cul-de-Sac for the removal of my head objects. There was no ceremony to this. Téoline kept what she was able to remove from the tangled and matted roots of my hair, knotted the stuff in my headkerchief, and began talking of other things. I am told that a second pot tête referred to by my name remained on the altar of the houngfor until Téoline's death, and this may have been the repository of my lavé-tête leavings, the more serious sacrificial offerings being in my own pot. What Téoline couldn't remove from my hair in one afternoon Titine and I picked at and brushed out and washed out in my room at the Hotel Excelsior. There was no hot water in the Excelsior and I hadn't thought of it until then, water for bathing being constantly tepid from tanks open to the sun. But for this operation Titine was obliged to make the trip of three flights of stairs several times from the charcoal cook fire in front of the servants' quarters—surreptitiously, to avoid questioning by the Rouzier sisters or the Senator. Finally I was free of the remains of the initiation, which by now must have lost their mana. I thought of customs at New York when wrapping my head pot and ason in cotton to be packed later in a cardboard carton. But I needn't have worried. Téoline had promised no problems so long as the articles were with me, and true enough, of the many crates and trunks that were opened and examined when I returned to the United States, those of sacred objects were left untouched. Perhaps it was by the law of averages, but I choose to think otherwise.

Dumarsais Estimé remained unfriendly for some time after my initiation. I missed him, even his aloofness, his caustic attitude toward my social unawareness, my political immaturity; the sarcasm with which he tolerated my adventures into the folk, the cult, and the occult. I knew that his career as a politician was taking form, and rapidly. I also was involved with a personal career.

Preparation for a dance program at the Rex Theatre in Port-au-Prince and the writing of over a year's notes into presentable form for my sponsors took most of my time. The rest of the time I saw some of Haiti, as yet unexplored by me, with Fred or Doc or alone. The struggle between science and art was fermenting even then and the nearest I ever came to a solution to this conflict was perhaps this period when I divided my interests as I chose between the two, and saw no real incompatibility.

In retrospect, I must have been, in my way, in love with the Deputy, and he, in his way, with me. I must qualify for both of us because now I see clearly the force of ambition, not for personal gain in either of us, but expressed in a drive for knowledge and experience and achievement through which to serve some cause, which cause would, if possible, encompass the black race. As I see it now, we were one with the avant garde of negritude. This ambition kept me from too much vexation at Estimé's prolonged absences and him from too much concern over my frequently incompatible behavior. In retrospect I also realize a strong tendency of mine to submerge a large part of emotional sensitivities in the image of my brother, and in Dumarsais Estimé I found many resemblances to him, physical as well as in other ways. This identification with my brother Albert Millard the second in no way diminished the personal and physical magnetism Dumarsais Estimé had for me. To the contrary, on reflection, I might admit that it probably served in some Freudian way as a stimulus. We argued bitterly over my initiation, more bitterly over my mulatto friends, over Fred Alsop, and over the imminent public appearance in a dance concert at the Rex Theatre in Port-au-Prince.

The very things that irked him most were the things that would have prevented our relationship from becoming more serious, that is, conventionalized by marriage, and this the Deputy was wise enough to realize though I was not. At the height of our arguments I might burst into tears of anger, feel comforted at the slightest sign of tenderness, suffer remorse, then continue to do as I always had, which was more or less what I wanted to do or felt destined to do.

I am not sure who originated the plan for a concert at the Rex Theatre. Perhaps the manager, M. Philippe Charlier, who had just built the place and had hopes for it as a concert hall rather than a movie house, and maybe still has. He has since retired from management but is still owner of the Rex. Perhaps the idea was communicated to me by people to whom Melville Herskovits had given some background of my extra-university activities, perhaps it came from me in an effort to compensate for so much involvement thus far in scientific research with so little of the reward I had begun to taste in public appearance. Whatever the impetus, I found time after my initiation to do scarcely more than plan and rehearse the program, the anticipation of which as the date approached took on nightmare proportions.

I have never liked the idea of solo dancing. I suggested to M. Charlier support by a corps de ballet of my friends from the Cul-de-Sac. I could see no reason why traditional material done by those most accomplished in its execution could not be presented at the Rex Theatre in Port-au-Prince if Ruth Page, then ballet mistress of the Chicago Opera, had chosen to rally untrained dancers from the south side of Chicago for group effects in her ballet *La Guiablesse,* in which she starred and in which I danced the supporting role. The management of the Rex Theatre was eloquently opposed to the introduction of this rustic element and I proceeded with my solo program, which opened, as nearly as I can remember, with De Falla's *Fire Dance.* I had thought about performing the *Fire Dance* for a long time and had even started to choreograph it with Ludmila Speranzeva, my teacher and collaborator in efforts to form a Negro dance company in Chicago. I had discarded the idea, finding the music banal. In my search for solo material for this program in Port-au-Prince I was delighted to fall back on De Falla, in spite of my earlier disdain.

I had always admired a Russian Gypsy number of my friend and teacher Ludmila which was convincingly authentic and brilliant when she performed it for us in class, gold hair in two braids, costumed in remnants of her *chauve-souris* theater days. I found the music in Carmen Brouard's vast repertoire —the Gypsy Dance from the operetta *Countess Maritza*— and the costume was made of pieced-together multicolored market handkerchiefs. I wore a kerchief instead of braids, and a number of strands of gold bead necklaces, also from the market. I felt the result to be neither authentic nor brilliant, but the music was played in a stirring manner. I whirled and leapt, and the audience liked it. For a Chopin étude I wore a white full-length tutu, the long dress helping to camouflage my ineptness on point. I had brought my pink toe slippers with me for assurance when feeling too far away from accustomed ballet disciplines, and had won a large audience in the yard of the cottage where I lived with the Maroon people of Jamaica when I clung to the doorframe of the Colonel's house and did échappés or bourrées across the termite-eaten sill. It was quite something else to attempt a full solo number of my own choreography. I wonder now if I didn't have secret hopes of some day joining the corps de ballet of the Chicago Opera, a brown nymph in *Les Sylphides*.

One of Villa-Lobos' *Saudades do Brasil* was accompaniment for a slender mime designed to evoke the image of a distracted nurse trying without success to put a baby to sleep and ending by tossing the baby in all directions, the nurse losing part of her clothing as well as her composure. I cannot now understand the inspiration for this particular kind of farce, but if I am not mistaken the number was a favorite with the spectators. The sensation of the evening, however, was Ernesto Lecuona's *Malagueña*, complete with red ruffled train, tortoise-shell comb, castanets, and purple shoes with Spanish heels made by the shoemaker across from the Boulangerie St. Marc. My share of the program was approximately two thirds of the evening, and in this a section was reserved for Carmen Brouard to appear as instrumentalist. She also played through the intervals when my costume changes were difficult, which turned out to be each one.

Haiti being one of the carnival centers of the world, there was not the problem being costumed one would have thought; add to this a long tradition of fine French dressmaking. Fortunately, because of my vaudun obligations, I had begun preparations and fittings for the dance concert well ahead of time. The main problem was a financial one, and, being at the very end of my already once-renewed fellowship grant, I was obliged to coax the Rex Theatre management into advancing enough money on my "contract" for costume material, and the two seamstresses executing them into waiting until after the affair for their pay, a precedent that went into effect then and hasn't varied in my long theater career since.

My castanets had been given me by Argentinita, greatest of all Spanish dancers. (Only Carmen Amaya could be spoken of in the same breath, and the two were so different that the comparison is hardly worth making.) I was back-stage at the Auditorium Theatre in Chicago after a performance on what turned out to be Argentinita's last tour. She died shortly thereafter.

At this performance I was with two dear friends of hers, my teacher Ludmila, and Vera Mirova who had studied with Argentinita and who shared the Auditorium Building studio where Ludmila and I were striving to forward the idea of equal dance training opportunities for everyone, Negroes included. Some nice things were said about me, backstage at the concert, and, already emotionally upset by the performance of the incomparable dancer, my eyes became moist, I blushed, then suddenly Argentinita had thrown her arms around me, kissed me on each cheek, and pressed a pair of castanets, still wet from her palms, into my hands. She had heard from Vera Mirova that I wanted to study Spanish dancing. Perhaps she was moved by the idea that someone in this far country, someone so near her own color, because her Moorish ancestry was evident, wanted to play castanets. She must also have been sensitive to the trials besetting some-one of that color searching for learning in this particular field in those days.

Before I had seen Argentinita, Quill Monroe, one of the enthusiasts for the pioneering Negro dance company, some-times visitor to the Cube Theatre, had told me of his days touring as partner to the great Spanish dancer. I must have met Quill with Ruth Page or Mark Turbyfill, ballet master of the Chicago Opera. In his northside apartment, literally overrun with some of the first specimens of Siamese cats bred in Chicago, Quill played recordings of Albéniz, "La Niña de los Peines," and, over and over again, especially for me, a sentimental German tango, "Ich Küsse Deine Hände, Mad-ame," entitled in Spanish "Yo Beso Sus Manos, Madame." Whenever visiting Quill I toyed with the castanets he had used while touring with Argentinita, and pored over photographs of the very tall, very thin, very shy young man who had been born somewhere in the midwestern part of North America, had toured Europe as a classical Spanish dancer, and then settled in Chicago to specialize in haute couture for the elegant heiresses of the North Shore. Quill is now living in Switzerland, where I was delighted to see him on the last European tour of the Dunham Company in 1960.

After seeing Argentinita in performance, and even more so after being in close proximity to her backstage at the Auditorium Theatre, nothing would do but that I devote my life to Spanish dancing. Vera Mirova, who had already aroused my interest in Oriental dancing, became my mentor. With her I learned the principles of the painstaking techniques of castanets and heel counterpoint. Perhaps my actual life of theater has not been devoted to Spanish dance because of the wealth of material and inspiration gathered during my first Caribbean experience. Periodically I have returned to its study or private enjoyment but I have attempted to perform it publicly only once since the Rex Theatre in Port-au-Prince.

I didn't know until almost the last moment that the Rex Theatre program was to be shared by a true vedette, a French singer in retirement in Port-au-Prince, billed as from the Opéra de Paris. At first I protested at sharing the program but later was grateful for support on a venture that I felt was beyond my depth. It didn't once occur to me to ask M. Philippe Charlier for the use of the theater for rehearsing. Heretofore I had thought of it only as a motion picture house, or, as one of my companions on excursions into the Haitian hillsides described it, a discreet cover for unfaithful mulatto wives.

I saw little of the historian Dantès Bellegarde during this stay in Haiti, though he and Melville Herskovits were dear friends. I did become friendly, as a sister or companion, with one of his sons, much younger than I. Sometimes, either when I was abandoned by my steady town escorts for some misbehavior or another, or when I myself sought freedom from their shepherding, I might go for long climbs in the hills above the capital with the young Bellegarde, usually accompanied by one of his friends of the same age. They seemed at first unknowing, but from them I learned much about Port-au-Prince élite social behavior, especially the clandestine. For instance, concerning the Rex Theatre as locale for the meetings of some mulatto wife or mistress, "bored to death" in Port-au-Prince, the strategy was so simple as to have been childish. I cannot believe that Haitian husbands were as naïve as their wives and consequently my young friends made them out to be. There was one example of a young man whose practice was to arrive surreptitiously while the family was at lunch and hide under the bed of his mistress until after siesta, at which time the husband would return to his office. This would leave the young man his hour of pleasure, as afternoons seemed safest from surprise returns. Sometimes these closeted waiting periods were enlivened by the disturbances of a husband claiming his marital rights; then the scroundrel under the bed would fume with anger or fight to suffocate bursts of laughter, depending on his relationship with his mistress. Another system was to bribe a 'ti moune, one of the small indentured house servants, who could be counted on to stay awake at night after the household was sleeping, who would give some all-clear signal, open a garden door, and lead the young lover to a latticed balcony or staircase. There, if by chance the master awakened and went seeking his spouse, the culprit could hide in the shadows while the lady led her husband back to bed, finding all sorts of excuses for her night wandering.

The system for clandestine meetings making use of the Rex Theatre was the following. A young matron would ask her confidante or chaperone to accompany her to see a film. Once inside she would leave by the side entrance, tip an usher to be sure the door would be ajar later (because of demand the door was permanently ajar), meet her suitor at a fixed rendezvous, return by the side entrance just before the film was over, and exit with her confidante. As they walked through the aisles, between greeting schoolmates and neighbors the young woman would extract from her companion the details of the film, and chatting and smiling they would walk out into the bright sunlight or gathering dusk and meet a chauffeur, father, brother, or husband to be conducted, still chattering about the film, to the seclusion of a Bois Verna villa or Kenscoff retreat. I thought of these escapades whenever I went to the Rex Theatre, more so because the side door was always slightly open, as though expecting a returning culprit. I am inclined to think that there were few scandals or public accusations because many husbands or fiancés had affairs of their own to attend to, perhaps under circumstances similar to those related by my young friends, or perhaps they simply didn't care enough to activate themselves into a position that might label them cuckolded. It is hard to believe that sooner or later they would not be aware of these goings on. The country is very small, and most of those of one class not interrelated are friends from childhood.

I pleaded with the Rouzier sisters for use of a room for my rehearsals, and for days the salon of the Excelsior resounded with the clatter of castanets and heel beats. The floors were customarily polished every morning by a 'ti moune with a frayed half of a dry coconut husk dipped in beeswax and they shone like tabletops. But underneath the beeswax they were termite-eaten, and here and there holes bored by the hungry insects decorated the pale surface like pockmarks. The first day of my rehearsal of Lecuona's *Malagueña* went well enough because at last some curiosity about my private life was gratified. Pensioners, visitors, and staff crowded to the door of the salon, so absorbed that no one noticed the dust seeping between the antique floorboards. Afterwards Titine and her squadron of 'ti moune did their best to cover the damage for me with coconut husks and beeswax. By the third day the Rouzier sisters asked if I couldn't rehearse without shoes, and by the end of the week I had cloth mufflers over my castanets. I couldn't very well complain about the Rouzier

sisters, as it was a great act of generosity on their part to un-
lock the upright piano, a family heirloom, and permit my
concert pianist accompanist, Carmen Brouard, to touch the
yellowed ivory keys. Pianos in any tropical country are rare,
and Port-au-Prince is no exception. Before long, doors and
shutters were unceremoniously closed by order of the pro-
prietresses as soon as Carmen Brouard tripped up the
veranda steps with her briefcase of music, and gradually the
pensioners who had been delighted by my antics stopped
even nominal greetings in the dining room, hallways, and
stairways. The Senator alone was on my side, asking on every
occasion possible and always in a loud voice how the prima
ballerina was making out and how the ticket sale was progress-
ing. I firmly believe that had it not been for Zépherin my
rehearsals would have been stopped and my presence in the
hotel would have been seriously *non grata*. The Chopin sessions were less trying, and De Falla and Villa-Lobos could
be played half volume and were danced without shoes. So, in
measure, fittings, rehearsals, and a certain amount of ticket
selling, press releases, and public relations took the time that
had heretofore been devoted to research.

The gala evening approached and I put Doc and Fred in
charge of a small group to come in from Pont Beudette. In
the end only Cécile came, sitting by herself in the balcony in
the middle of a dozen seats which had been reserved for my
houngfor friends. Doc and Fred helped carry my costumes
from the hotel two doors away, then stood around backstage,
by curtain time more nervous than I. So often an act or incident in my life has come and gone before I am aware of it.
Earlier I spoke of my attitude toward time and my incapacity
to realize fully the present, of how I feel myself to be like
Alice in *Through the Looking-Glass*, lamenting over a pierced
finger days before the happening, then wondering about all
the fuss others make over it at the actual moment of occurrence. This is the way it was the night of my appearance at
the Rex Theatre. Before I realized it, the evening was over.
There were moments of trauma, of finding myself on stage

going through motions, responding to cues, changing costumes with the help of Titine, and again finding myself on stage going through motions, responding to cues, changing costumes with the help of Titine, and again finding myself on stage. The wait during the program of the former vedette from the Opéra de Paris I remember well. As much as I wanted my part of the program to be on and over with, I felt sorry for her when M. Charlier came backstage, intercepted her rushing through the wings for a third encore, and pointed out that she had long overstayed her time, even her welcome. The plump little singer burst into tears bordering on hysteria, but the front-of-house curtain was lowered with its poster paintings advertising Port-au-Prince shops and businesses—reading material for the public during the intermission.

It was now the moment before my assault on bourgeois Port-au-Prince. Through a crack in the front curtain I could see that they were all there, the only empty seats being those reserved beside Cécile. During the intermission my blood remained congealed in spite of stretches and warm-ups between backstage and my dressing room. With the experience I have now had with audiences such as this one, which I peeked at every two minutes, I know my anxiety was well founded. There is no public more difficult to please than that composed of a society satisfied with itself. There can be nothing new because everything is already known by them or their kind, and any sharing, emotional or otherwise, is reserved for this "in" group. Any sign of enthusiasm is considered ill-bred unless by some automatic response the enthusiasm becomes an expression of herd reaction or follow-the-leader or group solidarity. I have seen audiences hold back on applause, squirm with a desire to express pleasure, but suppress this desire until dynamited into action by some catalyst, some force too strong to resist. This sort of public usually attends gala or special performances to be seen by friends whom they have attempted to outdo in dress or decoration, to be identified with things of "culture," or because of simple curiosity about the performers. Many times

I have smiled into binoculars, even field glasses pointed into the stage from the front row and marveled at the need to penetrate the performer, not by what he imparted, but by drawing him into the orbit of a magnifying lens.

Perhaps I was innocent then of what audiences can be like. That night at the Rex Theatre that innocence or naïveté communicated itself to the assembled élite, engendering sympathy; or perhaps Doc or Fred sneaked into the auditorium and started applause at strategic points. Whatever it was, and it could conceivably have been that my performance satisfied some esthetic or cultural need in that out-of-the-way capital of the Caribbean, after the first number my worries about success were over. I do not remember how the program ended, but there were many curtain calls and for the first time during my sojourn in Haiti I felt that a common denominator had reached black and mulatto. The Lion of the North, Zépherin, was there, smiling and nodding in the front row, and Dr. and Mrs. Price-Mars and the Lhérissons and friends of all colors who in the final analysis must have tempered the accustomed frigidity of élite gatherings. There must have been also at that time the beginnings of a democratic intellectual group, because the next morning bright and early René Piquion, then starting his writing career as reporter for *La Nouvelliste*, woke me for details to complete a brilliant review of the night's performance. René is still a good friend, a brilliant writer, and, although an international diplomat, is the essence of patriotism.

When I next returned to Pont Beudette I asked Cécile how she had liked the concert. Those in our compound who had been reluctant to face the unknown in the capital had heard such lively descriptions from Cécile that it was hard to convince them that they had not been spectators. Cécile exposed in a wide smile a tooth already gold-capped—and the others that one day would be—while 'ti Joseph, Marie Claudine, and Céleste, who sometimes helped keep house for me in the plains, nodded corroboration of Cécile's enthusiasm. They were all in a state of transport and the awed esteem with which they eyed me made me wonder what Cécile had told them. Later I found out that Cécile had returned to wake them with glowing accounts of my long golden curls, my full, high, laced-in bosom, the high, sweet voice with which I had charmed a large collection of people gathered at a special *service*. They were convinced that La Sirène had manifested herself in me. Cécile had left when the front curtain came down for the intermission. She had continued to clap with joy long after others of the audience had descended from the balcony, and then she had taken the camionette to Pont Beudette, thinking the *service* was finished. I explained about the French singer and her wig of golden curls, her gold lace *grande robe de style*, but no amount of persuasion could move Cécile from her story that Mademoiselle had been transformed into La Sirène, goddess who lives at the bottom of the sea with her grandmother Nana and her consort, Agwe, and who sings to sailors, causing storms so that they drown unless offerings are made to her.

It was after the Rex Theatre that I began to feel I had a place in Haiti not confined to research or to my friends of the Cul-de-Sac. These latter have always remained closest in my affections, and are often the reason for my returns to the island; but the mulatto class which I had heretofore eyed with suspicion, aside from a few individuals whom I considered exceptions, became less remote, less enigmatic. People I did not know phoned the Hotel Excelsior the following morning to congratulate me on the performance, and after the article by René Piquion in the morning paper I knew that my position was no longer ambiguous, that my nonconformist behavior would be attributed to artistic temperament. This was not the case with the President of the Chamber of Deputies. He proved to be far more conservative than the class most despised by him, and not until long after was the performance forgiven. In some numbers I appeared lightly clad—word of which had reached him—but more than that I had entertained members of the opposition party, had misused his friendship and courtship. By the time I was forgiven

I had left Haiti, toured Europe and Mexico, and returned at the request of Dumarsais Estimé, President of the Republic of Haiti, to be decorated in the name of the Haitian Government. Estimé's attitude was reminiscent of that of my family. With Albert Senior and Annette Dunham it took years of achievement and public recognition before the stigma of public entertainment as a profession wore off and the artist was once more accepted as a person.

The strongest motivating force beneath Estimé's rancor was the common Haitian *maladie*, the sickness under the total social structure of Haiti today, insofar as it has not changed due to the present dictatorship. This is the mulatto-black dichotomy, which approximates a caste system. I have referred to it earlier without explaining its proper background, but the composition of the audience of the Rex Theatre, my compulsion to perform there at that time, and the reaction of my Deputy friend, who was at the same time intellectual guide, made me attempt to understand a system that is hard for an American to grasp, even though living close to prejudices of color and religion at home.

With the Haitians' freedom from the French and therefore white colonial domination, the hatred which had served as a unifying force of tribes and nations scarcely able to communicate with each other turned inward into the country itself. The drama between the mulatto and the black slave, who had played a leading role in freeing the country, began. The mulatto was in an embarrassing position because of a history of recorded illegitimacy, but at the same time he was in a superior position because he had been franchised and given financial security and education outside the country by the white slaveowner who was his father. The blacks had the advantage of not bearing the degrading epithet of "sang mélé," but they were automatically judged inferior because of having been born into and retained in slavery. The one small group that perhaps prevented this classification of Haitian society from becoming a caste system in the strictest sense of the word was the freed blacks. But in a looser sense of the word "caste," and allowing for a reasonable fluctuation, the mulatto has been endogamous, inherits his position and guards it as a sign of social superiority. Manual labor, tilling of the soil, open practice of the vaudun are for the black masses. Before emancipation it was the custom for a franchised mulatto to own black slaves, but a freed black seemed to feel a certain fastidiousness about owning mulatto slaves and there is no such case on record. Alike to the mulattoes in aspirations and ambitions, the small group of freed blacks managed to maintain an equal though separate social and economic position. The ambivalence of these groups may account for the continuous unrest of the country, a personality separation which some psychologists are inclined to call a national psychosis.

The mulattoes of Saint-Domingue were off to a bad start because of the example of the white colonials. A few of the resident plantation owners were of French aristocracy, the rich bourgeoisie, and the military, and directed their own properties, living in elegant town houses in Cap-Haïtien, Port-de-Paix, and later Port-au-Prince, or on the plantations themselves, the main houses of which emulated Malmaison or St. Cloud near Paris. A larger part of the plantation owners were represented on the island by intermediaries or caretakers and lived in Paris or its suburbs—as did Joséphine Bonaparte whose vast Beauharnais properties were managed for her by Toussaint L'Ouverture during his governor-generalship—or in the provinces of France. The majority of the landowners, however, were white creoles, born on the island, direct descendants of the lowest class of adventurers, pirates, and filibusterers. These were known as grands blancs, were crude, with no education themselves and no plan for the education of their progeny, extravagant and vulgar in taste and incredibly cruel to their slaves. Because these grands blancs formed the pressure group in segregating the freed mulattoes from white society, their mores became the mores of the mulatto population, as though the fact that they had embraced libertinism, debauchery, despotism, ostentation, and the popular slogan that "to be free is not to work" would place them automatically above slaves and give them social equality with the whites. It was this separatism between white and mulatto which won the freedom of Haiti, because, as blacks of divergent nations united in hatred, so in the end, when it became clear that the re-establishment of slavery as ordered by Napoleon would not improve their situation, mulattoes who had fought bitterly against the black generals sided with them to expel the French, who by then had suffered heavy losses, having left more than fifty thousand dead behind them in the effort to reconquer the island. This collaboration was for a brief period and was solely for the purpose of freeing the island from French colonialists. During the years since the victorious revolution the black Haitian seems never to have forgotten the mulatto dictatorship established by André Rigaud, mulatto, or the fact that the intention of mulatto landowners was that while whites were to be abolished, blacks were to remain subordinate. Even of Toussaint, then Governor General of the island, Laveaux, the mulatto governor of the southern part of the divided island, is reported to have said:

> "All mulattoes and free Negroes of long standing are enemies of emancipation and equality. They cannot conceive that a former Negro slave can be the equal of a white man, a mulatto, or a free Negro."

The above quote is from Ralph Korngold's *Citizen Toussaint*. Further illustrating mulatto betrayals of mulattoes, and blacks of blacks, the author quotes from Robespierre what is applicable to another anomaly of the Haitian people, an explanation of many failures in attempts at invasion by exiles today—a mistrust of one's own class:

> "Men would rather submit to masters themselves than see the number of their equals multiply."

The mulattoes planned that they, not the Negroes, were to

be the inheritors of French authority. Toussaint, on his part, never failed to press home to the mulattoes their betrayal of the ideal of total freedom. He accused:

> "Your intention is to exterminate the whites and subjugate the blacks . . ."

When one realizes that on the eve of a liberation that set an example of freedom and courage for the rest of the world the mulatto leaders were ordering their soldiers to fight to the death rather than collaborate with the blacks, one begins to grasp better the happenings in Haiti since that date. The legacy was not an easy one to live with. The creation of the privileged mulatto class as reassurance against slave revolt may have given the governing colonials some peace of mind but it seems to have proved inadvisable for the evolution of a homogeneous society. The drama of mulatto and black began in Haiti with the struggle for equal rights and is probably closer to resolution than ever today, deplorable as the methods may have been, being founded on violence and despotism. More isolated each day from the civilization which we call "developed," Haiti seems to have blended hatreds of color into hatreds of class. In a historic struggle the army, which since Independence has known as many black generals as mulatto, has been shorn of its strength and, like Samson, made ineffective, fettered to the pillars of the National Palace by the Ton-ton Macoute, President Duvalier's militia. Because the percentage of mulattoes in the country is less than five percent (it may have been higher before the exodus during the Duvalier regime) one would expect to see, and does see today, more black than mulatto functionaries. Once this was not so. Even so, in spite of what has been called a "purge" of the élite, a large percentage of mulattoes remain, and one wonders, now that the target for hate has been removed, if it isn't fear that binds the pact. The natural consequence of such concentrated fear is hatred, in this case of the foreigner, of the color white, as in the days before 1804, of any one threatening to bring about a return to colonialism, as some feel happened during the American Occupation. There is bravery in the struggle of the tiny black republic to keep a voice in the events of the world in face of overwhelming economic odds and isolation, self-imposed or not. But there is something deeply sad in the regression to terrorism for political control.

9

I have always associated Haitian Presidents
of importance with "culture heroes." I say "of importance"
because since independence from the French, Presidents have
come into office by vote and gone by natural death, un-
natural death, revolution, timely flight, forced exile, but only
a few have achieved importance in the social and economic
evolution of the country, or even remained a full term. From
1936 to 1966, the period that I have known Haiti, there have
been three Presidents whom I would consider of importance,
no matter that this importance may be considered from positive and progressive to negative and regressive. It may be that
the present President, François Duvalier, will be noted in history simply for the length of duration of term and reinter-
pretation of existing laws to bring this about, and all else
will be forgotten or put to one side as a part of the politics
and turmoil of the world in general, or he may be remembered as an activist of negritude whose culture hero is Jean
Jacques Dessalines. I call these hero references "culture heroes" because, though the heroes were real ones of flesh and
blood in man's history and memory, they became riders of the
hills, phantoms, men wrapped in obscure African mysticism,
unreal because their deeds grew by word of mouth in a country where few could read, and because the deeds themselves
were outside the comprehension of actuality, and were even,

when examined dispassionately and much later, close to the realm of the supernormal. But more interesting than the associations that I have made, whether of identification or emulation, these Presidents themselves, all three of whom I have known to a lesser or greater degree of intimacy, give every evidence of having been or of being aware of this phenomenon. The mixed tenses are because one is dead, one is in exile, and one is currently President of Haiti.

The child Estimé one can imagine poring over what history has recorded of Toussaint L'Ouverture. Both were inclined to be sickly, ruminative, self-educated beyond primary training, and imbued with the idea of disseminating humanism. Paul Eugène Magloire, President of the Republic from 1950 to 1956, I have seen stand balanced beneath a portrait of Henri Christophe, man and portrait exuding authority through sheer African male impact, physical charm, personal dignity, both drunk at the height of power with the good things of material wealth, of pleasure excess, that European-inspired manipulation of the Haitian peasant had bought for them. For François Duvalier, Dessalines is the mold that cast him. Identification is more obscure, emulation the driving force, to say nothing of deeper, more esoteric covenants rumored to have been pledged and executed through the incarnation of the essence of Dessalines, betrayed by a trusted officer and murdered at Pont Rouge outside Port-au-Prince, his body brutally desecrated. These rumors soon die down in Haiti, but it is by order of Duvalier that the date of the death of Dessalines has become a national holiday and a ceremony is performed at Pont Rouge. A flame burns day and night before the tomb of Dessalines, the contents of which were once removed and placed elsewhere. That is, the contents were supposed to have found a new resting place, but rumors go even further and say that they have since been disinterred and put to ceremonial black magic use. This sort of story runs rampant in Haiti at all seasons and must inevitably reach the attention of wandering news reporters. It takes some time in Haiti to know what to discard of the lurid word-of-mouth scandal sheet, typical of any community living in insecurity and confined by illiteracy.

All three of the culture heroes dealt in blood, but of the three, Toussaint L'Ouverture, Henri Christophe—later King Henri I—and Jean-Jacques Dessalines, the first was the only one free of despotism, from savagery, who did not revert to the primitivism that keeps Africa from being a body of united nations today. When speaking of Toussaint L'Ouverture we speak of an educated man, but more than this, we speak of a man of culture. Toussaint, a coachman, a house servant, was self-educated. Another part of him must have been inherited from a past of which we know nothing excepting rumors of royal parentage; a great deal of his charisma was that mysterious thing which makes for unelected culture. By knowledge, by passion, by brain he created an army for the French out of fragments and engineered it to such discipline that he became a menace to the security of the empire-minded French. (The fact that he met his enemy as gentleman to gentleman on the fateful night of his betrayal, the fact that his sensitivity of spirit, his belief in some essential core of goodness in man would not arouse his primitive, in the sense of intuitive, self-protective nature, is to his credit as a man.) He preferred to think well of men, even his enemies. Somewhere, somehow, in his inner being, having lived among and known so well these white men come to claim friendship and take him as prisoner, he must have been aware of his imminent betrayal, and been prepared. He must have known that so far as he could go the battle was won. White would die here, black there; black at the hand of black, white at the hand of white, to say nothing of colors mixed, as there always had been and always would be. And seeing ahead—because if any of these three was gifted with the prix-des-yeux it was Toussaint—seeing the ignoble fall of Christophe, the never-ending blood lust of Dessalines, the continuous revolution and constant hunger of his beloved people, until they didn't know that they were hungry but thought it a natural state of being, and the murder of statesmen by poison or witchcraft or ambush or trickery, he must have felt his heroism slip from him like the chrysalis of an uncertain victory as he left his battle cloak on the quay of Port-de-Paix and with some relief moved forward toward the guest warship which waited to take him, instead of to a fête on board, to prison. With this same clairvoyance, in his prison cell in the *Jura*, he must have seen his beloved island as it is today, witch-hunted from without and within, with fear so a habit that people who read, educated people, speak of not buying *foie* at the best markets because it "comes from the public hospital." Such a man as Toussaint was Dumarsais Estimé, as I knew him, but let us talk about the last of the triumvirate, the one in power now, François Duvalier.

A chemical change seemed to have taken place between my first meetings with François Duvalier in 1956 and the last time that I saw him, which was in 1962. This change produced a physical and, I would suppose, a personality change which may explain the enigma of the man. Most photographs of him are highly uncomplimentary, which is a privilege the press of the system seldom waives when making a point. The thick lenses of his dark glasses, his full lips, a gray coloring which films a natural color and which, it is true, seemed to seep through his pores at our last encounter, make ample material for photographic detracters. In his pictures one wonders at times if Duvalier goes out of his way to *be* Baron Samedi, not just possessed by him or by Dessalines, or is he just that good a comédien? I wondered this as I watched him enter the Palace auditorium where I sat on the rostrum and he in the front row at a dedication in honor of the Haitian poet Carl Brouard. During the endless reading of eulogies I had time to examine squarely and closely the man just then taking definitive steps toward creating the breach between Haiti and the United States, who was creator and sponsor of a band of hoodlums not so skilled as those of Adolf Hitler but every bit as zealous, and in a way more ruthless. The President of the Republic seemed like a relative sev-

eral times removed from the man who had visited Leclerc
with Madame la Présidente and his army guard four years before, and who had so graciously received me at his Palace offices, talked national health and anthropological research,
finally decided that I should graduate from the post of Chevalier in the Haitian Legion of Honor conferred on me by
Dumarsais Estimé in 1949 to Commander *Grand Officier* in
the same order, and arranged for a wide ribbon and heavy
cross to be placed around my neck by my old friend the
psychiatrist-statesman Louis Mars, Minister of Foreign Affairs, later Ambassador to the United States from Haiti and
now Ambassador to France. Here before me was the man
chemically, physically, and in personality, from what I heard,
so changed as to be in effect another man. But at least he was
there in the flesh to deny current rumors that the final payment at the tomb of Dessalines had left the body but not the
soul, or that he had been done in by his own creatures and
zombie-ized—that is, made into a controlled robot, the dead
come to the fringes of life. This was a man all right, but a man
who had been extremely ill, physically, perhaps, and I had
heard about that, but mostly morally and spiritually. Not ill
with a broken heart for home and country as Estimé had been
when he died in the Henry Hudson Hotel in New York but
ill with the Faustian bargain and its price; and I see no difference when the changeover of chemistry and personality are
made whether they are due to real or symbolic acts; the effect
on man and society seems to be about the same. My glances
in his direction were not acknowledged.

For two years I stayed in Haiti, planning and planting and
digging and building at Habitation Leclerc, and though I
sent more than one letter requesting an audience, for reasons
which at the time seemed crucial, the Chief of State maintained a stony silence. Uneasiness was mounting to hysteria
among most of the people I had known outside my circle of
houngfor and plains and mountain friends, and they were
leaving the island as fast as they could and under any pretext,

abandoning goods, position, sometimes family. It was as though the man in the Palace had only to be there, and his high-buttocked, gun-hauling phalanx only to walk through the streets, and a hush would fall, or a store go out of business, or a bar close. Boats were fewer and fewer in the harbor. People would get off them for only a few hours, sometimes for only a few minutes, tourists in outlandish getups cackling and fluttering and clustering together, drawing away in fright from beggars, from yaws, which had had a resurgence due to the wiliness of staphylococci in dodging penicillin, melting into terror when taken out of their courses by Ton-ton Macoute taxi driver guides who made a confidence game of pretending to be out of the class of simple taxi drivers but insisted on playing guide, procurer, gigolo, escort, and business manager to the helpless tourist.

On that visit in 1962 uneasiness crept to the very boundaries of Leclerc, and I too might have joined the panic and closed shop had not a strange thing happened. Whether due to the magic of Habitation Leclerc, which abounds in springs reputedly seeping up from the sunken continent of Atlantis, or because of some respect that scholars have for each other or that sorcerers have for each other, Leclerc was left out of the figurative tidal wave that stripped the Hotel Roosevelt, vandalized villas and plantations, bankrupted thriving businesses, impoverished the rich in providing comforts for the newly created, ever-hungry machine of strong men. These men are known as Ton-ton, or "uncle," Macoute, "big stick." In anger and exasperation, before I had been made aware of what I was dealing with, I had driven a band of such men from Leclerc while our constantly busy masons burrowed in their cement and rocks, carpenters found reason to begin frantic hammering, and guardians found reason to scale palm trees to test ripe coconuts just to avoid being called to the aid of the mistress of Leclerc. Only much later did I realize how often I had committed the unpardonable, said the unforgivable, done the unacceptable. But it was as though Habitation Leclerc lay in a circle of protection, and being reasonably de-mystified at the time, I could only attribute this protection to the awareness and delicacy of the President, graciousness and sentimentality going hand in glove with the reportedly ruthless extermination of enemies, real and imagined. This character juxtaposition I consider one of the strongest traits of Duvalier. I am not important enough to be afraid of, nor interesting enough to be wooed as some American tycoon might have been. I was simply left alone, as were all of mine, as was Habitation Leclerc, and it was as if this circle of protection emanated from the Palace on the Champs-de-Mars, unsolicited. There must be until now some Haitians who, I suspect, regard this untouchedness as collaboration. Others have told me that the only group that might be called "opposition" in Haiti today is the Estimistes, followers of and believers in and disciples of the teachings or at least reform measures of Dumarsais Estimé, and that this group has always respected the long and deep friendship between the former President and me, and acts as a buffer between the new psychosis and some few who represent the old and good way of thinking.

One thing can be said in favor of François Duvalier, and I believe that even bitter enemies will substantiate this. Unlike Christophe's dauphin, Paul Magloire, he is not nor ever has been motivated by avidity for material things or good living at the expense of the populace. Today there is so much to hide behind, so he may have the largest bank holdings in Switzerland or Montevideo, but I doubt this. For one thing, I have had too much experience with the costs of supporting an "extended family." In my case it was a theatrical company, in Duvalier's case it is a private, newly established army, or, one might say, a whole class split off from upper proletariat and lower bourgeoisie and made into an army police power structure. This takes whatever financing might be filched from within or extracted in handouts from sources without. If this does not go on—and I have no personal evidence, only testimony of those claiming to have been burned—I would be surprised because that would make Haiti indeed unique. So I would say that while Haiti's present President may have been driven successively by need for personal aggrandizement, then power, then to hold the power, then fear of losing it, then fear for life, he has not been one of those to commit whatever the syndicated press and expatriated countrymen attest to his having committed for material gain. And while there has been a dehumanization in process at one level, we might ask of this new class recently created, were they ever "human," in the sense of knowing or experiencing humanism. It seems likely that the dehumanization began with the revolution and carried on through independence and until today. I am not speaking of the Haitian peasant, who seems reasonably untouched by this *folie* of the governmental superstructure, but of those who are periodically brought into the inner structure of the government to execute deeds of violence for some insecure, fear-ridden, hate-filled or essentially brutal leader. Dessalines surrounded himself with a militia of laborers rather than have to depend on the Army, which, though respected by him as a general does his soldiers, he did not trust and he mistreated. Duvalier's mistrust of the Haitian Army stems from its "betrayal" of Dumarsais Estimé, in whose cabinet Duvalier served.

Modeling after heroes seems to be inherent in the nature of man. The total change of personality evidenced, whether in the houngfor possession by a loa, or in a communion such as Duvalier is rumored to have been having with the ghost of Dessalines, becomes pathologically dangerous and risks retrogression. That Duvalier himself, scholar and scientist that he is ("Papa Doc" is a true medical doctor, graduate of Cornell University), must have recognized the dangers of drowning in another man's image I do not doubt, were it a fact, just as I feel that he was coming out of the shadow of the valley of death the day that I saw him, in a state of recent resurrection from some deep and soul-shaking experience. If the identification and emulation of Duvalier with Dessalines is as complete as I have indicated, it might have been in the culture hero sense, then it would only be reasonable that this would carry through to fear of, and therefore every effort to protect himself from, the kind of betrayal and violent death that was Dessalines' fate. Thus he would justify supporting a private army made up of non-military men.

There is no doubt that Haiti was left with strong revenge feelings after the Magloire regime which preceded Duvalier, leaving out the brief revolution governments in the interim. The inheritance of Dessalines was the aftermath of a period in which the slaves had been all too aware of the libertinism and frivolity of the colonials; there had been a brilliant but superficial society, built on suffering and inhumanity. The worst legacy was hatred for the former tyrants. After Magloire the situation was essentially the same and the material with which Duvalier had to work was, if considered objectively, much the same. There were three governments within as many weeks, bloodshed, witch-hunting, revolution, and the fear that governs all Haitian mass feeling, that of a change in the Constitution, particularly the part of it designating powers of the Chief of State and a restricted mandate. Whether or not it is true that Paul Magloire built a private fortune during his tenure of office I do not know, but it is highly rumored, and certainly the country had been impoverished economically and to some degree culturally when Duvalier took over. The world at the end of the eighteenth and beginning of the nineteenth centuries, the time when the Haitian revolution was won and Dessalines became Emperor, was in a state of turmoil and violence. The pattern of the French revolution had its effect on the Haitian people, as did the American revolution, in which many of them fought. Voltaire's ideas of the rights of man reached even the freed slaves, but it is my impression that it has never been digested by most Haitian leaders or fully understood in its reciprocal obligations by the people. Freedom became a reality by violence, and this "took" like the most successful of vaccinations.

Of physical comparisons between the first black ruler of

Haiti, Jean Jacques Dessalines, and the present President there is not much similitude excepting that both were of average height. Dantès Bellegarde, who later became President of the Constitutional Assembly but is better known as author of the most dispassionate current book on the Haitian people, *Histoire du Peuple Haïtien, 1942–1952*, describes Dessalines as being tireless of body, with the "élan and speed of a lion." Duvalier must have an iron constitution, but gives the impression of being phlegmatic. Perhaps this physical dissimilarity has led me to classify Estimé-Toussaint, Magloire-Christophe kinships as identification, while Duvalier's seems a confusion of identification and emulation. The conditions under which Dessalines and Duvalier came into office have some similarity, as I have pointed out above; both natures follow the lines of fanaticism, of immediate and unequivocal retribution coupled with generous sentiments. Dessalines could not alone fill the mission of organizing the political and economic life of the nation, and while the same is indicated in present Haiti, the results of Duvalier's tenure-for-life remain to be seen. Each surrounded himself with an untrained coterie, reducing the moral and material strength of the established army and creating a militia from the proletariat. In each régime the predominant classes are two, the militia and the laborer. Each man requires dictatorial power without limit. Like Dessalines, Duvalier is aware of the corruption and pillaging by his functionaries, but the downfall of Dessalines came when he threatened to break the control of his entourage, and this Duvalier has chosen to do and more than likely he will never risk the attempt. Both allowed no dominant religion by law, and both allowed liberty to cult worship, participating themselves, according to rumor. Both reserve the right to judge by a special council anyone suspected of treason or plotting against the Chief of State, the Constitution, or the public order. Each had admired greatly and been influenced by a person of intellect, even culture, Dessalines by Toussaint, Duvalier by Estimé.

But each strayed afield from the original precepts of his mentor, and fell into ways of control by uncompromising force.

Both hated white people, especially if associated in any way with endangering the freedom of the country. Dessalines massacred all the remaining white colonials as a first act; Duvalier fostered an anti-white anti-Americanism that I almost fell victim to when dealing with petty functionaries, in spite of my color, honorary decorations, honorary citizenship, and years as an adopted daughter of the country. Both have what Bellegarde has described, in Dessalines, as the "fury and cunning of the race," though, I repeat, it is hard to imagine Duvalier giving external evidence of this rage. He simply issues orders that must come from fiery inner torments or convictions. Both acquired the houses and plantations of the rich and distributed them at nominal rentals to the functionary class newly created, many of whom were illiterate. Both dreamed of isolation, Dessalines constantly fearing attack from the French; Duvalier, and rightly so, invasion from Haitian refugees backed by finances that may or may not have their source in the American system, as he claims. (It is hard not to listen to his argument, given the Cuban Bay of Pigs incident as a precedent.) Both have allowed a feeling of insecurity to take hold of the populace, and each let flourish around him pure anarchy and despotism. Bellegarde specifies in Dessalines' case a "dispersed, impersonal despotism; the worst of all tyrannies," which was certainly the kind current among the Ton-ton Macoute when I was last in Haiti. Dessalines notoriously loved only himself, and my reaction to François Duvalier when I last saw him was that preoccupation with self had risen to the surface as a dominant part of his present nature. But again I cannot help but make every effort to see the man as a product of his times and pressures, as so many have seen Dessalines, despot though he was. The American press stresses political murder, torture, and assassination; but then are we not, as the French have pointed out, *tout assassins?* And the Haitian peasant seems to have been left with his dignity; also, there has been no mass extermination. So in spite of the psychosis that has pervaded the country as long as I have known it, perhaps there is hope. At any rate, since this writing, I have resolved to cry out to the next complaining expatriate, "This is *your* monster! You have created it, live with it, don't be afraid to die if you feel it pulling you and yours into the dark ages!" But I know that I won't say it, because when I am there I know the feeling, and am sick at heart, if I step outside the boundaries of Leclerc, simply because I have known less troubled times and have been so close to one who shared with me his hopes and aspirations for his country and his people. It is impossible for me to think of what is happening in Haiti as due to one man, and this is why this comparative history interests me.

Dessalines, wooing the mulattoes, some say, but surely wanting to solidify himself with the disgruntled army, proposed his daughter, Célestine, in marriage to Pétion, general first under the French, then under Toussaint. Pétion, aware of an ill-fated liaison between a subordinate of his and Dessalines' daughter, and for reasons of his own, declined. Recently the daughter of Duvalier was married in considerable pomp and splendor to an army captain. There will be more about my encounters with President Duvalier when I describe Habitation Leclerc.

Colonel Paul Eugène Magloire, one of the three of the military who had "denounced" Estimé, that is, "advised" his resignation as President of the Republic, which resignation and subsequent exile was effected May 10, 1950, resigned from his military and ministerial offices in time to become a successful candidate for the presidency. His tenure was for a single term, but like his predecessors a taste of power and in his case good living led him to suggest constitutional reforms and re-election. Six years after taking oath of office the President fled the country with his immediate family and has since lived in New York, at times, gossip says, masterminding dreams of invasion of the island, and in a pretty continuous state of fear for his life. Whatever the truth of the matter, I am sure that he is living well, because that was one of 'ti Paul's talents. There is no doubt that Paul Magloire meant what he said in his presidential speech, that regardless of any personal sacrifice he would execute the "heavy privilege which had been confided in him," that his plans and aspirations were for the evolution of the Haitian people. Though accused by his detractors of misuse of government funds, libertinism, and excesses due to alcoholism, Paul Magloire brought about some incontestable improvements. What pothole-weary traveler hasn't welcomed the asphalting of the new road to Pétionville, the highway just short of being completed to Cap-Haïtien. Like Christophe, Magloire believed in overland communication; like Christophe, he believed in the land as the ultimate hope for economic stability. His electoral speech included some lightly veiled allusions to the predecessors who emphasized other solutions. Undoubtedly some of these referred to Estimé, who believed in the importance of public relations with other countries, in tourism, in preparing the country for this as an asset. Agricultural loans and aid to peasants were a part of the Magloire platform. He fell short of his dream partly because of the people with whom he dealt, partly because he was primarily a soldier and being a soldier is not always being a statesman.

The Cité Magloire was one of Magloire's dreams. I am not sure that it has ever been completed, at least not along the lines that the President intended. I visited it at a bad time—that is, psychologically—for me. I had just returned from a long, hard eighteen months' tour of South America, had undergone an appendectomy in Jamaica, and was recovering from the shock of guilt at having smuggled an innocuous letter from Dumarsais Estimé, exiled in Jamaica, to someone in Haiti who might be able to solve his really drastic financial problems. I was never able to overcome my feeling of apprehension about the smuggling. At the last moment the document went through customs formalities tucked away in the valley of the ample bosom of Ann Smith, then my Girl Friday and confidante. I felt that under the circumstances I shouldn't be making friends with a successor President, but like Henri Christophe, Paul Magloire was hard to resist. He was handsome of face and figure, black as was Christophe, personally attractive, and like Christophe he had a weakness for English and American people and language.

In addition to feeling apprehensive, I was still in a state of trauma after seeing Buenos Aires and Evita and Juan Perón, chiefly Evita. I had visited the Señora's public and social works at her invitation, but I was also a performer there, seeing much of the seamy side of their support of the "descamisados," having many friends among those of the class hated by Evita and consequently Perón, the aristocracy of Argentina. After a benefit for the "Benefactoress," a command performance at the Colón Ópera, I was literally ordered the following morning to review the orphanage, various nurses' training schools established in the confiscated homes of some of my friends, the refuge for prostitutes or mothers without husbands where one or two complained bitterly to me as though I could waive their, literally, prison sentence. Evita was anathema to prostitutes, whose profession is practiced with great dignity in most Latin countries. The result of her cleaning up was a scourge of male prostitutes, but that was after her death, which was not so long after our departure from South America and the Magloire period of which I am speaking. The Cité Magloire, and many of the social works of 'ti Paul and his actively religious, strongly Catholic wife (as was Evita Perón until denied papal nobility, reportedly because of obscure birth and questionable behavior prior to her marriage to the President of Argentina), made me think of the appeasement-by-building pattern that so many countries fall into today. The architecture is there as a monument, but surely the pyramids fulfilled their intention more completely. Though my thesis here is Haitian Presidents and culture heroes, I have never thought of Paul Magloire and Madame la Présidente without associating them with the Peróns. There was that same error in thinking that doling out pesos or gourdes personally would endear one to the population—the attempt to buy a people. I had been too close to that in Buenos Aires to appreciate it in Haiti. And, strangely enough, this is said with a real sentiment for Evita Perón. I could not agree with her, often questioned her actions, but I understood her and, in a way, mourned her death.

Paul Magloire and his wife were good friends to me and my family, to my entourage, which then consisted of secretaries, ladies-in-waiting, fifteen members of the Dunham Company and business managers visiting from New York, Argentine orchestra conductor, pianist-composer, and others. Habitation Leclerc had just been acquired in 1950, I was there ostensibly to recuperate from the appendectomy which I have mentioned before, and, while rallying to the defense of Dumarsais Estimé, then in refuge in Jamaica, had announced my intention to ask further protection for him and his family from the Governor of Jamaica—named Dunham, if I am not mistaken. The President of Haiti must have known of my friendliness with his political enemy, but at no time mentioned it. My recuperation period did not keep me from renewing my old acquaintance with Cécile, seeking those who couldn't be found or were dead like Téoline and Dégrasse, rehearsing the company for a benefit performance for the charitable works of Madame la Présidente (I feel sure that more of the receipts went as promised than in the case of the command performance at the Colón Ópera in Buenos Aires), and taking some interest in the public works of Madame Magloire.

Most striking of my experiences in these public works was when I had gone to the Saute d'Eau at Ville Bonheur for a vaudun reaffirmation. In July the protectress of Haiti is venerated at the cathedral of the small village where she is said to have appeared in miracle form, and at the same time, a half mile away, the multiple gods of Haiti come forth from the highest waterfall in the Caribbean to talk to their devotees. I had dared to spend two nights beside the waterfall on territory reserved for the loa, not able to sleep for the sound of the fall, soaking from the spray that reached at least two hundred feet from the water, eaten by mosquitoes that seemed to be having their first meal of the season, and more shaken by periodic visitations from the loa than I care to admit. I rode from the waterfall to the village on the white horse of a guide-chauffeur vaudun friend who had also been an Estimiste and who for this reason felt some protective interest in my welfare. The village was all in festivity as much for the loa as for the Virgin. The presidential entourage had arrived, and hearing that I was there, Madame la Présidente had asked for me. I regretted leaving the fall, because pilgrims were arriving, but I well understood her need when I arrived at the Social Works dispensing station, which happened to be this time the front gallery of a modest caille.

Madame Magloire was, and I presume still is, a woman of a beauty combining worldliness, *chic* as the French use the word, wit, and with it all a virginal and childlike quality that made everyone rally to her during the decline of her husband's popularity and sympathize with her when 'ti Paul's escapades became embarrassingly public. This day she was in a state of utter confusion, and I thought immediately of one of the times when I had assisted at the distribution of peso notes by Evita Perón. The small gallery was surrounded by suspicious, incredulous, demanding peasantry from the village and its isolated countryside. That the wife of the President, whose name I am sure many of them did not know, would in person be distributing blue denim pantalons and jumpers, straw hats, and gourde notes was in a sense more than they could believe, but in another sense something to be approached warily, as a miracle such as is attributed to the Virgin of Ville Bonheur or a "happening" of the loa, which would be taking place right then at the Saute d'Eau. To be so close, and in the presence of this person of grace and dignity, small, plump, with soft black eyes, dark brown skin, and black curly hair of the "marabou" classification and decide whether to choose between the clothing or the gourdes

was a little too much for them, and also for Madame la Présidente. When I arrived she was perspiring, nervous, and a little undone. I stepped to the balcony of the house in my best
Chautauqua manner, and together we stood pressed to the
wall by dusty, sweating humanity, the sick, old, poor, and
finally children not waiting to be asked but snatching the
goods when the paper notes had given out. I have never had
occasion to ask Madame Magloire her impressions of this experience, but knowing her to be a truly sensitive person, I
would believe that there must have been by the end of the
day some doubt as to the validity of the Magloire methods
of elevating the poor. I only know that as time went on she
turned more to the Church for refuge, and as for myself,
when I think of her I associate her more with the miraculous
Virgin of Ville Bonheur than with the parties at Leclerc or
at the Palace or her house at La Boule, to arrive at which one
had to pass a cordon of army privates and lieutenants.

The Magloires were an active part of what I call my
"middle" Haitian period, between Estimé, the days of research and initiation and becoming acquainted with the island, and the long period of many visits which is this present
period when I refer to it as home, yet am away most of the
time.

Paul Magloire and Henri Christophe had much in common
in looks, stature, and appeal. Both were soldiers of high rank
and both had served in army or government the men whom
they followed. Christophe's wife, Marie Thérèse, must have
had much the character of Madame Magloire, and in their
union she frequently was the pacifier of his unruly temper,
which otherwise might have led to cruelties. Both men were,
though black, beyond the prejudices of color, and were at
home with mulattoes, whites, and blacks. Christophe loved
ostentation, as did Magloire. Both were vain, and both had
along with the qualities of a military chief those of an organ-
izer. But both lacked the true democratic spirit. Some doubt
always surrounded the good works of Magloire, as I see things.
Both saw the family as the basis of human society, though

Magloire is reputed to have strained his ties of family to the utmost during his last days as President, the days reported as those of libertinism. Both took particular interest in public roads, construction and upkeep. Each needed private property for self-aggrandizement, Christophe in palaces, each more ostentatious than the other, Magloire in villas, mountain retreats, town houses. There was about the two an absolutism, an insistence to help people in spite of themselves; and both thought that happiness of the people could be arrived at by the exercise of physical force. Both were bon viveurs, fond of regalia and magnificent receptions and parties. Each by autocracy created discontent in the army that had supported him. Christophe was led to his death by believing flattery, Magloire to exile. Though Magloire's election speech would lead one to think the contrary, I would say that like Christophe his methods of government were not inspired by a "humane conception of the needs and aspirations of the country." The quote is from Dantès Bellegarde. The fall of Christophe left a large number of superior officers without employ and with discontent at a loss of prestige. Duvalier inherited this same situation after Magloire.

The fatal error of Haitian Presidents seems to be the continuous effort to impose changes of Constitution involving the most delicate and vulnerable point in Haitian character —re-election, or prolongation of the presidential term. And yet this is just what François Duvalier has achieved, though two days after Paul Magloire proposed this he was in exile.

10

Legends of zombies—the dead come to life or the living so anesthetized by drugs as to appear dead—are among the commonest of surrealist tales in Haiti. My initiation and the Rex Theatre concert safely over, I began to take interest in life in the capital and spent days listening to stories and exchange of gossip at the meeting places of porteresses and at stalls in the Iron Market. At night I would drive with Fred to the waterfront, stopping along the way at one of the many stands where we would drink tiny cups of hot, sweet black coffee. Until Senegal I have not found coffee comparable in flavor and excitement—even in the smell of it roasting—to Haitian coffee. We would sit in the parked car at the waterfront, where boats from Gonaïves, Les Cayes, Port-de-Paix, Jérémie, Jacmel, and other coastal towns anchored, families living on them for hours or days depending on the time it took to make the trip and wait for a cargo for return. The boats would creak in the gentle motion of the waves, which, chastened by the bay, had spent almost all their energy by the time they reached the mainland shore. On the boats there would be charcoal fires, laughter and small talk. If we were so fortunate as to be included in a storytelling we might hear of the cunning of the trickster 'ti Malice, a Haitian Br'er Rabbit, of pacts made with the White Witch of Trou Forban, of strange practices of sects frowned on by the

Arada-Dahomey vaudun—the Congo Moundong, for instance, which was supposed to claim human flesh for ritual banquets.

Seated by the charcoal fires of the waterfront, I learned many things not to do if I were to survive, remain healthy, ensnare a lover, and become rich in the possessed island, and antidotes were I to make a mistake or be taken advantage of, possibilities not too remote in view of my lack of instruction in these things. A mapou tree, for instance, is always dangerous at night; in the day, bacalou, the evil little man-eating sorcerers who frequent mapou trees, are inclined to rest or wander the countryside as animal embodiments, chiefly pigs. At Leclerc it has always been difficult to raise pigs. In the forests surrounding the Habitation they soon run wild and with the least display of personality are labeled bacalou and left to fend for themselves. Then one day they are reported missing and everyone is certain that they have taken residence in a mapou tree. This is the report of my former gérant at Leclerc, but at times I wonder if the fate of the missing pigs isn't more simply explained, since grillot is a favorite Haitian dish.

At any rate, in my waterfront education I learned that the bacalou haunt mapou trees, which, with their buttressed trunks and thick overshadowing spread of branches, are reminiscent of, or may be a relative of, or may be the fromager of West Africa. The fromager is a favorite meeting place of the Diola of Casamance, mentioned before, who gather in male and female initiation groups to drink palm wine with what mixture I wonder, in view of ethnological gossip about Diola food tastes. Inside the huge trunk of the mapou trees of Haiti the bacalou hold forth, carousing, singing—which has been described as blood-curdling howling concerts—and conferring over their evil deeds as they feast on the night's victims. Passing the tree late at night, one can clearly hear the crunching of bones and mortars being pounded in which are more than likely human parts mixed with magic herbs to be used in potions for further witchcraft. There are protective devices against the bacalou; potions to drink, thunderstones, Congo sachets of powdered herbs, or a stick to be carried and brandished when passing a mapou tree. The stick is cut from a special palm tree and is called cocomacaque. The bacalou are unholy and should never be confused with the loa. But I had heard of a Congo-Guinée loa named Baculu Baka and the idea of associating this loa with the human-flesh-eating "little men" intrigued me.

The persistent recurrence of intimated anthropophagous practices among branches of the Congo pantheon made me almost regret the months spent in familiarizing myself with the Arada-Dahomey cult. Like most researchers, the more unusual the phenomenon the more attractive for investigation and documentation. Congo Zandor, known in the Cul-de-Sac but a rare visitor, is supposed to be malevolent, sanguinary, and a regular consumer of human flesh. Also the commonest remark about Congo Moundong was that "l'ap mangé moune," he eats people as his sacrificial food. No one was willing to commit himself seriously as to the source of this alimentation, nor was I able to ascertain what loa or spirit required this dish ritually killed and prepared, as in the case of four-legged animals and fowl, or whether the need was simply gustatory, in which case a profane corpse would serve the need, or whether the loa or spirits were necrophagous, as stories of the removal of the dead from graveyards for nourriture would indicate.

My initiation, which by now was known from one end of the island to the other, engendered respect, but when Fred and I told of our trip to Trou Forban the effect was sensational. We had not much, after all, to tell, as compared to the classic stories of politicians who had pledged their children to insure success in elections, after which the children died or disappeared one by one, or Doc's favorite one of a rich mulatto landowner known to all of us by name who had tried to deposit a quantity of old Spanish coins of rare vintage at the bank shortly after his wife died. But we all agreed that the White Witch, or diabl' of the mountain needed no

advance notice for rendezvous, that he invariably knew
ahead of time and sent his silent horseman to meet the person come to make a pact or *engagement*. The fact that we
had dared to climb to the cave raised our prestige consider-
ably, as the average Haitian peasant will have nothing to do
with affaires of the devil, leaving this to people who are
better equipped to defend themselves. Also, most of their
needs can be gratified by a bocor at a much more modest investment and, thus kept within the doctrine of cult, no more
is required than, as I have already described, periodic
sacrifices, services, or promises. But a good deal of time must
be spent in insurance against the evil doings of others or the
capriciousness of nature, and for this protection magic is often
resorted to, in the spirit of fighting fire with fire. There are
loups garous, cigouaves, diablesses, all more or less invested
with the same powers, caprices, and appetites as the baca-
lous. There are gris-gris to guard against ill health or loss of
property, ouangas, or charms, hung on doorposts or buried in
a property (we find many at Leclerc), for negative or positive
control, love potions and powders. Each bona fide houngan or
mambo is supposed to have some control over disasters
caused by black magic, but if a ceremony pouin—ceremony
to prepare protective or retaliative ingredients—is unsuccess-
ful, then the conscientious houngan or mambo should with-
draw in favor of a bocor, or doctor of feuilles or curative and
magic herbs.

Periodically—and I would like to chart the recurrence of
this phenomenon—Port-au-Prince will fall into a state of
hysteria over the report of some incident impossible to be
measured by any standard other than mass hypnosis. A cow
has been led to the abattoir and, as it is about to receive the
coup de grâce, talks, either petitioning a stay of execution or
holding its keepers spellbound with some discourse or proclamation. Or a fish talks when caught in a net and from then
on follows the same routine as the cow, or a fish is caught on
a hook and when hauled in turns out to be a dog, and so
forth. Having been a victim of this sort of hysteria when try-

ing to start a small zoological garden during my latest stay at Habitation Leclerc and having had the poor judgment to include in it a display of reptiles, local and imported but all harmless (this was the idea of Dick Frisell, then guest at Leclerc, and was in no way associated with my affiliations with Damballa), I now see these tales as usual in any animistic society.

During my last stay in Haiti, a neighbor a kilometer away from the property of Leclerc, who in reality objected more to the threat of vaudun drums playing for tourists, now that the Habitation was open to the public, than to danger from an invasion of poisonous snakes, published a complaint in the *Nouvelliste* charging one Madame Dunham with importing venomous serpents with the subversive intention to destroy the government by overrunning the island with them, an island which had been free from such a menace since historical times. I of course replied to the article. One thing led to another. Victims of political feuds were reported to have been victims of serpents loosed from Habitation Leclerc, children on the way to school were reported to have been swallowed by the snakes now become dragon size, and a woman complete with donkey suffered the same fate. The whole thing ended in a mess of near loss of friendship with the neighbor, an architect whom I had always admired for both his work and his character, in calumnious essays in daily papers, scurrilous announcements every five minutes on the local radio, around which, before the affair died down, porteresses and peasants would gather to listen at every country store. It also ended in the relegation of a group of carefully selected Amazon, African, and Haitian pythons to the government farm at Damien, where they probably died of starvation. At Leclerc they had been well taken care of by Dick Frisell, sponsor of the whole idea, and were regularly fed a diet of home-grown white mice, lizards, and guinea pigs. The destruction of these reptiles might have been immediate had it not been for the direct intervention of President Duvalier, who decreed their banishment instead.

My disenchantment about Haitian tall stories had not begun when these waterfront hours with Fred were spent, sometimes until one and two in the morning, listening to and exchanging stories with the boatmen, some few of the dock hands who would join us, and now and then a wandering musician, a guitar or accordion player. These latter might lounge on the deck of the boat where we had gathered, play softly all through our conversation, humming or singing and seeming lost in a world of their own, then surprise us all by adding some comment or correction to what we had been talking of. Favorite stories beyond those already discussed were of people believed dead but buried alive, which led to the dead coming to life, which inevitably led to the word which never fails to interest tourists in Haiti, zombies. Something about the persistence of my storytellers, and the sincerity with which they told of the long history of recorded cases since colonial times in Haiti, made me put the zombie stories out of the category of tall tales and take a real interest in the macabre subject. It seemed less likely as fact than was anthropophagy. Nevertheless, when speaking casually with friends of any class or color, there was some tinge of credulity at the mention of zombieism.

The first definition of the creature is that of a truly dead person who by the intervention of black magic has been brought back to life, but by such a process that memory and will are gone and the resultant being is entirely subject to the will of the sorcerer who resuscitated him, in the service of good or evil. Fearing this possibility, many Haitian peasants keep watch over the bodies of their dead until there are signs of disintegration; others hammer a long iron nail into the forehead of the dead person so that all bodily functions are interrupted beyond revival. Another version of zombie-making and probably the one most believed and indeed the most likely is that some person selected by a bocor practicing this black art has been given a potion of herbs brought from 'Nan Guinée. The person falls into a coma resembling death in every pathological sense. When the body is buried the

bocor waits an occasion to disinter it, administers an anti-
dote, and the subject is his to command. The difference between the two types seems to be that the former is without
a soul, and if given salt, which is strictly forbidden in alimentation for all kinds of zombies, the zombie who is a resuscitated dead person disintegrates or falls dead, whereas the
zombie which has been revived from a drugged state returns
to life as a normal human being. The latter seem preferable
because they have souls and if by chance salt should enter
their diet the sorcerer would be able to re-enslave them; there
seems to be also some intangible preference given the zombie
with a soul. His actions are, by report, similar to those of the
dead ones, he works the fields as hard, shows no interest in
the life around him, never sweats even when working in the
hottest sun, is tireless, without emotion, without changes of
facial expression, but is somehow related, in the minds of
the living, to the living by the fact that he has never really
died. These zombies are not used for evil deeds generally, but
are put to the serviceable work of tilling and cultivating
fields. They work slowly but thoroughly, and for no one but
the person who is responsible for their state.

In Haiti the dead are apt to reappear for brief visits of
their own accord. These are simply unquiet souls such as are
common in many countries of the world; these do not fall
into the classification of zombies. The tales and reports of
dead come alive may have been strongly influenced by or
may be direct hand-downs from Africa. Melville Herskovits,
in his comprehensive two-volume book on Dahomey, writes
of the zombie concept: "They were soulless beings, whose
death was not real, but resulted from the machinations of
sorcerers who made them appear as dead, and then, when
buried, removed them from their graves and sold them into
servitude in some far-away land."

Recently here in Senegal I have begun a habit that is surely
bothersome: asking soothsayers who pass by my doorway,
or bush priests who earn a living predicting the winning number of a lottery, why they don't extract bank notes from in

front of a bank teller's nose, or break the national lottery bank for themselves or their families, which remain constantly needy. The answers are always the same. We can do this for you, but not for ourselves. It comes to my mind when reading Herskovits and thinking of zombies that if this was the practice in Africa during the slave trade, there should have been no reason against these desensitized persons with no remembrance or feeling replacing those multitudes who suffered the physical and moral indignity of bondage. These are the things we think about in our moments of incredulity and speculation, but they are not the things that necessarily advance scientific investigation.

A song about the zombies of Léogane was sung on the ocean front one night by our visiting musicians, and after we had listened to it I made up my mind to trace what I could of the legend. Léogane, next town of any size south of Port-au-Prince, was where I had heard about a bush priest who was not only a houngan of the cult Congo Moundong, but who was supposed to have as wives seven women who had been converted into the zombie state. He was called 'ti Couzin and was widely known as a bocor, houngan, and practitioner of black magic in a number of forms. He was also, according to rumor, a partaker of human flesh.

Titine had been chambermaid at the Excelsior Hotel for ten years. She was short, plump, a hard worker, and very serious in her checkered uniform and white head scarf. When serving in the dining room in the evening, she wore white cotton stockings and flat one-strap pumps. These set her apart from the rest of the house and yard servants, but she carried her advantages well, feeling no particular superiority over the others, especially since the stockings and slippers did not really belong to her and were kept in the locked linen closet of the hotel and were issued only for the occasion. We had become friendly over my months of going and coming at odd hours of the night or day. She was a person who, like many people of African and Oriental extraction, would never show her true age but because of her size and her round face, almost always smiling, I thought of her as quite young. She, on the other hand, considered me her charge and became quite matronly when scolding me about late nights or careless handling of my friends. When the Deputy had not been by for some days this, of course, in the eyes of Titine, was my fault.

Titine was from Léogane, and one day I asked her about 'ti Couzin. Her alarm was genuine. She knew of him but had never seen him and hoped never to. She also hoped that I was not planning one of my visits in that direction. When Titine took the camionnette on visits to her family in Léogane she always closed her eyes tight when nearing the compound and houngfors of the houngan, not opening them until well past. There were, according to her, seven wives in the compound, all zombies, and this corroborated the stories of our waterfront friends. Each of 'ti Couzin's houngfors was for a different Congo god, each more bloodthirsty than the other. Moundong ruled, but Maît' Grand Bois was often there, and Baganda, Zandor, and Baculu Baka had sanctuaries and separate altars. Stories were told of young girls who had entered the sanctuaries for initiation and never come out. Surely Mademoiselle would be made into a zombie wife or, worse still, sacrificed to one of the bloodthirsty gods and eaten by the priest and his chief hounci, all of whom were men. Some part of me would be left unsalted for the zombie wives, perhaps not even cooked. I did feel uncomfortable as Titine elaborated on what might happen to me, once in the hands of the bocor priest, but I laughed at her fears and assured her that I would be safe. I would carry my own protective thunderstone, my baptismal beads, wear my marriage ring to Damballa, and bathe beforehand with a special ointment given me by Téoline to use against ill-wishers. Also, I would be accompanied by Monsieur Fred.

I did not tell her that Fred would deposit me, continue on to Léogane on business for his garage, then return for me an hour or so later. This would give me time enough, I hoped, to find out whether or not the wives were zombies, take a photograph or two if I were clever, and visit the houngfors. Verifying rumors of human sacrifice and cannibalism would be a different matter and I scarcely hoped in one visit to confirm or discount the rumors surrounding the priest, which had reached legendary proportions. When we were packed and ready for the day's trip, Titine again begged me to reconsider. All of my Arada-Dahomey protections were nothing against the combined Congo forces. She wept as we drove around the glorieta and waved good-bye. The Senator had come to his balcony to greet us, and as we turned out of the driveway, maneuvering past the Pierce-Arrow, I could see the sun glint on his black glasses and protruding teeth.

During the two-hour trip over the bumpy road to Léogane, Fred and I discussed 'ti Couzin. The distance was not great, not over fifty kilometers, but at times we were forced to the side of the road to wait until a truck or camionnette worked its way out of a ditch or a pothole in the middle of the narrow road, and at times we were the offenders. With each mile my curiosity about 'ti Couzin increased. After thinking things over I had decided that I was basically skeptical of zombies as a concept and preferred to believe 'ti Couzin was simply a peasant, somewhat educated, and shrewd enough to use divining powers, extrasensory perception, and mother wit to elevate himself to the position of an important landowner, a capitalist in Haitian peasantry terms. He may also have secured his several wives by personal charm or aptitude and by the same means secured their services as aides in cultivating his property, an answer to another widespread byword that his wives were seen planting and reaping in season day and night and were never seen at ceremonies or at market. Fred told me that 'ti Couzin made a weekly trip to Port-au-Prince in a touring car undoubtedly left over from the Occupation, went to the bank to make deposits of hundreds of faded gourde notes, did marketing for staples, and returned the same day to Léogane, not stopping to take part in market gossip and encouraging no intimacies. He had seen the bush priest in town, but he thought it not too strange that 'ti

Couzin should own a car and put money in the bank, though he did agree that it was a little unusual for a man, and a houngan at that, to do marketing. This was not and still is not usual in Haiti.

We had been told to follow the Léogane road until within a mile of the town, and at just about that distance we saw the landmark of a giant mapou tree and a barrier of poinsettia and spiny sablier posts sheltering a compound from the road. On the left of the dirt road was a complex of freshly whitewashed houngfors and tonnelles, on the right beyond the barrier we could see a caille built of stone blocks instead of wattle and plaster, and forming a semicircle on each side, and behind that were other huts, presumably for the "wives," and beyond these a stretch of well-cared-for cane fields. 'Ti Couzin's compound was immediately set apart from our clean but poor compounds at Pont Beudette by its air of prosperity. As we descended from the car a tall, strongly built man rose from his chair on the veranda of the caille. This was 'ti Couzin. It is difficult to describe his appearance because one felt rather than saw the man. He must have been fifty years of age, which heretofore had always seemed to me to be well advanced in years. I remember making a mental note that his skin color was blacker than that of most Haitians who do not originate in the north or in Léogane, that he was dressed in khaki trousers and blouse, that his feet were bare, that the pupils of his eyes were outsize, the iris the color of his clothing and the rest of his eye, the part which ordinarily is white or near white, was red. The rest of my impression was taken up by an overwhelming sense of personal magnetism which left me stammering introductions and blushing. I could feel Fred looking at me with surprise, and let him precede me as we followed 'ti Couzin up the steps to his veranda and into the house. My confusion did not hamper my curiosity about several women who could be seen walking slowly about the back yard or squatted in front of their huts. Two were pounding millet, and I had the feeling that even though they were some distance from us, there was no sound from the heavy pestle as it fell into the mortar. None of the women looked up or seemed by the slightest sign to be aware of the presence of strangers. I was not able to count them because Fred turned, indicating that my dragging behind was a little obvious. The behavior of the women must have seemed strange to him too. Haitian women of peasant class are not under the same disciplines as the élite, and at any compound I had so far visited mangy dogs, pigs, goats, and at least the wife in charge would have been falling all over themselves welcoming us.

'Ti Couzin looked at me as though reading my thoughts. We were in a small, immaculate parlor, and we were motioned toward wicker chairs that might have been relics from some plantation, salvaged before the razing of the great properties during the days when Haiti was known as the "Pearl of the Antilles." The floor of 'ti Couzin's house was covered with brown and red ceramic tiles, old ceramic rare in Haiti then and impossible to find now. Through the voile curtains separating the salon from the next room I could see the corner of a high poster bed and an altar. The salon was pleasantly cool and I should have felt comfortable after the hot dusty ride, but I didn't. 'Ti Couzin sat in a chair near the corner table, picked up a canework fan from it and began to fan himself. Then he turned his strange eyes on Fred, who lost some of his usual aplomb under the scrutiny and fumbled lighting a cigarette. There was an awkward silence, during which I realized that the next initiative was mine, but I did nothing. The houngan excused himself and went to the veranda to signal a woman in front of one of the compound huts. It was one of the two pounding millet. She dropped her pestle and walked slowly toward our host. We could see this from the open shutters, and we could hear 'ti Couzin ordering fresh coconut water. I looked at Fred uneasily. Titine had said above all not to eat or drink in 'ti Couzin's compound or houngfor. Fred was even more skeptical than I of the zombie stories and gave no help. At last 'ti Couzin spoke:

"You are the American," he said, and in English. By now

I was more or less accustomed to surprises from renowned bocors, so I nodded and began my story about wanting to know more about my people and how I had traveled to the other islands of the Caribbean in the search, and how I had lived with the Arada-Dahomey worshippers in the plains and now wanted to know something about true Congo ceremonies, having only been to Congo dances and not being satisfied that I knew all that I could to take back to my people. I stopped myself abruptly from adding Moundong after Congo, not because it wasn't a perfectly respectable cult but because the words mange' moun', "eat people," hung in the air between us. The Moundong are a tribal group today reported in three areas—the eastern Gambia River, the Congo, and the Upper Volta. 'Ti Couzin gave no sign of sensing my quest of the sacrifice of the "goat without horns." He nodded and turned his discomforting gaze again at Fred. Fred blushed under his Haitian suntan to the roots of his curly blond hair, crossed and uncrossed his legs, lit a cigarette, and explained his presence in Haiti and his interest in knowing more about such an important person as Monsieur. He did it all very well, and I felt relieved not to have to carry the conversation further, not trusting myself to avoid the subject that had drawn me there, which surely was a delicate one.

I should say now that in spite of repeated reports of cannibalism among Haitians there has been no substantiation for them except once: the ritual eating in 1860 of a small girl named Claircine at Bizoton, not far from Habitation Leclerc. All of the culprits were tried legally, convicted, and executed. But to arouse my curiosity I had been witness to a Petro ceremony the preceding Christmas Eve at Croix-de-Missions, after which I was left with some reservations about this subject. Doc was with me for the first part of the evening, but soon he was driven by Guedé into mounting the bullock which had been set apart for some special sacrifice, I do not know which; not Petro, in any case, because Petro gods prefer pigs. Petro ceremonies are perhaps the most spectacular of all Haitian folk worship. There must always be gunpowder, a trough of a hollowed-out log filled with special leaves and herbs, pounded with clairin and mixed with gunpowder, and in the courtyard the iron staff to the god Petro Simbi or Kita burning red in a charcoal fire. At a given moment the trough of herbs and raw alcohol and gunpowder is lighted, cries of ecstasy accompany the burst of flame, then the trough is paraded before the congregation and carried off amid possessions and the frenetic earth-stomping, shoulder-shaking dancing that characterizes the Petro pantheon. The trough is usually brought into the houngfor, still flaming, or it may be carried into some nearby wood where the fresh-water god Petro Simbi may be waiting.

On this particular Christmas Eve I had sat through endless dances and songs and praises to the god Petro, and was tired, lonely for familiar things and a familiar Christmas, and had no taste for the freshly killed pigs that were being grilled in the fires of the red-hot iron staffs. I sat inside the peristyle, not really a stranger to the Petro worshippers because I had been there many times before to dances, but feeling an outsider at this ceremony, the meaning of which was obscure to me. There were small children of both sexes sleeping in blankets in corners of the tonnelle. Earlier they had danced, sung, eaten, but now they were tired. Parents sat over them or near them, joining apathetically in songs, rising now and then to dance. I was tired and sent someone to tell Doc that it was time to go back to Pont Beudette. Doc appeared soberer than I would have expected him to be, somewhat shaken by his ride on the bullock. We made our farewells and left. It must have been near midnight.

On the road I used our flashlight to keep from falling into holes. We passed no one and I felt lonely and afraid, not of people but of those disembodied spirits or demons. There was no sure way to identify them. There was no moon on the black road, but this was territory familiar by now. Suddenly Doc seized my hand, turned off the flashlight, and pulled me into the shrubs of poinsettia at the side of the road.

I thought that he had had a seizure or a return of his loa and jerked myself away and back to the road. Then I saw the reason in what he had done. The road was dry and covered with the white chalky film that stays on roads and byways of the plains of Haiti from the beginning of the dry season till the end. A cloud of dust was approaching us from the rear and I heard the beat of horses' hooves, horses moving faster than any that I had seen outside the Pine Forest. Suddenly I was alarmed. There had been something mysterious, inimical about the whole evening, and it had been evident toward midnight that I, sitting alone in a corner, and Doc, roistering outside, were no longer welcome in the true sense of the word, were scarcely being tolerated. I had danced Petro, but it was tiring and too aggressive for what I felt comfortable in when dancing. The others seemed interested in some activity which excluded us, the only visitors to this special Christmas Eve ceremony.

My apprehension was not for physical harm, because I felt perfectly safe alone, and Doc was there, surprisingly enough more alert than ever. It was simply a reflex preparation for the unknown. This must be part of something special and unclear that had gone on all evening, that was reaching a culmination in this whirling band of horsemen that I could now distinguish against the star-lighted sky. Doc dragged me farther into the fringe of dry brush. He forced me into a squatting position as the horsemen approached, galloping, crouched on the wiry little horses. In front or in back of each horseman, huddled under a pointed hood was a child. There was no way to know which were boys or girls, but I could feel their collective terror as the nine horsemen swept past. They were gone in a cloud of dust and Doc released his hold on my arm. I had stepped into a rivulet and was wet to the knees. I was trembling and at the same time annoyed because Doc had saved me from some disaster, I wasn't sure what, and I felt foolish at my ignorance. We scrambled from the ditch, torn by brambles, dripping water, caked with mud when we clambered into the dust of the road. I wanted to turn around and walk back to the ceremony, to ask people what was going on and why this, the most exciting part, had been left until our departure. More than this, there had been efforts to have us believe that the ceremony was about to end when we had left. Doc called me some unpleasant names because of my insatiable curiosity and this shocked me more than what he had to say. His explanation of the cavalcade was as follows: there was every indication that the children were being taken to a woods on the road to the Pine Forest where there was a sacred spring, Petro Simbi's dwelling. The children had been ritually fed, probably given some opiate, and while I sat inside bored at the dances, which must have been dull especially for my benefit, to tire me no doubt, in the adjoining houngfor Doc had, while indulging in his well-known Guedé possession, seen the children bathed, dressed, and instructed in last-minute dogma which they must already have been acquainted with at some earlier session. Then they had been led out to the tonnelle and left as if to sleep, but I remembered as he spoke that above the blankets bright, beady eyes were following each dance and that instead of being sleepy the children were in a state more than likely close to trance.

Doc wanted to go home. He had assisted at numerous New Year's Eve Petro ceremonies, and was irked at the cool rejection by the houngan and hounci of his overtures to become more intimately acquainted with them. He had brought me as a special favor, but this was all there was to see. Not even the good friend or extended family member could go further than we had that night. We trudged our way toward Pont Beudette. I began to complain of fatigue, sore muscles, wet feet, till at last Doc agreed to stop for a rest, both of us seated on a ditch side, Doc smoking and reminiscing, I speculating. Finally our thoughts took the same road. If the horsemen had taken the children somewhere they would have to bring them back before they were missed in the village. It would be a strange procession to enter any village after daybreak. Also, if what we suspected was true, that there was some vestigial initiation or token circumcision taking place, as would seem reasonable in view of African heritage, the children would have to be returned to their parents or some guardian circle to be treated and cared for after this operation, or, if the "rite de passage" were not carried out in full, to some cloister where they could be re-inducted psychologically into their accustomed routine. The circumcision possibility seemed remote; I had never heard or read of it as a Haitian ritual practice. The most likely cloister, we judged, would be the houngfor. We climbed over the ditch and started the road back to Croix-de-Missions. Doc was not very happy about the whole affair. He had been trying since his first experiences with the vaudun to follow leads of puberty rituals, circumcision, and cannibalism, real or symbolic, without success. It was by now three o'clock in the morning and Cécile was waiting. He wanted to continue to Pont Beudette, but I wasn't to be stopped. Dusty, caked with mud, we approached the houngfor by the back road.

People were dozing around the iron staff, which had become gray in the charcoal cinders. Inside the tonnelle we recognized parents drinking tin cups of what might have been coffee or hot rum. In the houngfor all was silence, but we could see the flicker of candlelight and people passing in front of it. There were no children under the tonnelle. We walked into the circle of light of the dying charcoal fire, and a man with the air of a sentinel spoke to us from the shadows. We had not seen him. There was no friendliness in his manner, and companions joined him to stand around us, glowering. I thought of the caco camps during the Occupation, or filibustier hideaways during the Revolution. We looked around for some familiar face, but there was none. We made some limp excuse about wondering if the ceremony was over, excused ourselves, and took the main road away from the houngfor as fast as we could. We could see the black shadows of our interrogators against the fire, poised as though watching our flight and at the same time expecting an arrival.

An hour later, dragging along the road, out of sorts with each other and all things ceremonial, Doc again clutched my arm. This time it wasn't necessary to force me into the road-side bushes. By now everything seemed out of place and sinister. There was the dull beat of horses' hooves, then a kind of broken rhythm and they were upon us, slowly this time, the horses white with sweat and dust, the reins slack in the riders' hands. Children nodded on the necks of horses or clung to the riders before them. The smallest one was about three years of age, the eldest nine, and they were the same children who had danced all the night at the houngfor, who had lain half-asleep in blankets in the tonnelle, and who had thundered past in the dust several hours before. Again we counted. There were nine horses, nine riders, but only eight children. This time I squeezed Doc's arm, and he nodded, cautioning me to be quiet. A horse snorted very near our faces and I fell into the bushes. Doc was furious. I stayed flat on my back in a poinsettia tangle until they had passed. As we continued on our road to Pont Beudette the sun was rising, a mist covering the road ahead and turning the riders behind into ghosts. Doc was certain that we had come upon one of the child sacrifices that everyone talks of but no one can verify. He was also certain that had we been discovered my reputation for partisanship to cult practices and his reputation as the foremost "white" houngan in Haiti would not have saved us from great embarrassment, more than likely physical harm. The men on horseback may very well have keyed themselves to such a pitch of devotional delirium that one half-white and one white human obstacle in the early dawn would have meant nothing for them to eliminate. That is what Doc said and I, though later skeptical, was inclined to believe him as we trudged home that Christmas morning.

The voile curtains between the salon and the altar in 'ti Couzin's caille parted and the woman who had been told to serve us entered with a pitcher of coconut water on a tray with three gold-rimmed glasses. I stopped my monologue about why we had come to see 'ti Couzin with the unpleasant impression that I had been talking to myself. Our host had said nothing; had simply stared at me and puffed on a pipe which looked like ivory but was probably meerschaum. I overcame an impulse to find some pretext to leave as soon as possible without investigating zombies or cannibalism. The woman who entered was coffee-colored and the hair under her kerchief was smooth. There were no introductions and the woman looked at none of us, only at the tray. She placed the tray on the table beside 'ti Couzin and left slowly, scarcely disturbing the doorway curtains. 'Ti Couzin handed us glasses in which small flecks of gelatinous unripe coconut and shreds of brown shell floated. Fred and I held our glasses poised as though to offer a toast. This was to camouflage our discomfort while waiting for 'ti Couzin to drink first. The pose became too embarrassing and was surely not advancing the comédie. I excused myself, went to the veranda and somewhat ostentatiously spilled three generous portions of coconut water offerings to my loa at the foot of the steps. I certainly could not pour all of it in libation, but at least there would be less of whatever opiate Titine had told us was sure to be in whatever we ate or drank at the compound of 'ti Couzin. When I returned to the room Fred was at ease, discussing the merits of fresh coconut water as compared to milk from ripe ones, especially when used as a mixture with rum or clairin. 'Ti Couzin, his drink finished, was in the friendliest of tones lamenting the days of fine rum, the stores of which he claimed to have been depleted during the Occupation; now only in private caves in Jérémie or Jacmel could the real rum of Haiti, aged at least fifty years, be found. I emptied my glass and found nothing strange in the misty, almost tasteless nut water. Then 'ti Couzin turned to me. His English vocabulary was clear but limited and we found ourselves in a three-way conversation, each speaking the language easiest for him, helping each other with unfamiliar words. The tension was over and I wondered how I could have been drawn into the superstitions and common gossip of the capital. Our host wanted to know more about black people in America and whether or not they were aware of the existence of their brothers in the Caribbean and Africa, and if any of them worshipped the gods of 'Nan Guinée, about the cult practices I had seen so far in my travels and those I had experienced in my initiation. At first I talked of dances of Place Congo in New Orleans and vestigial motor behavior in the clapping, jumping, and whirling in storefront and sanctified churches in Chicago and the town where I had grown up, Joliet, Illinois. Then I told him of a study I had begun at the University before leaving for the West Indies. I had submitted the outline to Lloyd Warner, head of the Department of Social Sciences at the University of Chicago, the subject being the *Occurrence of Cults, Drugs and Magic Among Deprived Peoples.* (Once back in Chicago I was to continue the research for the Federal Writers' Project with such capable co-workers as Frank Yerby and Nelson Algren and years later to deliver a paper on the subject before the Royal Anthropological Society of London.) I had already investigated a cult known in Chicago and Detroit as Black Muslims, not to be confused with a smaller and less belligerent cult, the Moslems, but destined to achieve much more publicity with time. It was long before the day of Malcolm X, but I had attended several meetings in the temple with Mohammed Elijah presiding, and 'ti Couzin was interested in the military training, schooling, black nationalism, and secret-society aspects of the Muslims.

I was excited to find in Haiti a houngan, a wise though uneducated man, with whom I could discuss sociological and anthropological subjects beyond the horizons of his own background. He nodded in agreement when I explained my theory that people deracinated, denied full participation in a society in which they are obliged to live, inevitably turn backward to ancestral beliefs or follow any leader who can propose a solution to their immediate distress, who can offer a future if not a present. I mentioned the disorientation of the German people after World War I and their subsequent need for a leader such as Hitler, nonbeneficent as he was. Then I returned to the Black Muslims, American Negroes

seeking social and economic stability, first banded together,
my study showed, by a Japanese in Detroit but soon transferring their headquarters to Chicago and calling the new
establishment Temple Number Two. According to press reports Temple Number One was disbanded under pressure;
rumor had it that some of the Detroit members had been intercepted in a basement in the act of dismembering a white
policeman in preparation for ritual feasting. My thesis was,
talking earnestly without thinking of where I was or why I
had come, that people would not fall victims to such accusations were they not deprived of full benefits in the social
structure, their own or imposed, in which they lived. Unless,
of course, and here I laughed, there be some gustatory appreciation involved, as is said to be the case among certain of the
African and Polynesian tribes accused of anthropophagy.
Though not a member of the Black Muslims, I have always
respected their unity, faith, economic and spiritual ambitions
and recently their journalistic skill, as the weekly paper published by Mohammed Elijah is among the best in the country.

Fred began to shuffle his feet and lit another cigarette,
as though he wished I would change the subject. I had been
looking beyond 'ti Couzin, seeing before me the ghettos of
black Chicago and my classrooms at the University and my
eagerness to be partisan to whatever meant cohesion among
the deprived black people. In the middle of a sentence I became aware of the burning gaze of the priest. He had stopped
smoking and, to all appearances, breathing. Fred was unnaturally still, looking out the window. I rose and went to
the veranda. Now I could see all the women, seven of them,
because they had stopped whatever they had been doing,
whether carrying cooking pots, pounding millet, or just sitting, and had come to within range of the open window.
They were absolutely motionless, with faces turned in our
direction, faces with absolutely no expression and which
might as well have been the faces of the blind or deaf. There
was one difference; they were listening with every pore and
fiber and were seeing with sightless eyes and smelling with

nostrils distended like animals who have caught the first
scent of fresh blood.

I returned to the room and sat down. Fred and 'ti Couzin
had not moved. These women, I supposed, were the famous
zombies of 'ti Couzin. Fred and I sat looking at them, they
through the window at 'ti Couzin, and 'ti Couzin at us. There
was no sound at all, but the faint odor of vétivert drifted into
the room. Not far from Bizoton a spring bubbles year round
to make a small pool, and the damp earth around the pool
is covered with the grass and the intoxicating odor can be
smelled all through the neighborhood. But there was no possibility that the scent would travel this far, and I had not
heard of vétivert anywhere else in Haiti. This was the perfume, but mixed with something else which I could not define, something repugnant and yet attractive. I thought of
the odor of durian fruit, aphrodisiac of the Malayan penin-
sula described to us by Fay-Cooper Cole in one of our
classes, "The Peoples of the Pacific." At that time I had not
smelled durian fruit but imagined it to have the same heady
fruit and flesh odor that filled the room in which we sat. Had
this been the odor of Indian hemp I might have been able to
explain the air of lassitude, of euphoria that seemed to have
reached Fred, and which I was beginning to be aware of in
myself. But Indian hemp was unknown then in Haiti, and
little known now, and the odor was not from 'ti Couzin's
pipe. I wondered if this was the beginning of becoming
zombie-ized. I thought of what Melville Herskovits had
written me, following a cable of negative response when I
had asked if I could remain in Haiti to undergo the test
of fire, the canzo. He had warned me against trying to experience too fully the mysteries of the magic island. He himself
had known these mysteries in Dahomey, the country of origin
of many of them, and had stayed outside what was beyond
his reach.

There was, however, an absurdity to the present situation.
We were sitting in a comfortable Haitian caille, not far from
the third largest city in the republic, which even so should be

called town, by some standards, village. It was early afternoon, Sunday, and now and then, though screened from the
highway, we could hear the racket of dilapidated camion-
nettes, the lowing of stray cattle, and the horn of a car that
might well have been that of a government functionary passing within calling distance. All of this traffic raised a gentle
fall of dust that filtered over the veranda and drifted down
the rays of sunshine that splashed into the room. Under
these circumstances one should not start imagining things.
As I was about to ask our host if we could see his houngfors,
he turned to Fred and proposed we visit them. Through the
window I could see the women disperse, presumably to resume their activities. I knew that it was time for Fred to
leave for Léogane, but the last few moments had been somewhat shattering to my usual self-confidence and I hoped he
would stay. He could also cover for me if I could find an
occasion to photograph the wives. I nodded agreement to
'ti Couzin's invitation, and at the same time asked Fred if
he would wait for me before going on to whatever he had to
do in Léogane. Fred agreed more willingly than I had expected. I have never known if it was gallantry or curiosity.
I managed to take a picture of the courtyard as we left the
house, and somewhere in my archives is a photograph of a
lone woman with others behind her in ghostly attendance.

   The Congo houngfors were a complex of buildings joined
by tonnelles, and one could pass from one to the other always
under cover. Crossing the road, 'ti Couzin repeated what we
had already heard, that the Congo gods were jealous and
powerful, and that more than one ceremony could take place
at one time, and more than one initiation. This is how
he explained the complex of houngfors, the like of which I
had not seen before. Moundong was without doubt the controlling loa. Others of his family were there, and other
Congo loa, but if they entered—even the strong ones like
Zandor and Baculu Baka and Maît' Grand Bois—the most
powerful of all, Moundong, could send them away, demand-

ing extra payment if they hesitated to leave. By now we had
reached the first tonnelle. I wanted to know what extra payment Moundong required. The houngan evaded the question, telling me what the boatmen had said, that Moundong
liked roasted corn and goat and Congo peas, that he liked
dogs but did not eat them, excepting the clipped morsels of
their ears on special occasions. One thing I learned about
Moundong was that he might enter a ceremony and select
a "horse" or bosalle, and demand to be alone with his choice
in the privacy of his sanctuary. There, with no drums and no
dancing, he feasted with the acolyte, not on cooked sacrificial
food, but on the blood and viscera of freshly killed goats.
'Ti Couzin seemed to take particular interest in telling me
these details, as though to answer what I had been telling
him about the needs of my people. And for one very clear
moment I felt that he read the words "long goat" that flashed
to my mind, or that had probably stayed in my subconscious
since long before our visit.

Through the open door of the Moundong's houngfor I
could see the altar on which were Congo figurines of all sizes,
the largest at least three feet tall, with the round satin-
covered base as large as a basketball. From the roof of the
tonnelle hung rows of drums. They were in sets of four and
were mounted with wooden hoops top and bottom between
which cords were stretched. The tuning pegs wedged between
the bottom hoops and the drum for tightening the goatskin
heads had been slipped out of the hoops to slacken the resting drums. They were unpainted, varied only slightly, and
were all close to the size of the largest Arada drum, the mama.
The poteau mitan of the tonnelle was heavily patterned with
cabalistic designs, none of which I recognized, and against
it a standing drum, an asotor, reached almost to the rafters.
A red satin robe hung from the ceiling; cut-out tissue-
paper flags were strung from corner to corner, crossing in
the center at the poteau mitan. The doors to the other
houngfors were closed and 'ti Couzin made no offer to guide
us to them. Instead, he returned to the first houngfor and,

as we were about to enter it, turned to Fred and spoke in creole. He told him that there was no need for him to go to Léogane as the owner of the garage where he hoped to find an extra part for the garage in Port-au-Prince had just died and there was much confusion in his family. People had been sent out to notify relatives and it wasn't the moment for business associates and the garage would be closed until after the funeral. We stood outside the houngfor, Fred and I hardly believing our ears. The priest entered and I asked Fred what he thought of it all. At first he was all for going to Léogane to try and disqualify the story, then he shook his head, took my hand and started for the road outside the tonnelle. Fred felt that it was time to end our visit.

The Chevrolet coupe was parked across the road from the temples, was covered with dust, and still had a dent in the back fender not repaired since our trip to Cap-Haïtien two months before. A camionnette passed on the way to Léogane. The driver recognized our car and waved to us, and things seemed again too real for our growing apprehension. The strange morning could all be accounted for, if one took the time to analyze things, by clairvoyance, in which I firmly believed, and as to the affair of the wives, by hypnosis; but about hypnosis I felt uncertain, because in all my varied experiences and experimentations, hypnosis has never affected me. I decided that the women had behaved strangely and that there had undoubtedly been the odor. Now I felt it time to go to Léogane and verify 'ti Couzin's story. Before we could cross the road a camionnette approached, headed toward the capital. The name was familiar, Sacré-Coeur de Jacmel, and Fred apparently knew the driver. We stood on the roadside and waved. The driver stopped with a wide grin, nodding toward the old Chevrolet, which he had probably seen in trouble before now and thought was out of commission. Fred climbed to the step of the camionnette and spoke to him, and I saw the driver's face become serious, then frightened. The news was exact, but how had we known when he himself had just left the garage, not able to change a faulty tire because of the death which had been sudden and without explanation. He looked nervously from right to left, from the compound to the houngfors, excused himself and drove on, almost pitching Fred off the steps and into the dust.

I turned back to Congo Moundong's tonnelle, thinking that we should at least say good-bye, wondering whether we should tell the priest that we had doubted his story but that it had been verified. 'Ti Couzin was just behind us, leaning against a post of the tonnelle. He was smoking his pipe and I thought smiling, though I could not be sure. Everything seemed too confused, and in spite of feeling that there was little more to find out without taking up residence and becoming initiated, neither of which I had any intention of doing, I wanted to see the inside of Congo Moundong's houngfor, the sanctuary if possible, and this would probably be my last chance. Fred was annoyed at my persistence and showed it. I suggested that he wait for me in the car while I inspected the houngfor. Instead, he entered the tonnelle and sat on one of the benches, lighting a cigarette. I was grateful for his wanting to be near, though I still had no thought of actual physical harm, and doubted strongly becoming subject to either drugs or hypnosis, if these were the instruments of the priest. I was still reluctant to believe in zombies; on the other hand, I thought as I followed 'ti Couzin into Moundong's dwelling that such a complex must call for a wealthy community to support it, or else some kind of unpaid labor.

It must have taken days, even weeks to gather the herbs that filled the largest stuffed object on the altar, and hours of pounding after they were dried. The pounding and mixing are done ceremonially, and the mixture depends on the god or the needs of the circumstance. Tiny red-satin replicas of these objects are now for sale at most curio shops in Port-au-Prince, but when I was visiting 'ti Couzin they were rarely seen outside Congo houngfors. Those on Moundong's altar were old, stained, and draped with beads, none of which had snakes' vertebrae mixed in. They were red, dark blue, purple, dark brown. The pots têtes must have been for very important people, judging by their size and decoration, and many candles must have been burned in offerings, because most of the pots were thick with candle grease. The altar was draped with red satin, and a clay dog was surrounded with bowls of dried corn, cornmeal, and dried peas. In a plate sat the skull of a goat, a brown handmade candle set in each eye socket, beads draping its horns. The door to the sanctuary was closed. Unless some sign has been given a mambo or houngan that a loa favors a particular person, the sanctuary is closed to all excepting the higher grades of hounci. As lavé-tête hounci, we of the plains entered Téoline's sanctuary only for our initiation. I regarded 'ti Couzin's opening the door to the sanctuary of Congo Moundong as a challenge. He may have heard that at the priest Julien's at Descayettes I danced the Congo paillette or Congo fran (femme) many Saturday nights until Sunday morning, but these were borderline secular dances, and while sometimes venerating a loa had been so popularized as to be played at any time and danced by many almost as social country dances. He surely had heard of my recent initiation and marriage to Damballa, and knew that by loa code I would be severely punished for trafficking with Congo gods not friendly to our Arada-Dahomey society unless those Congo gods took it upon themselves to protect me, and this they would do only if I "broke" my marriage and entered into some deep, irrevocable pact with whichever had been audacious enough to "choose" me. This interpantheon jealousy, I have learned to my regret, has no time or space limitations. My Haitian gods continue jealous of my Brazilian ones and vice versa, my Cuban gods of both, and the animist genii of Senegal and Ogun and Yemenja of Nigeria figure somewhere in this ill-chosen assembly.

The altar and objects of Moundong's sanctuary were liberally stained with blood, some quite fresh. This is what I first saw as my eyes became accustomed to the dim light, which came only from the aperture between the roof and the supporting walls. The door closed behind me and I stepped forward and would have been ankle deep in a hardly discernible pool at the foot of the altar had not 'ti Couzin supported me. As I regained balance he struck a match on the cement border of the pool and lit two candles on the altar. In their light I could see the green slime of the bottom and sides of the pool, the tadpoles agitating the water in their effort to find cover under the slime. The priest touched the tips of his fingers in the water and crossed his forehead: this was an absolutely necessary formality and I did the same. He then filled a tin cup on the border of the pool with the vile-looking water, drank from it, and offered it to me. This was probably the most difficult moment of my months of research, and I saw only two possibilities: to refuse the water and incur the displeasure of the priest, arousing questions of my sincerity in this visit of inquiry, perhaps even jeopardizing my relations with the Arada-Dahomey vaudun, and close friendships with those who had been responsible for my initiation and research; or, as alternative, to ignore the consequences of the polluted water, the health cautions so carefully indoctrinated in me by Julian Lewis and Melville Herskovits, which until now I had somehow managed to adhere to, and drink at least a respectable amount of the offering. I chose the latter, and as I swallowed the water I felt all the Congo gods looking at me, with a certain mockery. I threw the rest of the water unceremoniously back into the pool and must have made a face showing my disgust. 'Ti Couzin began to laugh. I cannot remember ever hearing laughter in a houngfor or sanctuary. He threw his head back and laughed loudly and uproariously, like any man might do upon discovering a weakness in a woman who thinks she has it well guarded. Of course he had known exactly what I was thinking.

For this reason I decided not to waste time or words. I stopped his laughter by pointing to an object hanging from the crossbeams, just now distinguishable. It was an elongated bundle wrapped in a straw mat and after that with a few bands of red ribbon. Two poles running the length of the bundle made it resemble a narrow stretcher on the like of which dead are carried in country burials. I approached toward the bundle and reached up and touched it with the tips of my fingers. Dust fell from the poles and the bundle swayed. It seemed very light, and kept swaying after I had withdrawn my hand. I turned to 'ti Couzin and tried deliberate thought transference. By now he had demonstrated that he would be able to know that I wanted to know the contents of the bundle dangling above us, and I had an irresistible desire to force him not to ignore the other questions that were foremost in my mind; for instance, whether the Congo cult felt itself tied to Africa in the present or only in an ancestral sense; were there initiations more secret and more special than those taking place in the houngfor; and, above all, was there truth in the common belief that Moundong could not be satisfied for long without eating human flesh. I hummed a few measures of one of the waterfront songs:

> Nan Léogane
> Yo marre zombie yo
> Nan paille figue banane
> (In Léogane they tie zombies with banana straw.)
> Ah, Bobo! Waye, O!

'Ti Couzin took an ason from the altar and sang another Congo song about what Moundong eats. I followed and since have used this song in recordings and on stage without once—to my surprise as I write this—recalling the conditions under which I first heard it:

> Moundong oh, ye
> Moundong oh, ye ye
> Moundong yo mange cabrit bouilli
> Moundong mange cabrit boucanné
> Yé yé yé, o o o
> Yé yé yé o o o.
> (Moundong eats boiled goat, Moundong eats roast goat.)

By now we must have been in this close, candlelighted, death-permeated room for nearly a half hour, and I was not much further toward what I had come for than when we had entered. There was no reason that I could think of for 'ti Couzin to begin my instruction in the Congo cult. I can only surmise that he believed me to be sincere and he must have taken discretion for granted. As he explained the altar objects I felt we had known each other for years, even in some other incarnation. He spoke of the blood on the altar, of the meaning of returning blood to the earth at times to appease the unsatisfied souls of ancestors, at times in honor of great chiefs or noble men dead far from 'Nan Guinée, and at times to ensure fertility of the earth and therefore protection to men. When the gods demand blood it is not for themselves but so that they will have the necessary strength and magical power to do good or evil. Nature has no will of its own but reacts according to how men act and the gods are the embodiments of natural forces. Those priests who are in direct contact with the gods may control them to some degree by the necessary propitiatory acts, but the vital essence that is blood is the most powerful, and only the priest can keep the thirsty gods from demanding greater and greater quantities. The gods, he continued, must eat, but most important was quenching their thirst. Some of my queries he answered as fully as I could have wished, others would be answered when I made my decision to become a part of the Congo, which until now I haven't.

On the altar, draped in strings of beads and covered with dust, was a book that the priest told me left nothing unsaid. I could not touch it or open it, and I did not know the book then, but now I am convinced that it was the *Petit Albert*, textbook of medieval European magic still banned in Haiti, and in Spain too, for that matter. A mortar so patinated as to have been deliberately polished and a pestle in it were hardly visible in one dark corner. I went to examine the contents of the mortar, and the same sweetly obscene odor that had entered the houngan's caille rose from it. 'Ti Couzin dipped his fingers in a powder that half-filled the mortar, touched my forehead in the vaudun cross, and spoke to me or rather at me in "langage." For a moment I wanted to tell him that I was quite prepared to stay there, to "couche" in the sanctuary of Congo Moundong, to read the *Petit Albert* by candlelight and be inducted into the cult. This was while bathed in the insinuating odor and almost suffocated by the magnetism of the man whose physical self by now seemed to have grown to the proportions of the room. Whether my restraint was a University classroom or Protestant upbringing I cannot say, but I turned from the priest and made my farewells to him and to the altar, unconverted.

In reporting this close, even intimate experience I am aware of what other researchers must often feel. That one may spend one year or one afternoon, as I had, and the result—a profound experience—may be the same. Much depends on circumstance, part on formal training, but most, I believe, on a conjunction of personalities destined to meet under conditions and in places not planned or foreseen. Living with the Maroon peoples of Jamaica, I waited weeks to find one drum or see one dance. Then on the eve of my departure all that I could have hoped for fell into perfect order, and in abundance. People and nature have a way of testing us before giving up their secrets. As a personal problem I have never known just how far to go in adding to the archives of truth, of knowledge, or what must be withheld in respect for a society or of a trust. I firmly believe, however, that only the one involved can decide these things.

This is some of what Fred and I talked about on the way back to Port-au-Prince. I had promised the houngan that I would return to Léogane before my departure, which was imminent; he answered only that the Congo gods would be near in time of need. I did not return to the compound or houngfors of 'ti Couzin, and when I would have, some years later, I was told that he had died and that his houngfors had fallen into ruin, there being no successor ordained.

At the Hotel Excelsior, Titine was waiting to hear about our trip, but when I told her that I had drunk from the sacred well at the altar of Congo Moundong she looked at me strangely, wanted to hear no more, and from that time until my departure from Haiti kept a distance from me, respectful but wary. I am sure that she considered me completely zombie-ized.

The night of my experience with the Congo houngan I was unable to sleep in my perch on top of the Excelsior. It was cool; a breeze from the bay passed through the open shutters and down the corridor, and another from the plains bringing the faint sounds of a bamboche, some country fête or dance. I had the reaction that most conscientious students of people and their ways must suffer from when coming upon facts exciting in their documentation yet ephemeral; unreal, and unbelievable when put into words or on paper. At four in the morning I made my last notes for the Rosenwald Fellowship report. From now on I would see what I could of Haiti, enjoy my friends, present my long-delayed letter of credentials to President Sténio Vincent, and reluctantly prepare to leave the country that had done so much for my development as a scholar, an artist, and as a person.

The thoughts that kept me from sleeping were somewhat the following:

"I now understand why the study of man is a thing apart, and why it becomes a passion. Heretofore I have taken my professors and their years of research for granted. To experience everything and to tell everything is not our mission; it is rather to be drawn to, to define, to examine with all of our equipment, moral and intellectual, the ways of other people, but to do so with an essential kindness toward humanity that has driven us in the first place to want to penetrate, with as much objectivity as possible, into every aspect of it, of its oldest and its newest customs, its most obscure systems of thought and action, its perversities, its deviations and its norms."

At about four o'clock in the morning I wrote:

"The excursion to the compound of the Congo priest known as 'ti Couzin was the result of interest in and curiosity about rumors current in Haiti of zombies, commonly called the 'living dead.' This, particular priest undoubtedly practices bush magic and hypnotism and may also make use of bush drugs known to induce trance or hallucinations. I was accompanied by an English friend familiar with the folkways of Haiti and am convinced that while neither one of us was either drugged or hypnotized, the following (I enumerated the instances already cited) are examples of unusual clairvoyance, divination, highly developed extrasensory perception. The priest being endowed with an unquestionably magnetic personality, it is not difficult to believe that his reputation would have extended into all classes of Haitian society, to have inspired 'myths' of his zombie wives and of his command over the supernatural. The system of ritual used by 'ti Couzin is evidently one in which a major part of Africanisms have persisted, with less syncretism or reconciliation with Catholic or other European religions than found in other Haitian cults and similar sects in the other island a part of my study.

"As to the common belief that one of the instruments used by 'ti Couzin to invoke and control the supernatural is ritual sacrifice of or partaking of the flesh of human beings, I can make no comment with authority. I left the houngfor of Congo Moundong feeling that whatever the bocor priest's device, he could and probably did use this for good as well as evil."

11

Something is always going on in Haiti, and whatever happens to be going on gives one the impression of constant motion. Earl Leaf called the Caribbean the Isles of Rhythm. I have, when away from Haiti or when there, tried, always unsuccessfully, to put on paper this rhythmic progression taking place always and all around, whether near sea, in mountains or on plains, to capture the ebb and flow of its tide. There are Saturday night country dances and "get togethers" called bamboche. Music at these gatherings is heavily influenced or wholly borrowed from nearby Cuba or adjoining Santo Domingo, a constant exchange no matter what the political atmosphere between the countries may be at the time. At the bamboche the dancers are for the most part couples and the usual orchestra is a guitar, Cuban style, or Congo drums, maracas, two gourds with enough hard seeds inside to produce a percussive resonance, or a rattle or tin tube in place of the gourds, and a marimboula, a wooden box with tuned steel prongs of different lengths fastened over an opening on the side of a box large enough for the player to sit on. The pegged Rada-Dahomey drums or baptized Congo drums are never used at these dances. The derivation of the marimboula is undoubtedly from the sansa or lekembe of the Congo, which instrument is much smaller, hand-size, and soprano in tone, whereas the marimboula gives much the sound and percussive effect of a bass violin. At the country social dances there is always a lead singer, usually the guitar player, and just as Cuban and Dominican rhythms mix with the Haitian méringues, so the songs and dances fuse into each other so that at times one could just as well be in a thatch-covered clearing in Cuba or across the border in Santo Domingo as in Haiti. But there is something special about the Haitian méringue when it is played in its pure form on rare occasions, and when one has for a partner one of the older cavaliers in the starched white national uniform. Then the méringue becomes a mixture of polka, the "balancé" of the quadrille, and the sensuous hip movement of the Cuban bolero.

An imposing villa set far back in a grove of palm and mango trees on the Martissant road was the town house of some high functionary during the latter part of the nineteenth century. When I was first in Haiti it had been converted into a house of assignation by a Dominican "madame." Prostitution was rare in Haiti, as the selling of sexual pleasures seemed out of keeping with the African polygamous pattern. The ladies of these houses were imported, and most of them were from Santo Domingo, that being nearest to Haiti and the Dominican women being willing and apparently excelling in the expertise of their merchandise. (The same villa is now a school for training secretaries.) But since I wanted to know what was danced in Haiti at all levels, and if possible from whence it came and what the musical accompaniment was, it seemed to me reasonable enough to make every effort to see these popular dances wherever they were to be found, and to participate in them if possible. There must have been many other gathering places of this kind, especially after the Marine Occupation but La Paloma Blanca was my favorite. When the wind blew from the bay I could hear the méringues of Haiti and Santo Domingo and the rumbas and boleros and guajiras of Cuba; finally I worked my way around to spending most of my last Saturday nights in Port-au-Prince at La Paloma Blanca, the villa in the grove. I was often with Fred or, if not, with some one of the young lieutenants of the army, which latter proved more useful for my purposes. At first the ladies entertaining at La Paloma Blanca were suspicious and on guard against competition from an outsider of their same sex. I was used to this from Martinique and Trinidad, where I had not spent as much time in folklore, but rather in popular research. But it was not long before I had made friends with almost all of them from Santo Domingo, with a few from Cuba and a few from Puerto Rico, and when they were at ease and aware that there was nothing to lose by my presence, they became the best of my professors for popular secular dances. My Haitian escorts were not hampered in their pursuits of pleasure and were willing to regard me as a companion, sometimes confidante, enjoying my eagerness to learn. Strangely enough, older women, plump and showing the unmistakable mark of time and hard living were more popular with the male clientele than young girls. These latter would dance together, first one then the other of the couple taking the lead, mascaraed eyes roving from tables to doorway, waiting for some customer to intervene, to make his arrangements with the proprietress and lead the fortunate one up a curving staircase which once must have been the pride of the owners, or to one of the cubicles behind the villa which one could imagine to have been, in colonial times, slave quarters.

The older women would sit at our table criticizing the dancing of the younger ones and sometimes insisting on getting up to dance with me to demonstrate how a step should be properly done. At first I was embarrassed to dance with these duennas, most of whom, with unnaturally high bosoms, wide hips, and thin legs resembled pouter pigeons. But as I realized the objectivity with which all matters of intimacy are regarded in such establishments, I was grateful for their attention. And were I there with the young Haitian lieutenants I might very well be alone at our table for long pauses, during which the men one after another melted into the upstairs or outside shadows, leaving me listening to the life story of one of these friendly, almost motherly hostesses or trying to master a step or combination under her tutelage. The impression of American young women left by me must have been a strange one.

Haiti is preoccupied with carnival from January until Ash Wednesday. With the first day of the year, bands which may have been practicing for months, or which may have been associated in societies for years, clothe themselves in outlandish costumes and roam the waterfronts, hills, and plains of the island. They are not as tightly organized as the samba societies of Brazil, nor do they, until now, have the same political importance. But instead of ending festivities with Ash Wednesday, as in most countries where carnival is observed, there is no break whatsoever in the streams of dancers roving town and country long after Mardi Gras. The seven weeks following Mardi Gras are devoted to Rara, a festivity borderline between religious and secular. From the study written after my return to the University of Chicago, I quote the following notes which, as I recall Mardi Gras that year, are remarkably accurate:

"In addition to vaudun ceremonies Haiti dances also for special springtime rites. During days and nights the roads of the country are transformed into arteries of white dust which converge in rhythm on the capital and the larger towns to celebrate Mardi Gras. These are 'seasonal dances of the crowd.' All year long, except during Holy Week, Haiti dances under the innumerable tonnelles covered with banana thatch to music of Dominican, Cuban, or Haitian origin. These are social dances of smaller groups called bamboches. Also Haiti dances at funerals, during wakes and work and sometimes only *pou' plaisi'*, or for pleasure, with no other reason.

"Dances consecrated to certain specific seasons are danced only during that season. A characteristic of these seasonal dances is that they cannot be interpreted by a single individual because their existence and their essence is based on the crowd, the impulsions of which create the form of the dance. They are created by large crowds, as in the secular Mardi Gras dances.

"Between sacred and secular dances is a subdivision of marginal dances which take from both categories. It is to this group that rara and banda belong. At the time of this study there was some confusion among my informants about where to place rara and lalwadi; should they be identified with Mardi Gras or be set apart, because while their exterior aspects were similar their significance was different. Among older people the prevalent opinion was that rara, though now almost totally incorporated into Mardi Gras, had originally been a celebration of the ascension of Christ and was still so performed in certain remote regions. An effigy of Judas would be carried and burned on the morning of Holy Saturday. Most of the movements are extremely sexual and no doubt attest the need to stimulate procreation of a new life to replace death; often funeral dances among primitive people have this sexual character. The banda is officially a funeral dance and it can be open, secular and public, depending on the wishes of the family of the deceased.

"As opposed to sacred and social dances which take place in permanent establishments, seasonal dances always take place in the open air and the groups of dancers are characterized by their tendency to roam. Rara orchestras can cover a distance of twenty to twenty-five kilometers in two or three days traveling across the plains, through cane fields and plantations of bananas, through little settlements. Once in a town their route is the main street, and here, as in the country, they stop from time to time so that their leader can dance in competition with other leaders. Evidently such dancing cannot take place under shelter.

"Sometimes rara may be executed by the same people who make up a combite, or work group, for example the Congo society which invaded the fields of our territory in the Cul-de-Sac on Holy Friday, but in general carnival bands are conglomerations united for a brief orgiastic demonstration of a seasonal need. When I find rara and Mardi Gras interchangeable as terms I think it necessary to repeat that the confusion of two names for a single dance is superficial and, in my opinion, quite recent. There is no doubt that formerly the rara was of a religious character as evidenced by bands that one meets when Mardi Gras is finished, during Lent. The rara has been improperly incorporated into Mardi Gras and since the two terms have been used interchangeably the idea that they are the same has become accepted. Actually the Mardi Gras begins weeks before its climax of Palm Sunday, Monday and Tuesday of Holy Week. However, during Lent one still encounters groups along the dusty roads that are rara, not in the festive spirit of Mardi Gras, but seriously celebrating the Ascension of Christ. (Vaudun seems to be completely forgotten. Services are suspended during Lent.) In this study I make a difference between the rara bands of Mardi Gras and those of Lent.

"A major-domo in short trousers, shoes and stockings, a jacket heavily encrusted with beads, mirrors, and trinkets, an enormous crown of paper flowers, mirrors, and ostrich plumes on his head, a baton in his hand, leads the Mardi Gras group. Ordinarily the lalwadi or leader of this rara of Holy Week carries a red-robed figure of Judas hanging from the end of a pole. During the carnival season joyful burlesquing revelers liven the streets of towns and villages, sometimes four or five hundred at a time, as is the case with bands in la Grande Rue of Port-au-Prince; groups called 'orthophonic' or gros-bouzain. The leaders, or rois, of these bands challenge other leaders of rival bands to very complicated competition dances. Years ago there were similar 'kings' in Jamaica, but they have now disappeared. They were called 'John Connu,' and according to old accounts they wore the same elaborate headdresses as do the Haitian 'kings.' The Jamaican headdresses were sometimes complete miniature houses mounted in small boats."

The day of Mardi Gras I stood on top of Roger Anselm's

car and filmed hours of gay madness with my old sixteen-millimeter Kodak. It was a pleasure to use it again, because aside from carnival in the country and a trip to the Citadel at Cap-Haïtien I had had little use for it, being busy with my vaudun activities. I returned to Chicago with hundreds of feet of limpid ocean beach, palm trees, cane fields, secular dances and now and then sacred ones from the other islands. But during most of my stay in Haiti the movie camera would have been strikingly out of place. Perhaps I was also traumatized by an experience in Trinidad. A Shango priest heard the clicking of the camera from the cabin where I was supposed to have been in sanctified seclusion before entering the ceremony. Shango dances were fairly common in Trinidad, but not the ceremonies, and this one had been arranged in strictest secrecy. I have a few feet of film of a desperate white rooster, head down, wings flapping, beak open in a last gasp for air as the priest's knife descends to cut its throat. Then there is the surprised face of the priest turned toward the cabin door and, after that, kaleidoscopic disorder, part of which is the priest catapulting toward the door, flinging chicken and knife into the air in his anger. My camera was snatched away from me in an embarrassing episode from which only the intervention of the friend who had arranged things saved me.

For photography nothing matches carnival. For days and nights and weeks, towns, villages, crossroads, and the smallest collections of compounds prepare for the event, which never reaches the orgiastic proportions of carnival in Brazil or the studied decadence of carnival in Venice, but which has a combined rustic and baroque quality that is almost ritual. Perhaps it is because Haiti is poorer and those able to afford the glitter and glamour are a small percentage beside the swarming black population of dance and music societies, jugglers, acrobats, major-domos, and the "kings," who are in effect the vedettes, the featured performers of the bands. The ciseaux, a twisting foot exercise resembling a restrained spastic Charleston, is the main competing dance of the "kings," and at intervals, while moving from village to village, kings of two encountering bands compete in the ciseaux, varying the footwork with quivering shoulders and low cross-legged turns, blowing cheap store whistles all the while, disdainfully refraining from looking at each other, intent on outdoing themselves in exaggerations of the steps. It was up to the crowd to decide the winner, encourage the kings, insult the competitors, to pass the clairin or to toss coins in the dust to be picked up by the régisseur of the society.

This carnival, my first, was the happiest I have seen in Haiti. Perhaps there was still an exuberance over the departure of the Marines. Perhaps even while the praises of Sténio Vincent were being sung, plans were being made for a new President and there were those ever-recurrent hopes for prosperity. Vincent had, after all, instituted laws controlling ownership of retail business, until then almost completely in the hands of Syrian merchants. So this year the prize-winning méringue, a thanks to President Vincent, was sung from corner to corner of the island, and on all roads leading to the capital. Long after Vincent had lost his popularity, accused of pro-mulattoism and negligent handling of the massacre of Haitian workers by Dominicans at the Dominican border in 1937, one could hear the méringue in street cafés, élite salons and at country fêtes:

Merci, Papa Vincent,
We know a man who loves us, who has given us the right
to retail commerce.
It is up to us to say, "Thank you," Papa Vincent!

During one of the performances of the Dunham Company, years later, a Haitian singer refused to join in this song, part of a production number which we had created to reproduce a Haitian market place. I had forgotten for the moment the massacre of many thousands of Haitians invited to Santo Domingo as laborers which had taken place under Vincent, and that his retaliation had been so feeble as to have been considered by some as collaboration, all the more plausible because the grandmothers of Vincent and Trujillo had been of the same parentage.

This day the streets of Port-au-Prince glittered with satin and spangled floats on which cream-colored and honey-colored queens stood draped in satin and lace and bowed regally to the cheering crowd. I thought as I stood with my camera that whatever Charles Seabrook, incautious author of *Magic Island*, may have said to offend the Haitian government, he had certainly and rightly sung the praises of the Haitian mulatto woman. She is of a blend of beauty hard to find elsewhere. There is also in Haiti another kind of beauty, other than the golden-skinned, wavy-haired mulatto. I am speaking of conventional beauty, leaving out the kind that means appreciation of essentials, conventional or not, and that is the marabou. One of the queens this day was this particular mixture, admired by black, white, and mulatto. In earliest accounts of the island, Moreau de Saint-Méry has given the complicated ingredients of the blood mixture which produces the beauty known as marabou. The result is a satin-smooth black skin, fine features, large, heavily fringed eyes, and wavy, silky black hair. This day the float of the marabou queen was a kneeling camel, on the saddle of which she sat in a cloud of gold cloth. The effect was so dazzling that mulattoes parked in cars or crowded into the front lines of crowds that pressed in from the Champs-de-Mars or Club Bellevue applauded and cheered for her as loudly as did the bands of black peasants. There is, after all, a meeting place when esthetics are involved, or there was that day. Under drums, singing bands, orchestras mounted on floats, and gramophone records, we could hear the shuffling of the chairo pié, the trudging cohesive step used equally in combite or work groups, or rara or carnival, or funerals; always traveling, always in bands, a coordinated restlessness leaving observer as well as participant with the feeling of ecstatic urgency.

There were societies of Carib Indians resplendent in colored feathers and striped face paint, of Moors in satin robes and jeweled turbans. Some of these bands are of long

standing and their clothing is furnished, refurbished, and issued by the society to which they belong and pay dues.
Among those making up the bands at that time were town
proletariat, peasants, small shop owners, taxi drivers, students, mulattoes, the beginnings of the middle class that
now exists. The nephew of the Rouzier sisters passed with
a group of Mexican charros wearing sombreros and serapes,
some of them carrying guitars. Young girls of the élite,
dressed in the period of Pauline and the Empress Joséphine, rode in flower-decorated carriages, and devils painted
red and flaunting horns and tails circled the carriages or ran
leaping into groups of children, who screamed, fell to roll on
the ground in mock terror, then ran back for the same thrill.
There were professional stilt walkers wearing top hats and
tail coats and long black trousers, and bands of school children wearing the colors of their schools. I thought of the
Deputy when I saw the band from St. Marc—new shoes, however ill-fitting, neat blue denim uniforms, red neckerchiefs.
They were the children of peasants, street merchants, fishermen, farmers, seeing the capital for the first time, wide-eyed,
knowing somehow that they were special and were the fore-
runners of social, even economic, change. There was applause
as they passed, and I felt proud to know the man who was
already in the process of making these changes.

By the night of Mardi Gras I was in a state of complete
exhaustion. I felt obliged to put on my carnival dress, a
leotard and tights with assorted bandannas sewn around the
waist line, and go to the masked ball at the Club Bellevue.
Before midnight I had slipped away from Roger Anselm and
into the streets of Port-au-Prince. From time to time in the
crowded streets I would see a familiar face, but before we
could meet, we were separated by the churning, intoxicated
crowd. This was a new experience for me, and my first reaction was to struggle against being crushed. Then I found that
complete nonresistance was the simplest way to survive, and
was shuffled like a rag doll from dancing partner to dancing
partner, out of the arms of Mephistopheles into the arms of

a Moor who had lost his turban or a peasant with a red neck-erchief, straw hat and jug of white rum. Sometimes I would find myself locked in a chairo pié band about to start on a trek of forty or fifty miles. The concerted shuffling, unbroken rhythm and clairin seemed to keep the bands going for days without stopping to eat or sleep. Then I would be out of that and into a pelvis-grinding grouillère knot, face to face with some man, woman, or child too far gone in the sexual ecstasy of the official carnival dance, the mascaron, to pay the slightest attention to the sex or age of a partner. There are somewhere statistics which verify an increased birth rate after carnival. I would imagine this to be so, but what I made note of then in carnival was, as in the frenetic dances of the vaudun, stimulus, even sexual, in the highest degree, but not necessarily with an end in consummation. It would seem that the Haitian peasant can be characterized as reluctant to par-ticularize his feelings of sex in public. Allegory, the prover-bial, the metaphorical are important, and while the entire community may be aware of the object of his or her desires, this is handled obliquely, as are most African relationships. So in this mass dancing I have never taken sexual gestures or close physical contacts as a direct advance. For this rea-son I shuffled, swayed, trudged, pressed against others and was embraced by them, drank rum for which I had not yet acquired a taste and, finally, climbing onto a car trying to force its way through the crowd in order to throw a limp streamer at my last reeling partner, found myself pulled into the seat beside Fred. Doc and Cécile were asleep in the rum-ble seat. Roger Anselm had given up looking for me, had found Fred and turned the task over to him. Roger never quite forgave me for my behavior that night and was added to the list of suitors unwilling to carry torches over the hills and valleys of Haiti—in the sense, that is, of putting up with my vagrancies. But we remained friends and I have missed among those of his class, on my returns to Haiti, a quality that he had which is so rare in any society where the élite is based on nonessentials: a sense of humor toward himself, his social status, and toward life in general. Roger Anselm died before Estimé became President.

Doc and Cécile and Fred and I threaded our way through the thinning crowd to one of our favorite coffee shops and sat until dawn watching bands forming for the chairo pié back to wherever they had come from. We watched couples finally moving off toward the shadows, and marveled at the rocket burst of the sun as it catapulted from the ocean, where those fishermen who had missed last night's revelry hoisted sails in the morning breeze and made their way to the deep waters between Port-au-Prince and the island of La Gonâve to begin the day's work.

Carnival in small towns, villages, and the country has a flavor quite apart from the three days' festivity in the capital. It was my impression when seeing the carnival in Port-au-Prince the last time, in 1962, that poverty might have been leveling things, and élite and peasant, city and country were finally arriving at a cultural agreement. The floats were more than modest, the street bands were of either country people or that newly established class to which I have referred earlier, falling somewhere between upper proletariat and lower bourgeoisie. For days before the last carnival I have taken part in, the one of 1962, electricians were installing a mammoth portrait of President Duvalier above the double archway that Estimé had constructed years before in the center of the rond-point of the exposition grounds, an area still surrounded by exposition buildings, which now serve as various embassies and the Pan American Airways office. I had sat on the second floor in a window of what would one day be a ballet room of an attempt to establish a Dunham School of dance and theater in Haiti. I found myself reviewing some of the same carnival costumes of twenty-five years before: societies of Moors and Carib Indians, devils and goblins. But they were worn and soiled with spangles hanging by threads and mirrors tarnished. There also entered this year an element that had been there before, which was familiar to all of us, but which had never been previously exploited to such a degree in either representation or caricature: the transvestite. They were there in bands and singly, in couples and intimate groups, a few girls dressed as boys, as girls have always done, but boys and men costumed as clowns with exaggerated breasts and buttocks, or simply parading in frayed silk dresses, wigs, careful makeup, now and then a pair of high-heeled slippers; blatant homosexuality, sorry residue of the bargain-rate Caribbean cruise.

The parade was hours late in starting and meanwhile we fortunate ones, on the second floor of the Dunham School to be, sat inside and on balconies and watched the unfortunate ones standing in the hottest sun of the season. We watched a sorry display of horsemanship, arranged by the Army to amuse the spectators, watched the Militia take out their own discomfort and concerted vile dispositions on children who broke through the cordon on each side of the road, and on plain citizens trying to park where functionaries had reserved spaces, which restriction it seems one was supposed to know by divination. Over it all the badly installed, unflattering portrait of "Papa Doc" traced in electric bulbs winked and blinked even though the sun was high.

Two hours after the announced starting hour, the ragged masses swarmed down the avenue singing the carnival méringue to "Papa Doc." The meagerly draped floats followed and I stormed over the niggardliness of the banners, floats, and costumes, acutely aware of the few tourists present; those not monied enough to continue south below the equator to the rich, decadent carnival of Rio de Janeiro, or those returned, as I, to recapture something from the nostalgia of other, surely gone-forever days of the Black Republic. I looked at my companions leaning eagerly over the balcony and no one seemed to be in agreement with my disappointment. Élifait, houseboy born and bred on Leclerc, and Emmanuel, head mason for several years, beaming over the tawdry displays of "societies," and Gâchelin, overseer of Leclerc, all took the bands of pederasts in their stride. Lavinia

Yarbrough, once a member of the Dunham Company, now
progressed in her own right to proprietorship of her own
school in Haiti, found the carnival what carnivals should be.
But then they live there all year round. I, for my part, felt
sad and sick at the increased poverty, distressed at the lost
melody of a wide-eyed scholar, unnerved at the lost rhythm
set off into epileptic spasms by the badly hooked-up portrait
of the President. In thinking things over, I may find or see
now a rhyme to the insane rhythm. These other days of
carnival were a catharsis in national spirit, a symbol of all
that could be hoped for in gilded escapism, and today there
is no place for such in a starving nation. The ragged carnival
of 1962 may have been the turning inward of the Haitian
people, their decision to make do with what they found
themselves with. It had all of that air. The sea sparkled as
always, dust churned under bare feet, but the blinking caricature of His Excellency dominated the scene, dulling any true
gaiety, changing everything that had heretofore meant carnival to me into a stark reality of the present.

A bush priest named Julien was the houngan at Descayettes, a small settlement above the hills of Port-au-Prince
going south toward Jacmel. The houngfor at Descayettes
housed a conglomerate of Ibo, Arada-Dahomey, and Congo
gods. The Congo gods seemed to be borderline, or with their
mana at a low ebb, because they seldom entered to take possession of potential "horses" but seemed to content themselves with being complacent spectators to the antics of their
associates, manifesting their presence mostly in song, dance,
and occasional demands for promises. One day not long before my departure from Haiti, after my lavé-tête initiation,
Dantès Bellegarde's young son suggested a walk into the hills
with a schoolmate of his. I agreed, provided they would escort me to visit the priest Julien. This was after the Rex Theatre performance, after my conquest of Port-au-Prince mulatto
society. I was certain that I was being put to one of those
"club de jeunes hommes" tests, a boy scout challenge to a

tenderfoot. My reputation for daring, curiosity, and resistance to query and criticism made me a logical prey for wagers on this level, but by now I knew how to be prepared, even for emergencies that my young friends might overlook. I wore cotton stockings, solid boots, packed a palm fan and hunting knife in my knapsack where there were already sandwiches for the three of us, bottles of kola, a small thermos of coffee, soap, a towel, a toothbrush, the everpresent eau de cologne, a tiny flask of rum, and a notebook. This was more or less my "bush" equipment. I carried my Kodak and between them they carried my movie camera and the knapsack, grumbling as we started at dawn and teasing me about my tourist precautions, sometimes calling me "Dr. Livingstone." They felt differently when we stopped under a mango tree on the mountain path for lunch.

We had as yet come across no crossroad shops or porteresses carrying cooked food or kola; besides, I knew that they had counted on tiring me and returning much sooner. This was, so far, my victory.

Since it was a test of endurance, I had chosen the most difficult paths, skirting around Descayettes and climbing higher into the fresh hilltops, from which we could see isolated plots of cultivated land, lone white huts, a valley here and there, and the mountain range ahead. From people whom we met hurrying in the direction of Descayettes we knew that a dance or ceremony was in full swing at Julien's. From time to time as the breeze shifted from ocean to mountain we could hear the drums and faint singing. My companions would gladly have stopped sooner, but I led them merrily on, leaning against a tree trunk to fan once in a while, grinning at their fatigue. I had learned to wear a bandanna under my straw hat and a cotton sweater under my shirt for hot sun or mountain climbing; my escorts, however, had worn sports shirts, and their curly mulatto hair—one's was reddish brown, the other's, black—offered no resistance to streams of sweat which coursed through the dust on their faces. They had started out in white tennis sneakers, which, by noon, halfway up the mountain path, were soiled and scuffed, and their feet, when we stopped to wade in a mountain stream, were obviously worse for wear. My old boots, on the contrary, were made for this sort of thing.

I sought ways to step out of sight of my companions long enough to sip a thermos cup full of heavy black coffee, and this also helped keep me ahead in energy. I at times used the pretext of changing film, or see or pretend to see a hidden offering to Legba or Guedé or Baron Samedi or Asaka, favorite loa and protector of mountain people. In the early afternoon we called a truce and, having proved my point, I agreed to a roadside siesta if they would spend the night at the priest Julien's with me. We lay on a dry mound shaded by a gnarled wild cherry tree. We laughed at my complicity, now evident, when I had so readily accepted the mountain trip and ate the mealy sweet fruit from the ground under the tree. Turning my cheek from one damp young shoulder to the other, listening to gossip and school tales and escapades in élite society, I fell asleep in what was perhaps the most comforting moment of my entire stay in Haiti. But it was not for long, because the insistent sound of Congo drums disturbed our rest and woke me, reminding me of my serious obligation at Descayettes.

The ordeal of lavé-tête being over with, I had set my next goal as trial by fire, canzo. Since Melville Herskovits was categorically against this at this time and observing a series of canzo rituals had made me also begin to have doubts as to my preparedness, I had decided to pass the next stage of initiation by making a promise to fulfill the *service* at some later date. At the same time I would discharge myself of the burden of guilt of my family toward our ancestors, a convincing excuse for my curiosity, and guarantee a yam ceremony on my return to Haiti, a return which, even then, I felt to be inevitable. I have often wondered whether my reluctance to attach myself solely to the houngfor which I had known best and which was responsible for my spiritual protection in the vaudun, was because of the never-ending quest for the novel,

the statistics-gathering of the researcher, or another reason,
which had troubled me, beginning as a doubt and developing
into a full-grown suspicion. I was, in short, not at all sure of
my sincerity in these pursuits and there seemed to be no way
to put myself to the test, to find out. Could Herskovits tell
me, could Erich Fromm, could Téoline or Dégrasse tell me
what part of me lived on the floor of the houngfor, felt awareness seeping from the earth and people and things around
me, and what part stood to one side taking notes? Each moment lived in participation was real; still, without arranging
this expressly, without conscious doing or planning or thinking I stayed outside the experience while being totally im-
mersed in it. After my "marriage" to Damballa I longed for
some inkling, some indication of "possession"; I thought
of returning to give myself to 'ti Couzin and the Congo
Moundong cult. I can now observe with some pity, even
amusement, the newly traveled, ethnic-saturated, homesick-
for-Chicago Iphigenia wondering what next to do to prove
herself a scientist to her Alma Mater; the true scholar to her
country; the selfless sacrificial maiden to her people. While
I might have been amused by such pranks as outwalking two
adolescent school boys that morning, I was still seriously
concerned about my moral position in this matter of trust in
making promises for future initiations.

As we neared Descayettes it was late afternoon and the
dull thud of the Congo drums indicated the dance in progress, a Congo paillette. Congo drums still evoke more sensa-
tions of pure sexual stimulus in me than drums of other pan-
theons of vaudun. They were circling around each other, I
knew, the men and women who had passed us on the hill
paths carrying reed chairs or stools on their heads, friendly in
greetings but with no familiarity and not even curious about
us, just intent on the single purpose of joining the mass
Congo dance taking place at Julien's houngfor, whether that
dance be Congo fran, Congo paillette, contredanse, or dances
to the loa. There they would be, circling, advancing, retreating, teasing, flirting in the true, primitive sense without look-

ing at each other, all parts of the body excepting eyes inviting, with throaty cries and murmurs and intaken breath let out in a long-drawn-out panting. They would be full of desire and ecstasy that would keep the drums beating and hips swaying and breasts and pelvic girdles undulating for hours without touching or caressing a partner, drums and sounds and body heat generating sex from collective, concerted, uninterrupted central body rhythm in motion.

We left the donkey paths that had led us into the higher ranges of the hills and, turning our backs to the sun, cut through the forest of sparse, untended breadfruit, mango, wild cherry, and coconut palm trees, following the sound of the drums. I could hear snatches of song:

> Congo Ibo Lele-o,
> Ouayoh, Ouayoh!

It was cool and the air was clean and fresh. As we walked we opened fallen green coconuts with my hunting knife and drank the cloudy water, scraping out the jellied interior with our fingers. We couldn't be trespassing, because under every tree were stacks of dried husks, dropped by others as emptied, and the trees were heavy with unpicked nuts. Before I knew it I was talking of my problem, as much to myself as to my two friends, not even expecting an answer and not at all sure they understood its crucial significance to me, or whether they fully understood my French, which was not geared for such complicated thinking. Young Bellegarde found a piece of discarded sugar cane and broke it into three pieces and we chewed on this, listening to the drums, stumbling over roots, laughing at each other or at some startled goat or pig or over-turned Legba roadside offering, following the Congo drums, joining in the songs until, as we stepped into the clearing, there seemed to be no moral issue involved and I knew that I would enter a ceremony, baptism, or classroom with the same free spirit I felt then, because to any of these I would be giving my total self, and the supply would always exceed the demand.

At the hill priest's compound, I slipped into the Congo line of women facing men, waving to Julien, who led my two friends to the stands where grillot and kola and roast goat were spread on banana leaves. The two ate generously, excused themselves, from those of us known to the loa, and fell asleep on a mat in Julien's hut. The sun was down and our tonnelle was lighted by charcoal fires and candles and kerosene lanterns. This was festivity dancing after some ceremony which I didn't bother to ask about. At Julien's one came to dance, not to talk or theorize. For my two friends the next morning meant school, for me a promise to Damballa. I went on dancing with the last of the crowd, far into the night.

At six in the morning I was brushing my teeth outside Julien's hut, the two boys were drinking coffee and eating bananas and watercress bought from a porteress down from the mountains and on her way past Leclerc to the Iron Market in the capital. The hounci designated to assist Julien in my promise were clearing the tonnelle of all signs of the night's revelry and preparing Damballa's altar for his offering. Weeks before, I had consulted Julien, who agreed that the trial by fire was not indicated for me at this time. Téoline and Dégrasse were perfectly willing to take me in hand for it, and had I isolated myself with them in all likelihood the act would have been accomplished. As it was I had paid Julien six dollars to prepare for the promise, which could be made at any time. But my days in Haiti were now truly numbered, so the occasion to spend a day in the mountains and night at Descayettes was fortuitous.

Damballa's altar was a cement-block circle around the base of a majestic tropical oak. Four times a year the tree bore tiny lavender sweet-smelling flowers and showered them over the compound and altar. This particular morning even the straw rooftops were a film of flowers. Julien felt this to be a good sign. The hounci placed bottles of orgeat, a bottle of Florida water, a dish of shelled peanuts, a plate of flour, and a dish of eggs on the altar. Through the early morning mist and leaf shadow I could see the sun on La Gonâve, the island in the bay, and in the foreground far below the dim outlines

of the Palace and cathedral, and the fishing boats starting out
to deep sea. My two friends were clambering down the goat
paths to the main road. They stopped once or twice to wave,
and it occurs to me now that I have not seen them since, as
important as they had been without knowing it, during our
walk to Descayettes, in putting at ease my anxieties about my
sincerity in delving into the mystère.

I had never before seen Julien's compound when it was
free of people and activity. At the base of each tree in the
scattered compound was an altar.

It would seem more accurate to call Julien's establishment
a village or hamlet rather than compound, as there were none
of the barriers ordinarily closing auxiliary huts around the
central one. Each faced where it would and had its own garden plot, and the nearest thing to holding the huts together
geographically as a community was the houngfor with its tonnelle. Some of the circular altars were old and were cracking
where tree roots had pushed through. Others were of fresh
cement, but each was painted a base color, that of the god to
whom it was dedicated, then decorated in the symbols of the
god. The hounci moved with little sound, murmuring to each
other, their dresses snow white, drifting from houngfor to altar to charcoal fire, to pour tiny cups of coffee to take to Julien's daughter's hut, where the priest had slept the night. I
was sipping coffee and marveling at the quiet beauty of the
place, listening to parrot calls and a waking donkey and ever-
challenging roosters. I was smelling the charcoal fire in the air
and feeling good where the sun's rays drifted through leaves
and reached my arms and face, and wishing there could be
a belonging and faith and creed without ceremony or ritual,
when Julien spoke. He had walked over the leaves and grass
to where I stood and he also was drinking coffee and feeling
the morning sun and perhaps even thinking some of my
thoughts as he greeted me and nodded toward the altar.
The houngan was a tall, slender man of perhaps forty years
of age, and we had seen each other only when I went to
Descayettes for Congo dances, or rare services, as when
Georgina was punished by Papa Guedé. Julien was a man

who seemed to have more than one life behind him and to be looking ahead into some other. Each time I saw him I was impressed by an ethereal quality not common to houngans and mambos, who, whether in a state of possession or conducting a ceremony, exude a kind of capable matter-of-factness which balances the unreality of the total experience. It was said that Julien had studied for the Roman Catholic priesthood but had become shocked at the amoral behavior of his superiors, and turned to the vaudun more as an instrument of moral guidance for the wide community that found its way to his houngfor than for profit or a religious or cult affirmation. Formal instruction beyond the ordinary was apparent in his speech and behavior, and he charged no fee for the elementary school classes to which young and old came every morning during the week. They were gathering now under the tonnelle, old ones on benches, children on the dirt floor, sharing soiled notebooks and worn textbooks, watching the altar preparations and eyeing the stranger taking part in their most secret practices. I felt that in confiding my vaudun promise to Julien my interests would be well protected. I felt both safe and anonymous, and as we talked realized how much I was in need of respite from the intense experiences of the Cul-de-Sac and the Congo Moundong priest 'ti Couzin.

I was called to the altar. There I made my obeisances and was then escorted by the mambo maison, a woman who must have been, by her appearance, a relative of Julien's, into the houngfor. Inside were no photographs of saints, no baptismal basin, no dusty objects of profession. There were only rows of spotless head pots, and among these would be one into which Julien would decide I must recite my promise. Then small portions of today's food offerings and a clipping from the center hair of my head would be added to whatever was there already, and the pot would be closed until I fulfilled my promise or until the houngan would have decided I had defected. (In the latter case the pot is opened, the material having to do with a particular promise is carefully removed, pardon is asked of the spirit that has been disturbed for no purpose, and the materials are thrown at some crossroads to be walked on, sniffed at by stray animals, and in general desecrated.) At this time the unhappy one who has failed his fulfillment suffers a seizure of malaise, business losses, or worse, wherever he may be. I have learned to think of promises as more serious than ceremonies and second only to "marriages" in contractual force.

Outside the houngfor there was no drumming, but the hounci followed the ason with handclapping and singing and the pupils of the tonnelle classroom stopped reciting from notebooks and joined the singing and clapping. My promises made in the sanctuary, I joined the swaying group of houncis. Then we danced to Damballa. Julien took a seat in front of the altar and the mambo maison brought a clean, embroidered sheet from the houngfor. Seemingly from nowhere a "la place," Julien's male representative, stepped into our small group and, taking me by the hand, led me to the houngan, then in the deep undulations of the yonvalou, lower and lower until I was on my knees. Then I knew that La place was both instructing me and observing me for signs of Damballa's entrance or approval. The singing was louder, even frenzied, and as my face touched the earth at Julien's feet, I tried closing my eyes, hoping that something would happen to justify this trust. When I opened them the sun had disappeared and my first thought was of rain. Then I saw the feet of hounci around us and the sheet held in their hands which had been lowered to cover us. I was looking straight ahead at Julien's denim trousers and sandals, then down at a plate of flour lightly sprinkled with orgeat scraped into a mound on which an egg perched. Under the sheet the same dish was before my partner, who by now was completely taken over by Damballa. Flat on the ground, his hands clasped behind his back, he advanced; smiling and undulating, he advanced toward the offering. His body rippled, his neck became elongated, his tongue darted rapidly in and out between his open lips, and the familiar ric-a-tic of the serpent god filled the improvised tent. I watched fascinated as he lapped at the flour. When he crushed the egg in his lips, however, sucking the contents, swallowing egg, then shell, then flour, I succumbed to one of my old taboos, a revulsion toward eating raw eggs. I turned away and in so doing, still on my knees, still with my face almost to the ground, looked directly into Julien's eyes. He had lifted his side of the sheet and was peering down at me with what struck me as malevolence but might have been anxiety. Whichever, it was not only disconcerting but frightening. I froze for a moment, then went into action, inching and undulating in rhythm toward my sacrificial plate. I reached into it and tilting my head away from the houngan to cover my face, crushed the egg with my chin, praying to some Christian or at least non-vaudun god to come to my rescue, to work some miracle so that the dish would disappear or I would be able to overcome my repugnance, which was augmented by the fact that the egg was not quite fresh. The miracle did not happen. Julien watched me. I rolled my eyes for aid to my companion, but he was oblivious to everything but the flecks of sticky flour still left to be swept up from the dish by his voracious tongue. There was no way out. I heard the singing come to an end and felt fresh air on my face as the sheet was snatched back. A kata drummer had appeared and the staccato beat introduced a shoulder dance. I stood up, my face smeared with flour and egg, Damballa's offering untouched. Julien lifted my plate and took it to the houngfor, and when he returned the hounci and La place were in a frenzied 'zepaules, but I stood where he had left me, feeling sick and helpless as tears streamed through the flour and egg. Someone handed me a kerchief, I wiped my face and started to dance. I danced more than I have ever in my life, before or after. I danced out all my anger at unknown things and at myself for trying to know them, frustration at the rotten egg and weariness with strange mores. I found myself alone with one, with another, or just by myself while others clapped and sang and it dawned on me that it was with affection and encouragement. I hadn't dared look at Julien, but at last I did. He was puzzled, speculative, but benign. He nodded to me, and seemed to be telling me that everything was well, that the gods were happy, that things were now in my hands, even the decision as to how long we should dance. I was tired: the sense of being easily emotionally drained had stayed with me since the day with 'ti Couzin. I nodded to Julien and the drum and ason stopped, the group of pupils who had come to the edge of our clearing melted back under the tonnelle, hounci embraced each other and saluted me, and for the first time the ground at my feet was kissed and I turned a waiting hounci around in the vaudun under-arm salute. It was impressive because I knew her to be canzo.

On the way down the mountain I passed Source Leclerc. Porteresses were squatted around the icy bubbling spring that supplies much of the water of Port-au-Prince and others were leaning against the giant mapou tree that marks a corner of the triangle that is Habitation Leclerc. Their laughter and gossip stopped as I slid down the last few yards, sending pebbles and branches into the road. Some of them I knew from town, and this put the others at ease at this strange apparition. The water of Source Leclerc was cold and sweet, and after washing my face I sat as some of the porteresses did with my feet and ankles in the running stream, looking into the dense forests of the Habitation where stories of Pauline Bonaparte Leclerc and Rochambeau and slave atrocities are still told. Then I dried my feet, put on my shoes and stockings, and walked with some of the porteresses the four miles to the Excelsior Hotel. We ate watercress and tender young carrots and sweet dwarf bananas and I talked about the boat that would take me back "up there."

A week later I left Haiti. There were a few tears—farewells to the closest of my friends, like Doc and Dumarsais Estimé and Fred Alsop. But deep inside me I knew that I would see the land again, and be a part of it, to what degree I couldn't tell. When the little Royal Netherlands boat left La Gonâve and the pink cathedral behind I could still see the tangled jungle of my future home, the property Leclerc and the mountains hiding Julien's village, where my dancing had saved me from disgrace.

12

We were sitting at the bar at Kyona Beach, its owner, Pierre d'Adesky, and I, drinking Pierre's Kyona Special, which had a little nutmeg flavoring in it but still wasn't as good, I told him, as our rum drinks in the Geisha Bar at Leclerc. The sea in front and the mountains behind gave Kyona and its shoreline to the left and promontory to the right the impression of being sheltered, yet of being suspended over water clear as glass. There seemed to be no separation between the beach and a small deserted island, Île Cabrites, which is in reality at least a half hour away by motor boat. I was watching my swimming companion, Dick Frisell, snorting and playing at being a whale some distance out to sea when I decided to think about what Pierre was saying.

"The master of Leclerc will never be happy," Pierre said, and I realized that he had made the same statement for at least the tenth time that lazy day. I had probably as many times that day hinted at exchanging a small portion of our Habitation for something of interest at Kyona. There are no beaches immediately adjacent to or in the capital, and beaches such as Pierre d'Adesky's are at a premium anywhere.

Pierre is Haitian-Italian and looks Scandinavian. Before building Kyona he had been, among other things, apprentice to, and seconded, another Italian Viking type who called himself Tarzan. Tarzan is best described as an underwater deep-sea guide and circus master who had drifted into Haiti at the beginning of its tourist epoch, who had fallen under its spell, and for a living and to stay in this paradise went out of his way to emulate, in appearance and behavior, the then current film representation of his namesake. Instead of conquering land jungles his prowess was combing coral caves, leading eager scuba divers through tips of porous volcanic mountain formations which encircle the island, and cultivating friendships with myriads of multicolored fish, small and large. For revenue from nondiving tourists Tarzan had equipped a glass-bottomed boat for trips into the bay and through this one could see the 'spectacle of the golden-skinned, golden-haired giant plunging between coral branches with sun sparkling through his shoulder-length hair, sea flora gracefully making way for his passage. Tarzan would often carry a piece of biscuit or bread between his teeth, and the fish would swirl around him like delirious birds nibbling, kissing, waiting to be recognized, brushing affectionately against him. With time the good rum of Haiti began to tell on Tarzan's figure, then on his underwater endurance. I have never seen him wear diving equipment and his underwater sorties of several minutes were real feats of physical fitness. The last I heard, Tarzan had retired to California. This was during the Magloire regime, before the real decline of tourism in Haiti. With him went a good deal of glamour. Before leaving, however, he had trained Pierre d'Adesky, who was, beside Tarzan as I last saw him, a slender underwater bronze arrow. But when I knew Pierre at Kyona Beach, history was repeating itself and there seemed to be no point in his keeping fit for tourists, especially since these were fewer and fewer. Pierre married, lived well, charmed American tourist ladies, and bought what is now Kyona Beach for, he says, the proverbial song. Then singlehanded, again quoting Pierre, he planted palm trees on the beach, built the central conical thatch bar and small pavilion for weekend dances, built beach huts and guest quarters. He clipped his Tarzan-style

hair, sent boys to dive for crab and lobster while he tended
the bar, once in a while conducted special friends on tours
of the coral palaces near the deserted island, and was now
trying to talk me out of Leclerc while I bargained for only a
small corner of Kyona Beach.

There may have been and there probably was and still is
some hotel or gambling syndicate behind Pierre d'Adesky,
reaching as far as Puerto Rico and Florida, and of course
that would mean Las Vegas. There would have been a great
deal of logic in having affiliated with this unbelievable magic
beach the believable magic of Habitation Leclerc, now in its
full bloom of reconstruction. Apart from this bargaining,
however, there was an unmistakable note of sincerity in
Pierre's comment about the predestined unhappiness of the
master of Leclerc. I thought of the afternoon. Kyona is an
hour and a half from Leclerc and would be about forty-five
minutes if the roads were what they should be. Leaving the
capital going north there is nothing but countryside after
Croix-de-Missions; great plantations devastated by the sisal
crop; a few cane fields leading to mountains or sea, sulfur
marshes specked with flocks of aigrettes perched picking ticks
from the backs of cattle, the cattle themselves so undernour-
ished that it seemed unfair; tiny cemeteries with lime mauso-
leums or crosses. There is nothing after Croix-de-Missions in
the way of villages excepting Duvalierville, which was once
Cabaret. There is also between Port-au-Prince and Kyona
Beach the unpleasantness of being stopped for inspection
at Duvalierville, just to be made aware, it seems, of how important the Ton-ton Macoute are and how many rifles and
holstered pistols they have at hand. By now I had learned to
sit patiently and answer briefly but politely when stopped
for questioning or a search of the car. There seemed to be
something offensive to these functionaries in anyone being
able to go to the beach on a weekday; still, in the end, we
were always sent on our way, though suffering the same routine returning. Sometimes we would see those voyagers un-
luckier than ourselves who might be waved over to the side of

the road with a rifle and left to sit until remembered much later and passed on. The thing to do was to fall into a Zen state, I had decided, and this took me through many travel aggravations, especially if travel was to or from the North, which mine usually happened to be this time in Haiti. It was better to think about the wonderful things of the island, which were and still are.

My thoughts returned to what Pierre had said. Pierre was right in the adage of Leclerc. The mistress of Leclerc was not happy, in spite of having bathed in almost motionless water so buoyant there was hardly any need to swim, lying on my back looking past sisal and sugar cane and marsh grass fields into the stark protective mountains where the cave of Trou Forban could be seen, unchanged in the more than twenty years since I had scaled it from the other side with Fred Alsop. That day Pierre and Dick and I had all visited the deserted island of Cabrites and plunged into the frescoed caverns around it and now, after three of Pierre's rum punches, I had to admit that the acquisition of Leclerc had brought some deep, insoluble sadness into my life which even as yet I have not been able to unravel.

It was just twenty-three years ago that I had boarded the little Royal Netherlands steamer with my pot tête and all the other memorabilia of more than a year of gathering the secret cult and ritual and dance life of the Caribbean. I was anxious to reach the University of Chicago before summer examinations and was already feeling guilty because I was certain then that I would abandon further work with Melville Herskovits if this meant leaving the University of Chicago. Much had happened in the twenty-three years. I had known and married John Pratt, our daughter Marie Christine was almost grown, I had known a large part of the world as a star performer and choreographer, trailing my degree in anthropology along as I could, and, following a year of retreat, writing in Japan, had begun a professional writing career. Since I had known Leclerc, two Dunham schools had come and gone and the Dunham Company, dispersed after an impossible season in Vienna, was just about to become a thing of the past, not because I wanted it so, but because I was the mistress of a property with a curse on it. This was one way to look at things . . .

From most of Leclerc one can see the bay when the heavy jungle of coconut and royal palms, mangoes, breadfruit, orange, lemon, almond, tropical oak trees and mahogany, bananas, manioc, and dozens of other lush plants are trimmed of heavy foliage. There are now two swimming pools and four fountains, one with a wide selection of local and imported fish. At one time John Pratt had begun digging into the crumbling staircase leading to the forest below the Habitation plateau. Iron carriage lamps were found which are now on iron posts in the driveway; also a copper ceiling lamp and cannon balls to add to those already lining the driveways when we first took over the place. Later, during the construction of an office in one room of a small villa said to have been occupied by Pauline Bonaparte Leclerc, I dug up a silver fork with a hallmark authenticated by the Jesuit fathers, who seem to be experts in such things in Haiti, as having belonged to the regiment of General Rochambeau, Leclerc's successor. A rather touching comment, when one thinks of the ravages of yellow fever during the French Army Occupation—one of our masons, who are now careful to bring any finds immediately to someone responsible, found, several feet under Pauline's bedroom floor, a bottle marked for castor oil and bearing the name of a Paris pharmacy then extant. General Leclerc's sword, the date of which, but not the ownership, has been authenticated, was unearthed and now serves as a main altar piece at vaudun ceremonies held in the open-air peristyle.

The last stages of the reconstruction of Leclerc followed a European and Near East tour of the Dunham Company. Influence of the temples at Baalbek may be seen in the circular peristyle which rises in stone terraces on one side of the vaudun dance floor to the height of the road where years ago

I scrambled down from my "promise" and the all-night dance at Julien's. A path leads past my private peristyle, past its houngfor and to the mapou tree at the far end of the property. Another path leads across a rock pool which Agwe and Simbi share if their "horses" are mounted on nights of dances and ceremonies. Then there is the main pavilion where seventeenth-century Venetian blackamoors give the dining and dancing veranda its name of Salon Guinée. In an apartment bordering a lower swimming pool, a fourth of one wall is a Venetian mirror, sixteenth century, delicately molded and flowered—a birthday gift to me from the Dunham Company as we left Venice and headed for Buenos Aires in 1950. In another poolside apartment, my own, a table from Pauline's palace in Paris and two vases from the period of Napoleon, said by Fernand Lumbroso, who gave them to me after a Paris opening, to have belonged to the Emperor himself. In my apartment there is also a Rosenthal portrait of Nefertete which I cherish as a first household gift from John Pratt. There is a winding paved driveway, some of the stones of which are pre-Revolution, staircases into jungle walks, and on a hill on the other side of the main property a tiny graveyard where the oldest headstone, dated 1789, marks the tomb of a German sea captain.

All of these things about Leclerc take a long time to tell, but while Pierre was discussing the master of Leclerc they were in panorama. There was so much beauty in the place, and yet it had been hard-won because it had not started out that way, and what he said I knew was true. I let him tell his tales of the various curses of Leclerc and made light of most of them. At the same time I felt more and more melancholy as the sun dropped behind the Île Cabrites and small fires began to dot the chalk mountain of Trou Forban. There was the inevitable story of Rochambeau in orgies and there was pretty good evidence that the General who followed Leclerc had lived near Port-au-Prince on the property now known as Leclerc. Thinking about the General I was almost sorry that I had found the fork engraved with his hallmark.

Donatien Rochambeau was the son of the Marshal of France, Jean-Baptiste Donatien de Vimeur, Comte de Rochambeau. At the death of General Leclerc, Rochambeau was ordered by Citizen Bonaparte to correct the situation in the rebellious island of Santo Domingo, otherwise Haiti. If reports of the conduct of the General toward slaves, freedmen, blacks, and mulattoes are true, and they surely are unanimously recorded as so, then he may be rated among the highest ranking of despots. By an English lady, Miss Mary Hassall, writing from Cap-Haïtien at the time of his arrival, he was thus described: "His uniform was à la hussar, and very brilliant; he wore red boots;—but his person is bad; he is too stout; a Bacchus-like figure." In an effort to reinstate slavery in Haiti and secure it by giving masters the right of life and death over their slaves, Leclerc's successor drowned, asphyxiated, hanged, fed to man-killing dogs, starved to death and buried alive as many Negroes and mulattoes, officers and slaves alike as time from other duties and pastimes permitted. His macabre midnight parties are said to have taken place at Leclerc—and some of the burying alive of slaves. The most popular version of the Rochambeau parties and the one Pierre seemed to appreciate most is that one night wives and daughters of black and mulatto officers were invited to attend a very imposing party, and on special command of the General. During the course of the evening these unfortunate women were given the special privilege of seeing a procession of coffins pass before them to the accompaniment of strange music and—historian Dantès Bellegarde has added to other reports—to the laughter of the white women present. In the coffins were the mutilated bodies of their husbands or fathers.

As soon as I set foot on Leclerc I felt its evil. I knew none of its history then, or, I should say, only the bright side: its gracious alleyways and staircases, the figures in baroque style around the pool graced by a bas-relief of Pauline Bonaparte Leclerc on Canova's sofa calmly regarding two awkward slaves offering the fruit of the country . . . This latter item was

enough to have verified Pauline's presence to credulous
visitors for many years, in spite of the fact that the Canova
portrait was not made until Leclerc had died of yellow fever
and been shipped back to France (ugly rumors say the casket
was full of confiscated jewels) and Napoleon Bonaparte's
sister had returned to Europe and married the Italian prince
Borghese. That was when I first became serious about Leclerc,
and that was twelve years before the day at Kyona Beach. I
was entranced by the glint of the sea through trees heavy
with fruit, the frame villa called Pauline's in which were relics
collected by post-Revolution landowners, fountains, a pro-
fusion of plants, small lizards, bougainvillea, and crumbling
walls. But under all this I felt a current of sadness, even
anguish. Sitting on a wall of bas-reliefs overlooking the forest
leading to the main road, I told my guide-chauffeur friend
Ton-ton Nord of my uneasiness. It was at the end of our
first South American tour and just after my Jamaican appendectomy. A number of the company would be staying on
in Haiti for a three to six months' rehearsal period while I
recovered. My brother had died and not long after, my father.
My mother, Annette, would be coming to visit. The place was
ideal for housing all of us in relative seclusion and in fact in
every aspect, other than the malaise which I alone seemed to
feel, and which came from the very pavements and huge
trunks of trees and overripe fruit and arrested motion of
small lizards, which seemed to be listening to some sound or
cry of death or agony. Later, when we were installed on
the place, twenty-four of us, I would sit near the edge of the
forest or walk at night to the mapou tree or down one of the
palm-bordered avenues to the road crossing the property. If
I stopped breathing for a moment I could hear things growing and dying and other things feeding on the death of these
until nature became a frightening, awesome thing and the
least small plant sprung up overnight an intrusion.

Fred had long since married Colleen and was father of two
girls in Jamaica. Doc was ill in Florida. Dégrasse and Téoline
were dead; 'ti Couzin was dead. Julien was alive and came

to see me one day, but there seemed to be no ties in spite of my "promise" of so long ago. I knew that there must be an exorcising, that whatever was evil in the soil and rocks and hidden streams under the property could, by the right person, be laid to rest even if it took years to do so. The forests would grow in happiness again, and the lizards in arrested motion would be without terror.

Now I can say that all of the restless, vengeful, agonized souls have gone peacefully to sleep or drifted back to 'Nan Guinée. It all came about through Kam, my Haitian prix-des-yeux godmother whom I met with Papa Augustin and Jean Brierre when Dumarsais Estimé sent me on a tour of Haiti, just after having pinned my decoration of Officer in the Haitian Legion of Honor and Merit over my left breast.

A great deal should be said about Henri Augustin, known to a large part of Haiti and much of New York as "Papa." I had not been long back from my first trip to the magic island —just time enough to turn in papers and finish with examinations at the University—when the Young Men's Hebrew Association in New York decided to institute dance programs, and a small group which I had gathered and trained with Ludmila Speranzeva in spare time was invited to be on the inaugural program. Nine of us in two undistinguished automobiles made the trip through snow and slept from Chicago to New York and back for this performance. Carmencita Romero (then Lily Mae Butler) and Talley Beatty—names needing no introduction in the dance world today—went along, and Archie Savage was on the program. That we arrived at all was a miracle; that we performed at all, arriving just in time after fifteen hazardous hours of driving to change into our costumes and dance, was another miracle. On the program with us a girl whose name I have forgotten interpreted Gauguin paintings, and Archie Savage displayed his world-famous Etruscan athlete's body in some sort of "primitive" dance, with a jovial, tall, dark-skinned heavily built Haitian playing rhythms that brought tears to my eyes as I stood on the side of the stage waiting for our turn to come.

The drummer was Papa Augustin, and it was perhaps thanks to him that I did well what I had to do that night, that Louis Schaeffer saw it and combined with Mary Hunter to bring me to Labor Stage and the Windsor Theatre, from which I moved into *Cabin in the Sky* and Hollywood and the rest of the world.

There was a party after the YMHA performance at Archie's mother's railroad flat in Harlem, and I who had thought I knew about hard times, knowing Chicago's South Side, was stunned at people taking shifts sleeping in beds and on boards over bathtubs that didn't work anyway, to have an extra roomer in order to make an extra dollar. But there was kindness and warmth all around for us, the weary travelers who had made a select, snob, intellectual, art-loving audience sit up and take notice, and there was a kind of food I had not known until then, but which now takes its place among gourmet treats the world over and is known as "soul food." We ate Papa's Haitian red beans and rice, and Mother Savage's neck bones and collard greens and pigs' feet and tails and black-eyed peas, and Archie's cornbread, which I watched him make, and helped by shaking roaches out of the meal and flour. Then Papa played his mama drum and I played the boula and Papa heard rhythms he had almost forgotten or which had been spoiled by the Cuban influence in Harlem. I danced vaudun dances and Papa sang in his off-key, gin voice (rum was hard to find and costly in New York). Our nine dancers slept somehow in an apartment already full to running over. Early in the morning I went downtown to Twenty-third Street and Second Avenue to finish my New York visit at the apartment of Chicago Cube Theatre friends, Mary Hunter and Jack Sullivan. But Papa and Archie were in my life to stay for a long time. There is much to be told about Papa Augustin, much of how our two lives were held together for so many years and through so many experiences by the magic of Haiti. As all good bush priests must be, and Papa was one whether in Chicago or Haiti or New York, he was deeply partial but at the same time aloof, elusive, impartial. I learned of Papa's death while on a second tour of South America, and mourned him deeply. I wrote in my diary: "Dear, dear Papa. Wherever you are I know that you are cooking Haitian rice and peas for wide-eyed angels of all races and creeds. And telling them tall tales, some of them a little off color."

In 1949 Papa was very much alive, and passing through New York on my way to Haiti, watching him in his blue Asaka blouse and straw hat earnestly teaching small babies at the Dunham School on Forty-third Street how to drum and sing children's songs in creole, I felt a need to try in some way to repay this closest of friends for the tie, which he had kept in me, with the country I loved so much, for the glamour and truth which he had brought to the Dunham School, from which I was all too frequently absent. His dearest wish was once more to see Haiti, which he had left as a seaman on a Cuban boat many years before. So I took Papa to Haiti to witness my decoration by President Estimé and to tour the north with Jean Brierre, and Papa listened and looked and probably felt much more of what was happening than I did, and finally decided that I must have the protection of his dear friend Kam, who lived in the north of Haiti at Port-de-Paix. Ton-ton Nord drove us, and, as I have said, Jean Brierre was assigned by Dumarsais Estimé to accompany me. Those must have been turbulent days underneath the festivities wherever we went, because not long after came the fall of Estimé, and I am certain that he must have felt it in the air, and Papa did also. But it had become an obsession with Papa that I meet Kam, and meeting her kept me too busy to think of politics.

Among the slaves imported into the New World many must have been of royal families sold by political rivals, just as many were sorcerers too dangerous to have around. Kam's mother was about a hundred and one years old when I first met her, and looked every bit the daughter of an African king that she was supposed to be. Kam herself was small-boned, fine-featured, and as elegant as is possible; barefooted, in cotton dress and foulard, she could have stood beside any queen and come off to advantage. Having seen something of Africa now, I would imagine Kam's family extraction to have been Fulah-Foutah, or from somewhere in the ancient kingdom of Ghana. We were feted in Port-de-Paix by the army and by the mayor, Frémance Bienaimée. But somehow for Papa and me the day centered around the small caille where Kam's mother sat in state and received visitors when she wasn't dozing off or studying her cowrie shells, and where Kam did small commerce and took care of the cult needs of her particular family unit and deprived herself of any luxuries to send three grandsons to school. Often we would leave Jean Brierre on the beach, where we would meet him later to tell stories by a fire built by friendly fishermen: Papa and I would stay closeted with Kam while she talked with Lenguesou on my behalf. I repented for not having fulfilled my "promise" at Descayettes, slept in an incense- and herb-filled room, ate ritual foods, and accepted Kam as my protectress in Haiti. There was never drumming, because this does not go with the god Lenguesou. But Kam was literate with her god and communicated frequently by writing messages and answers in script unknown to us, much as marabout, the holy men of Islamic Africa south of the Sahara, receive and distribute messages from the Koran. I left Port-de-Paix fortified with small packages of protective herbs, a hazy recollection of the many parties offered in the name of the President, a warm and fraternal friendship with the poet Jean Brierre, and a godmother. What was happening in the politics of Haiti I wasn't to know until much later.

Years later, as I have said, Ann Smith carried a letter from Dumarsais Estimé in the cleft of her bosom from Jamaica to Port-au-Prince. Ann and I passed through customs and immigration, and once in the center of town I delivered the perspiration-damp letter, still warm from its niche, to the proper persons, who were indeed pleased to have news of a dear friend, who, though exiled, was still for them leader.

Until now, knowing nothing of the new President, Paul
Magloire, I chose to think of him as a usurper. The forced
exile of Estimé was the rude and bitter beginning of my dis-
illusionment as far as state and political ideology are concerned. On the plane from Kingston, when I wasn't weeping
on Ann's shoulder, I was trying to adjust my thinking about
Haiti and see a country in terms of its historical realities. In
the case of Haiti it was constant revolution, constant suspicion between color groups, traumatic feats of invasion, and
slavery, and a governing class which claimed far more than it
merited as far as intellectual, social, and political development are concerned. What was happening in Haiti then was
what had always happened. I simply was not ready for it. In
fulfilling my own needs, in living with the people, the peasants, who, I will always feel, are the true people of Haiti, I
had overlooked much that might have prepared me for what
I was to know of the country in later years. In the end I decided that my uneasiness was unfounded, was due more to
the fact that I had barely recovered from my appendectomy
than to the shock of my last meetings with Estimé and the
political upheaval which had exiled him.

By the time we arrived in Haiti to take up residence at
Leclerc the Dunham dancers had been spoiled by uniqueness
in each of the many countries of the world where we had
appeared. This is, I suppose, a contributing factor to the
rudderless feeling I have observed most of the dancers to
suffer from, once separated from the company, and certainly
it accounted for their boredom with Port-au-Prince and
Habitation Leclerc. As people they were not startling to be-
hold in Haiti, as had been the case in Europe, Mexico, and
South America, excepting when visitors would come upon
some one of them, Dolores or Van, wandering around the
gardens in bikinis, or Claudia McNeil pacing beside Pauline's
pool in blue jeans, rehearsing her new night club repertoire in
her fantastically deep contralto voice, which one would
imagine could be heard in the center of town. We rehearsed
through the hot summer months, which for me were filled

with obligations of the past and the present, and with the pressing need to do something about the unquiet spirits of Leclerc.

The prankster of the company, Wilbert Bradley, found Lucille, Frances, and Dolores in hysterics our first night at Leclerc. Dormitories had been set up in the pavilion gallery, and La Rosa and Lucinea were installed in the parlor of Pauline's house, where they were so deep in courtship that I doubt if they noticed leaks in the roof and families of giant cockroaches scuttling in and out of cracks in the floor and walls. We had all forgotten to test the charcoal stove in the kitchen this first night and smoke rose to the ceiling and billowed out of doors and shuttered windows. Lucille had been the first to see one of the smoke-blackened rafters start to stir lazily, then separate into shiny ripples. A couleuvre, the local python, larger than any I have seen since in Haiti, peered down at the strange assortment of newcomers gaping at it, then decided to vacate a post occupied undisturbed for perhaps more years than any of the intruders had been born. Wilbert, whose Brazilian fiancée had been a lady who fondled a good-sized boa constrictor for a living in burlesque houses, cozened and cajoled the serpent into descending from the rafters, and by the time I had arrived at the scene from my quarters at the edge of the forest he was dancing a samba with the reptile and headed for the main road. Amid shrieks of protest from the company, now gathered to watch this opening night drama, I persuaded Wilbert to respect my relationship with Damballa and loose his find into the thickest part of the bush below. Since then, various caretakers have tried to observe this respect for the person of the snake god and the serpent population of Leclerc has in recognition of this consideration, or so I say, moved to other territories, only one or two turning up now and then as testimony to the continual courtship of my "husband."

In my need to exorcise the evil or disembodied spirits frequenting or inhabiting Leclerc I thought of my godmother from the north of Haiti, Kam. Kam could only be reached by writing or phoning Frémance Bienaimée, still mayor of Port-de-Paix, still a good friend. The exile of Estimé, with whom Frémance had always shown the greatest solidarity, seemed not to have affected the little mayor's firmly entrenched position in Port-de-Paix, where he had been magistrate for many years. I called Frémance one morning from the public station on the Martissant road near the former Exposition Grounds. It was after a sleepless night when every tree and plant in the forest seemed to be shifting position and struggling against its own roots and the soil that tried tenaciously to hold them in place. The Gran' Boeuf of Leclerc, a full eighteen feet high and with glowing red eyes, crashed through the vines and low trees and made his way through the forest, snuffling at the bottoms of ruined staircases, fouling the plants and stones with his fetid slobber, yet never daring to mount to the plateau of the main buildings and pools. During my sleepless nights I had learned to distinguish between the sounds of falling mangoes and breadfruit in the gardens and of overripe coconuts loosening to clatter through rotting leaves to a thud below the trees in the forest. I had gotten over my anguish at the night cries and squeaks of small things being caught in the claws or between the jaws of larger ones, and over a cold fright at the sound of larger ones scampering off in terror of the demons let loose by Rochambeau's unhappy victims. I felt relieved just talking with Frémance by phone and wondered why I had waited to bring my godmother to the rescue. Three days later Kam arrived by a camionnette named Fleur de Jésus de Port-de-Paix.

One of Kam's most endearing and imperishable qualities is a childlike charm, which I have never seen fail to procure for her whatever she happened to want. Papa Augustin swore that Kam had been in her youth a dashing smuggler on boats between Santiago de Cuba and Cap-Haïtien. Something shook her out of that and from one day to the next she changed from lady smuggler to high priestess and clairvoyante. This is figuratively speaking as far as time is involved, because though clairvoyance had come with no effort and no warning, Kam went through all of the stages of the vaudun initiation before considering priesthood as a vocation. Between initiations she raised children, her own and other people's, cared for her aged mother and, when finally a practicing prix-des-yeux or "prize of eyes" mambo, foretold political events with such accuracy that at the height of her career diplomats from all parts of her own country and even from Puerto Rico and Cuba sought out her small caille in Port-de-Paix and paid large sums in money and jewels for her prophecies and guidance. Though Papa was, as I have said, given to the most elaborate kinds of fabrication, I somehow believe most of his stories about Kam. And, seeing her as she arrived at Leclerc in answer to my call for aid, I could imagine also true the tales of Kam as a proud young beauty knowledgeable of her royal ancestry scornfully refusing in matrimony many a suitor socially classified as her superior, but ever ready to come to the rescue of blood brothers.

With her usual insouciance Kam instructed the driver of the Fleur de Jésus de Port-de-Paix to enter the winding driveway of Leclerc. From above the road we could hear the clatter of the straining motor and catch glimpses of the dusty camionnette, steam spurting from its motor, goats, chickens, pigs, and turkeys protesting at this last indignity after eighteen hours of tortuous and precarious transport, some of the dust-covered occupants complaining, some roused from sleep by curiosity at entering this much-talked-of sanctuary for disembodied souls. The Fleur de Jésus slid to a resting position at the upper gate of Leclerc, where I was waiting to meet Kam. A guard assigned to Leclerc by President Magloire helped her from the seat beside the driver, inquisitive Dunham dancers rose from sunning beside Pauline's pool or sloped down from the improvised bar at the Pavilion. I embraced my slender, bright godmother and, smelling the talcum on her skin, fresh as a child's after her arduous trip, felt immediately safe. Kam must have at that time been about seventy years of age. Her blue-flowered shift belted at the

waist was sun-faded but clean and starched, and white embroidered petticoats showed above her ankles and slender
feet in their one-strap black slippers. She carried a worn
flowered carpetbag and a red foulard tied at the corners. The
foulard contained a gift of millet in which four eggs had
rested safely the entire trip. The receiving of small gifts of the
land immediately places one on a family status in Haiti, and
I was deeply touched by this further affirmation of our
relationship.

Stretching his neck out the window to look beyond the
gateposts and shrubbery and into the gardens, the driver of
the Fleur de Jésus manipulated a turn in the courtyard, somehow leaving plants and walls intact, and rattled off down the
drive to the Martissant road. As far as we could see, the
camionnette people and, it seemed to us in the courtyard
above, goats, pigs, chickens, and turkeys craned out of the
open sides and from the rooftop to stare at the dark forest,
at the house bearing its inscription proclaiming not only
Pauline's presence in 1805 but also that of her distinguished
husband, and at the odd assortment of strangers turned out
to greet Kam. They were more than likely convinced that we
living there were embodiments of the victims of Rochambeau's atrocities. In the red foulard carried by Kam was also
the ten-gourde note—two dollars—that Frémance had advanced Kam on my behalf for her trip. She had so entertained the driver with her tales of smuggling and piracy that
he had refused her fare, therefore it must be returned to me,
as the trip had cost her nothing and she was my guest.

Kam's first move after dropping her carpetbag in the small
stone room put in order for her was to begin a scrupulous
inspection of Leclerc which was to take her three days and
nights. Kam was purposefully lodged in what was known as
the "slave house," distinct from the slave quarters, rooms
with thick stone walls and solid roofs where two singers of
the company stayed. The slave quarters along with Pauline's
house, the Pavilion, the summer house where my mother and
Miss Scott, my secretary, lived, and another stone slave resi-

dence where I and, on occasion, my husband lived, attracted ectoplasmic visitations. But the "slave house" where Kam had been stationed was a long, low airless room with walls two feet thick which I had entered only once, being convinced that this was one important center of evil emanation. The cell was supposed to have been the slave prison where the unfortunate culprits were chained to the floor and left to die of starvation. This fits in very well with General Rochambeau's reported behavior pattern, and is even a little mild by most records. But it must have been a miserable enough death and could even have been accompanied by his asphyxiation treatment should the General have needed the space for persons on his waiting list. (Several years later, on Kam's orders, we rebuilt the storeroom. Digging into the floor, we found two iron rings with short lengths of chain attached, authenticating at least its use as a jail room.)

The ectoplasmic incident was the following. One night not long before Kam's arrival the Habitation was awakened by shrieks from my mother Annette's cottage. My mother had always had a powerful voice when under stress, but this startled me out of my sleeping pill and quinine stupor by its urgency and by some accompaniment that was not hers nor belonging to anything else to be classified as human. John Pratt was halfway up the driveway on the way back from an evening visit to Georgette's, where, he assured me, he went only for rum and Georgette's good humor. Half the company came running to our quarters from the Pavilion and Pauline's house, and the rest admitted later that they had heard the cries but preferred to stay put. Boss Meus, our caretaker, fell down the narrow stairway leading from his caille at the top of the hill and our yard boy Éli-fait, then a child of ten, came running wide-eyed, flanked by his two protectors, Neg'esse, whom I feel worth mentioning for having thrown her last litter of puppies at the age of eighteen, and Toto, her German police mate. The dogs were not at all happy to approach the balcony of my mother's cottage, and as soon as they were in sight of it they broke loose from Éli-fait and disappeared howling into the forest. My mother was in her nightdress pointing at the empty balcony. A moment before, she insisted, a man, black, bare to the waist, hands tied behind his back, wearing only ragged trousers, had knelt in the doorway and pleaded for help. In what language? She didn't know and didn't care, she just wanted to move from there. Tears had rolled down the cheeks of the man and when she screamed he had taken off in the direction of the slave cell. My mother being totally innocent of the history of Leclerc was convinced that some vagabond or thief had tried to enter the cottage. We all slept, and still do, with screens or shutters unlocked, but while Annette stayed at Leclerc, which she detested, chiefly because there was no television and because people did not speak the American language, her cottage doors and shutters were kept closed and locked at night. Boss Meus and I conferred after the excitement was over. We had both seen the misty, ragged figure go off through the euphorbia bushes and bougainvillea vines making for the torture chamber. This would certainly be the best center of operation for Kam.

While Kam hopped, skipped, and climbed her way over hillocks, through matted undergrowth and across landscaped gardens, I tried to pacify my mother, who had forgotten or had become reconciled to the episode of the "thief" but who objected strongly to my warm friendship with Kam. She felt insecure in my affections, perhaps with reason, though one relationship had little to do with the other. During her stay, Kam ate with us at our veranda table. As I remember, Annette addressed not one single word to Kam at table and was irked if any one of us did. Fortunately John and Kam were the best of friends, and when I was obliged to coddle Annette he took over with Kam, who actually would have been content to eat in silence, look at the garden, and observe the drama around her. My mother must have been two or three years older than Kam but looked to be much more. To Annette, who had always been spoiled in her small, endogamous world of Joliet sycophants, this alone must have been disturbing. Through it all Kam was totally unruffled partly because that was her nature, partly out of respect for my mother's state of mourning, and a good deal, I like to believe, to ease tensions for me.

At the end of the three days it took Kam to examine Leclerc to her satisfaction, she sat another three days on the cliff edge of the forest, looking down into the thick bush or straight ahead through palm and mango and mahogany and feathery oak trees to sparkling glimpses of ocean. These days she spoke to no one from early morning until the evening meal. I would pass her and sometimes sit beside her waiting for some sign or seeking some clue as to her system of adjuration. She remained passive as the Gautama, much of the time showing no signs of breathing or being alive excepting for an unreal glow from her skin and eyes. She was communicating with Lenguesou and receiving and giving instruction. Through her body were passing many evils, and she was sending them far out into the sea. Fever sent me to bed again and I lost count of the days. I know that Kam spent some time closeted in the slave house with burning herbs, incense, candles, and pages of white paper which she filled with fine cabalistic writing. She then called on me one evening and ordered me out from my fever-soaked sheets. It was the hour I had heretofore most dreaded, just after the night rain with soil and humus stirring and everything alive gloating over the death of something while in the process of feeding on it. But instead of apprehension and the nausea and chills that had kept me in my room most evenings, a great calm filtered in shafts of light through leaves damp and fresh from rain and I felt well and free of fear and oppression. The fountains sang, an almost sacred hush blanketed the forest, and all the small living things that had seemed to live in terror before went happily about their affairs, stopping to peer at us gratefully, it seemed to me, as we passed them. Other days there were things to do, and say, to the corners that have been accursed, incense to be carried burning into the forest in a charcoal brazier late at night, powdered herbs to be thrown to the four directions of the compass, and an all-night vigil in the slave cell with no drumming, only Kam singing and reciting from the papers which she later burned in the brazier. Lenguesou is said to feast on worms at times. If this is so, I have no evidence from Kam. There was no ritual food or sacrifice associated with her confrontation with Lenguesou at Leclerc.

The exorcising of Leclerc has not been as easy as it sounds, and was accomplished in several stages, the one I have just described being the first. In between times the master of Leclerc surely had problems and I have many times been inclined to believe the adage Pierre d'Adesky repeated so many times the day we sat at Kyona Beach twelve years after Kam's first visit—that the master of Leclerc would never be happy. Then I would return from several years of touring in far parts of the world, or even in Haiti from a day's sortie to the wild pine forest or to the cold, foggy red mountain heights of Furcy, and at the entrance to the driveway to Leclerc, which is about halfway into the property, I would begin to feel a thrill of anticipation, an expectancy always fulfilled of beauty, safety, and the love of the people who now occupy and service it as resident farmers, overseers, housekeepers, or just friends. Some of the friends went with the place, as did Éli-fait and his great-great-grandmother, who died recently at the age of one hundred and nine. Others became friends through a clinic I operated during one six months' stay. After their own cure or that of some member of their family they decided to stay near and put one or two, even three tiny cailles on some small plot where a garden of millet or corn could be started without being seen from the main residences. One of these resident farmers is Exumie, whose small child Kékette was cured of a groin abscess the size of a baseball. The entire family, including in-laws, moved in and Exumie now leads our ceremonies and dances at the peristyle on nights when tourists visit Leclerc, and in the forest at the sacred spring when there are serious and secret demands. A great red-skinned farmer named Alleman has been fired several times for mishandling of produce but always returns, and I am sure he has no intention either of moving or of mending his ways. I would consider it a great loss not to be able to look into the forest and see Alleman, who is near sixty-five, slither up a coconut palm as agilely as any of his young sons and whack off the ripe fruit with his machete, or, his legs wound around a perilous lower branch, reach into the top branches of a mango francise tree with a long stick to detach a prize fruit, skillfully catch it before it hit the ground to bruise, and bring it with pride to my veranda.

The legends continue about Leclerc, but they are melting into mild storytelling. Some of the stories are current and amusing. There are those who hesitate to cross the property at night, but the same people have been found by George, our gendarme guard, stealing coconuts and other fruit in the forest right up until nightfall. Then there was a gardener who had been sent for from Furcy; when he realized that he was to sleep at Leclerc, which was only logical, Furcy being four hours into the mountains by car, he flatly refused the job, which was a good paying one. I particularly wanted to develop a rose garden at that time and had heard that this gardener from the highlands of Furcy was a wizard with roses. No amount of persuasion could keep him at Leclerc after sundown, so I had to do the rose garden with what help I had.

A habitual apparition, a slender lady in a white trailing gown, white bonnet, and carrying a white pocketbook, was never again seen strolling around Pauline's pool at night after Kam's first visit. The only complaint against Kam, and this is more Boss Meus' than mine, seems to be that General Leclerc's treasure still lies unclaimed. Even finding the General's sword did not lead to the treasure. In search of it Boss Meus has dug pits all through the forest, and one friend and caretaker, Pierre Larousse, dug an immense hole near the lower entrance gate behind Gran'na's hut. Here, during one of our prolonged touring absences, Larousse buried a live bullock with much pomp, ceremony, and secrecy. The spirit of the bullock was to lead the way to the buried treasure. There were many wild night chases after the resurrected bullock, I am told, ending at dawn with worn shoe leather, torn trousers and shirts, scratches, but no treasure.

My first act when awakened by the restless animal for a few nights after my most recent return was to send for Kam. I was annoyed and horrified at the magic ceremony, attributed to Larousse, but since the deed was done there was no recourse but to treat it with whatever dosage had been successful in earlier exorcisings. Surely it is a kindness to put restless spirits to rest. This was not long ago and was, if instructions against the taking of any kind of life on the property itself are carried out, the final laying of spirits.

When Delcine, our laundress, was accused of smothering her newborn child it was across from Leclerc. She had made all plans to bury it secretly at Leclerc, but porteresses descending the hill from Descayettes saw pigs behind Delcine's caille feeding on the infant and reported this at the Poste de la Gendarmerie at the Porte de Léogane. This made it difficult to verify whether Delcine's story of stillbirth were true or not. Against many small evidences, I have chosen to believe Delcine but would have felt happier had the police in charge accepted my suggestion of psychiatric treatment. Delcine's small son, Vance, has long been one of the adopted children of Leclerc. He was a witness at his mother's trial, as the deceased child was born on the doorstep of their caille during the night and Vance was wakened by his mother's labor pains. I am afraid that the experience has left a mark on Vance, though Delcine, after serving a token period in prison, is again in the neighborhood. I have always liked Delcine, but the affair was dreary and I find myself avoiding her when she crosses the property now and then. The true fact of the matter is that she had been examined in our clinic by a visiting doctor shortly before, so that our records would show a full nine months' development, not seven as Delcine insisted to the end. For this reason I had hoped for a psychiatric examination, as there is now—quite different from my student days when Pont Beudette flourished under Doc Reeser—a well-run institute for psychiatric research in Port-au-Prince. The police were not quite ready for this approach. I felt that the whole affair called for a visit from Kam, her third to Habitation Leclerc.

What has been accomplished by my godmother and her co-worker, Lenguesou, has been sustained and elaborated upon by the magic of the place itself. I have worked on the premise that places of themselves are not given to evil, but man is, and man defiles the places. Over the years sacred streams have welled in the forest, sacred because they are clear and limpid and hardly a person nears them without feeling the presence of the water gods. The most forceful gods of the vaudun pantheon now feel at home at Leclerc. They enter, mount their "horses," prophesy, punish when necessary, are served, protect all and everything, and frequently entertain tourists. At first I felt small doubts at the damage done by hurricane Inez in 1966. Then I made comparative notes, and it wasn't so bad after all. The trees, as do all growing things in the tropics, have gotten back their "heads" in record time and the damage was not so great as it seemed at first.

Just after hurricane Inez passed through the Caribbean, Gâchelin, overseer of Habitation Leclerc, wrote the following, which, translated from creole, reads about like this:

> Dear Mme. Dunham
>
> I to write you for inform condition of Habitation Leclerc the 28 September at noon there was a tempest which pass Port-au-Prince which lasts one hour here at Leclerc we have no dead but for trees one had lost 15% and 90% without heads. Habitation Leclerc has lost its beauty even for 15 years After I to write more in detail.
>
> Robert Gâchelin

When I had last seen Gâchelin three years before, he spoke no English, little French, and had no idea of the working of a typewriter. I left mine, and the above note was type-written, which I felt to be remarkable self-training. I hope he makes carbons, as some of his letters are priceless, endearing.

One of the sacred streams was considered by old Gran'na to be her private property. Tepid water seeped into a pool from beneath a rock shelf of several layers jutting from the ruins of a stairway leading down from the front gardens. Crabs, most of the time found when soft-shelled, sent spurts of loamy soil into the quietly bubbling water as Gran'na teetered to crouch on a slippery boulder and dip her calebasse into the pool for drinking water. Then, outwaiting and outwitting the crabs, Gran'na would rake at the crustacea with her black, hooked fingers as they ventured from their hiding places. She always ended the victor and retired chuck-ling over a half-dozen clawing, fighting crabs, hobbling her way back to the mud and thatch hut near the entrance to Leclerc where she had been born, had given birth to more children than she remembered, and had assisted at the birth of her great-great-grandson, Éli-fait. Since there is never a shortage of wood in the forests, it pleased Gran'na to keep a marmite boiling most of the day in her small candle-cactus-fenced yard, and into this she would pop the crabs, which no one else in the neighborhood would think of eating until after the springs were cleansed of their evil spirits and sanctified, as they are now.

As to Gran'na's stream, the cleansing of that must be credited to John Pratt and to Cicéron, houngan, bocor, and once performer with the Dunham Company. Cicéron was more than a little jealous of Kam's relationship with Lengue-sou and of my confidence in this loa from the North who was not mine and who had made no manifestations directly to me, only working for me through his emissary. Surely, ac-cording to Cicéron, Agwe, Damballa, and that ambiguous Yemenja who had claimed me in Brazil and Cuba and later in Ibadan, but who nevertheless was known in Haiti were hovering about ready to do their share of protecting if given an opportunity. Kam, Cicéron reasoned, had taken care of

the misdeeds of Leclerc and Rochambeau, but long before
that, even before the coming of the French, there were creatures and beings mysterious and inimical hovering in the
rocky water and soil of Leclerc. John agreed to the cleansing
of Gran'na's spring and of an adjacent one which forced its
way to the surface practically as he and Cicéron were discussing the matter. Cicéron went about buying liqueurs, cakes
with bright little silver decorations, rum, imported fruit,
grapes, and apples, which were new ceremonial demands in
my experience and which resulted, I suspect, from Cicéron's
travels abroad with the Dunham Company. Pots of manioc
were prepared on the place, and yams and many other fruits
and vegetables, but no meat of any kind. All of this John Pratt
has told me. Meanwhile, he, my husband, was delegated to
rounding up a crew—not of the immediate environs for some
reason—to bring white coral sand from Mer Frappée at Carrefours as a bed for the springs. Then the banks were leveled
and the earth pounded hard and smooth. Watercress was
planted around the springs and in a small canal, where the
water formed a stream and wandered off under the guava
trees.

For the ceremony a houngan named Jacinthe came from
Croix-de-Missions with five hounci canzo dressed in white.
Boss Meus and Cicéron played drums softly, and sang, and
Jacinthe began the ceremony saluting the four directions of
the compass with General Leclerc's sword. Kerosene lanterns
and candles lit the clear waters of the two pools, and for an
hour and a half Meus and Cicéron sang and the hounci and
John Pratt danced while Jacinthe drew an elaborate vévé on a
smooth plot of earth beside the springs. Simbi, god of springs,
was most predominant during the night, which explains the
presence of Petro gods from time to time in our ceremonies
at Leclerc today. There were also Guedé, Cicéron's loa, and
Agwe and Damballa and the ferocious Ogun Feraille who
once mounted Egnoble, one of our caretakers. That was on
Christmas Day, my last visit to Leclerc, and Ogun Feraille
walked directly into the camera of a French television com-

pany, frightening the operator, who was filming the grounds of Leclerc, and sending the crew to the safety of the Pavilion, which gathering place of tourists seems to hold no interest for this loa. I hardly recognized Egnoble, whose already red eyes had turned to flame, and whose already flaring nostrils had opened wide as a stallion's. Jacinthe, at the height of the spring-cleansing ceremony, became possessed of Ogun Feraille and moved boulder-sized stones from place to place, sealing openings which only he could see, where evil and errant spirits had had access to the world outside. The sacred springs as I last saw them were placid, clean and joyful. One regret, however, is the scarcity of crabs, which were fecund when the waters were ridden by malevolent spirits. Since Gran'na has died, this makes little difference, as any edible creatures inhabiting these springs are still thought of as hers.

Trips to the Pine Forest, Furcy, Kyona Beach, and occasional ones to town for shopping are my only absences from Leclerc when I return these days. I have no intention of scaling again the vertical mountain path leading to the Citadel, having suffered the excruciating trip three times on the back of one or another wretched transport beast from San Souci—remains of Christophe's palace at the bottom of the Citadel —to the dizzy heights of that wonder of the world. I am told that there have been no casualties on these Citadel trips and this I attribute to some protective sorcery. When the miserably thin, sore-spotted horses are not trying to rid themselves of passengers by crushing them against the mountains on one side, they are trying furtively to pitch their burden over a cliff on the other. Being only skin and bones and with scarcely strength enough to hold to the path, much less keep to it if thrown off balance, the latter represents a hazard for themselves, so that almost immediately they return to the mountain side after showing the terrified tourist what might have been in store for him. Once at the Citadel, the view below and the majesty of the ruin itself are worth the agony. I repeat, however, that I have in all probability made my last Citadel trip. I cannot say the same for the Pine Forest, or for the heights of Furcy, and will never be satiated with the lone huts or far hills, the deep ravines; the green silence of the Pine Forest and red earth silence of Furcy. On Kyona Beach I have already reported.

Seldom leaving Leclerc in no way relieves me of obligations toward friendships, old and new. When I am not there, and John is, I am sometimes spared first meetings which might be painful. For several years I had had letters from 'ti Joseph, child of my Cul-de-Sac lavé-tête ceremony, all of them reminding me that I was his "mother," all of them requesting money. Of course I remembered him from my initiation, but I was most certainly not his mother then nor am I now, and much of the time when he asked for money my immediate responsibilities were so heavy that I simply put the letter aside for further consideration. I believe I answered once, and this is perhaps the reason for 'ti Joseph's visit to Leclerc for financial aid from his "father." He came with a letter written by his usual scribe, who probably worked on a percentage of hope. His letters were always signed "your favorite son" or "your cherished infant." On the first occasion, 'ti Joseph pointed out to John Pratt that he had no mother or father, was orphaned and depended solely on us. He was given all the produce from the place that he could carry but was not very happy about his reward. The next day he shamelessly appeared with a letter asking for money to go to Jacmel to see his ailing mother.

Worn down by 'ti Joseph's malign persistence, John Pratt found work for him as a mason's assistant on Leclerc. The laborers on the place were at once wary of the long-faced, bulletheaded, scrawny young man, as ugly as when he was a child but without the charm or pathos of that age. In spite of an attempt at pathos—a shirt so ragged as to be unrecognizable, mismatching shoes, on one foot an old brown sneaker, the other a sandal made of tire casing—the sum effect was what we found out later to be true: 'Ti Joseph had become a real "voyou," a vagabond, and in town, outside every tourist gathering place or at boat arrivals, provided no police agents were around, the other mismatching shoes could be seen on 'ti Joseph's young man companion, a half-Dominican Haitian. The two were operating what might have become a profitable confidence game had tourist trade stayed at par.

Cécile came to see me soon after my arrival on my last trip to Haiti. I had seen her once at Pont Beudette some years after my initiation, just after Doc left Haiti for Miami for what he had thought would be once and for all. Cécile had gone into a state of gentle semi-mourning, realizing that she would have no place in Doc's Florida life, but knowing somehow in her safe, unlettered Haitian mind that he would return. Return he did, a few days before she slowly climbed the drive to Leclerc. Cécile smiled and I saw that she had won the race for a full front row of gold-capped teeth. But her smile was sad. Doc was ill and wanted to see me. He was staying with a friend near Arcachon. I went immediately with Cécile and found Doc not as much changed as I had expected after two heart attacks. He was thinner, as red-faced as ever, refused rum, which to him must have been a great sacrifice, sang from his vast collection of vaudun songs and recitations, which I hope someday will be published, and talked of old days and of Cécile. There was no witchcraft in Doc's love for either Haiti or Cécile. As we talked that day for the last time—because shortly after, he died in the land to which he had come back to die—I saw an innocence in his brilliant blue eyes that I had not seen before. As I left, waving to him and Cécile, a tuft of hair, white, but looking gold in the evening sun stood up on his head, giving him, with his rosy face, the air of a naughty cherub.

There were important parties and receptions at Habitation Leclerc our first summer there, the summer of our rehearsals, of recovery from my appendectomy, of my godmother's first visit. Hardly a day passed but that some helmeted gendarme, even officer, would come roaring up the driveway with an urgent invitation to the Presidential Palace

or an announcement of a forthcoming visit to Leclerc by
Madame Magloire, or with a printer's proof of the program
for the benefit we were giving in the Théâtre de Verdure for
the social works of Madame la Présidente. Having recently
come from Buenos Aires, I was familiar with the benefit-for-
social-works operation. Here in Haiti it was well timed from
our point of view, as the company had begun dangerously to
weary of inactivity and boredom.

The orchestra for the benefit was recruited chiefly from
the army band and the elements were rehearsed for weeks
under our Argentine conductor, Bernardo Noriega, with the
help of the male members of the Duroseau family, Haiti's
best-trained musicians to date. There were multiple production problems but the two performances were brilliant. After
the second, with scarcely a half-day's warning beforehand, the
Colonel President, carrying himself more than ever like Henri
Christophe, preceded by guards, followed and surrounded by
guards, entered the Pavilion of Leclerc with Madame la
Présidente on his arm, stood at attention to the tune of the
Haitian National Anthem, then led Madame in the first
dance, a méringue of course, and after to the tables of honor
around Pauline's pool. It was an evening of great festivity,
with Lenwood doing acrobatic diving and Dolores, Frances,
and Lucille at their adorable best as hostesses. My mother
created problems about protocol seating, but that was to be
expected, and Vanoye came to my rescue as he has so many
times, acting as combined escort and social secretary for
Annette. I mention only these charter members of the
Dunham Company, but they were all there, and during the
evening all of them gave the impression of being as in love
with Haiti as I was. I was only happy that there was not the
added complication of Kam's presence to create further
problems with Annette.

Whether Paul Magloire was more soldier than President I
have never known. Being a staunch follower and supporter of
his predecessor, Dumarsais Estimé, I can only say that when
Colonel Magloire signed with two other chiefs of army the

enforced exile of Dumarsais Estimé he signed a crucial blow to the economic freedom of Haiti, to its evolution in the world of today. And in accepting the presidency he was accepting a task which might have been well done by his culture hero, Henri Christophe, but not by himself. I would be inclined to think that the present President of Haiti shares these feelings, although such a subject would not have been on the agenda of our brief meetings.

François Duvalier, his wife, and full escort visited Habitation Leclerc in 1958. This was when I had returned from a year in Japan—a vacation it could be called—after a strenuous tour of Australia, New Zealand, and the Far East. The company was sent ahead to the United States, to find whatever they had been yearning for all these months, some chimera or other, while I satisfied my yearning to write. After finishing A Touch of Innocence, the story begun in Japan of my first painful eighteen years, I fell into the idea of a clinic at Leclerc because of a tragically absurd happening. Boss Meus, Emmanuel, our head mason, and several workmen were in stitches of laughter when I came upon them one day under a mango tree in the main courtyard. When I asked what was wrong, each was so taken by the humor of the situation as to be unable to answer. The story, which made me decide to open the clinic, throws considerable light on Haitian humor. A young peasant couple took their only child to the general hospital with the trepidation all Haitians of this class feel about entering government buildings. The sick child was examined and a prescription given for twenty gourdes' worth of urgent injectable medication if the baby were to be saved. The couple had perhaps two gourdes between them, twenty gourdes—the equivalent of four American dollars—being unheard of to them as a sum in cash. They returned five miles to their caille on foot, gathered what they could from friends and neighbors, each poorer than the other but offering a sack of corn or meal if that would help, and sold from their plaster and palm thatch hut floor mats and furniture.

Somehow before hospital closing hours the unhappy couple had raised the twenty gourdes, returned to town and to the hospital on foot and bought the medicine. They waited for an hour in the emergency waiting room, the mother clinging to the small bundle which had become strangely uncomplaining. When the doctor finally saw them they thrust the medicine at him. He took the tiny bundle, shook his head sadly, as the baby was quite dead, and pocketed the medicine, explaining that there would be no further need on their part for it and they couldn't possibly sell it. This was very funny to the workmen and Boss Meus, but the next morning I wrote New York to my guardian angel and witch doctor, Max Jacobson, for medical samples and a week later received a mammoth supply of sample remedies for internal parasites of many kinds, for malaria, influenza, tuberculosis, yaws, and other ailments. Two doctors worked with me at the beginning of the "clinic" for all diagnoses and prescriptions.

During the most active days of the clinic I had, with this local aid and extensive guidance by post from Max Jacobson, effected some cures of malaria, paralysis, and rheumatic fever considered close to miraculous. One late afternoon during this period a blacksmith from the other side of Port-au-Prince was led to the clinic by a friend. The blacksmith was suffering intensely from what was easily diagnosed as compressed lumbar discs with resultant pinched nerves and contorted muscles. The man eyed our open-air hospital arrangement suspiciously, lay face down on our massage table shaded by an almond tree and allowed his trousers to be lowered sufficiently for me to make my diagnosis. Being not long back from Japan and not long over a siege of the same complaint, treated and cured by the Oriental touch point massage which I later studied, I instructed my helpers to bring boiling water for the application of hot towels before setting to work. As Dodo, cook when not clinic assistant, poured the water into basins at the foot of the table my patient arched his back, took one look at the rising vapor, cried as though he had been scalded, and vaulted from the table and up the steps, stumbling over his falling trousers, climbing on hands and knees through the back courtyard and up another set of stone steps past Boss Meus' house to the upper road. He was shouting in a creole unknown to me, or undecipherable. I stood with a steaming towel in my hand, mouth open, watching Boss Meus reel down the stairs laughing so that tears ran from his eyes. The man, Boss Meus explained, was convinced the whole affair was a diabolic plan to cook him alive, that we were Rochambeau's zombies preparing for a feast. I have heard that the blacksmith hasn't spoken since to the friend who brought him to Leclerc.

At the time President and Madame Duvalier paid us their visit, Clinic Leclerc was treating and curing, miraculously, as many as four hundred outpatients and a half-dozen inpatients monthly. From seven in the morning until seven at night energies formerly used on stage or at a typewriter went into therapeutic massage, injections, cleansing and salving ulcers, boiling needles, worming babies, and other clinic demands. The green forest below and sparkle of sea through the treetops seemed to be supplying me with more stamina than I had ever known, and if this ran low, I invariably evoked the image of my own culture hero, Max Jacobson. I should say that much encouragement and our first supply of penicillin came from a retired surgeon from Chicago, Dr. Ulysses Grant Dailey, who had come to Haiti as honorary American Consul and with a dream of being useful but until then had not found the way. Dr. Dailey left Haiti somewhat disillusioned, I learned from my last conversations with him, and he died soon after. For him the country was enigmatic and an adjustment late in life difficult, though both he and Mrs. Dailey were surely eligible for acceptance and were received and feted by all classes, especially by the élite. Madeline Preston, recovered from our strenuous Far East tour, came to visit and to change bandages, bathe babies, and check temperatures, and Nurse Smith—"Smitty"—dropped in as frequently as she could absent herself from her own private hospital to give advice. Smitty is no longer in Haiti, though to her it will always be home. One day she will surely return.

President Duvalier on his visit did not seem greatly impressed by the medical-service aspect of my activities in the clinic at Leclerc. Some anti-Duvalierists, insisting that the political strength of Haiti lies in its houngans and doctors, feel the Doctor to be wary of interlopers in both fields. It is true, and reasonable, that physical health is more important to the Haitian masses than new roads, telephones, clothing, or money in the Banque Nationale, which latter they have for the most part no occasion to know about. Because if a man is well and his family is well, do not all good things come, like being able to work on a small plot of land that belongs to oneself, like making love to several wives, like dancing to venerate the gods and ancestors or have a good time at Saturday night bamboches?

The anti-Duvalierists continued to whisper in my ear that "Papa Doc" was jealous and would either destroy the good work already done or use it for self-interested political purposes, but I was too engrossed in the clinic to think of these things. The evening of his visit to Leclerc, the President had been led to a terrace where a length of charcoal cooking apertures were built into a stone table. On these, needles and instruments were sterilized. There was under a banana tree a table of ready equipment, covered by gauze cloths damp with alcohol. In a wine cellar the basic supplies were kept in steel medicine cabinets and, if there was an overflow, on the stone shelves in cartons. The terrace hung over the back forest and it was all very picturesque, full of charm, and in off hours was used as kitchen and dining terrace for the lower residence. But it must have seemed a little amateur to the President, himself a medical doctor, no matter how many cures were reported to have taken place there.

One day, just before leaving Haiti for our last European tour, I was offered just the right person to revive the clinic and take it over during my absence. There would be funds for a separate building on another part of the property, with a feeding station for mothers and babies, a dream of mine as yet unrealized. The delicate subject of birth control might even be taken in hand, and, goodness knows, in spite of the high rate of infant mortality some kind of solution in this direction should be considered. One of Kam's guiding spirits, or perhaps Damballa himself, as I had been especially protective toward any serpents found on the place that year, prompted me to refuse the offer and to close the clinic definitively. Luck, or mana, has a way of running out, and I had no wish to tempt mine further. I later learned, after that person had fled the country, that the offer had come from political opponents of Duvalier, the clinic idea to be camouflage for a subversive munitions station.

Epilogue

When I first began a plan of this book I intended it to be concerned with all the gods who have walked through my life. I was going to call it *Letter from Rosita* because Rosita, Cuban santera in New York, has given me so many instructions and predictions, most of them useful and true, that I had allowed Damballa and Agwe and Yemanja and Guedé and Lenguesou and Simbi and the Congo gods to slip into something of the dim past. When I started writing, however, all these gods brought such fresh and delightful memories and vivid recall that I was willing to let them claim me for their own, at least for a time. It hasn't been easy, because the great baobab trees of Senegal—dry, aching stumps of branches extruding from gnarled bases as large as small huts, gaunt reminders of prehistory—house their own rab, governing spirits that must be appeased by sorcery and complex curing ceremonies. In Africa in all of nature, chiefly in the air and sea, there are the genii, life essences of the living to be controlled or of the ancestors to be propitiated. Cowrie shells are animated, if properly treated, and so are tips of goats' horns and hundreds of other fetishes, charms which have been slept with, prayed and muttered over, read to from the Koran, where the Koran is known, anointed and spat upon by the proper holy or unholy person, because some of my bush priests frankly treat with the devil. These charms are sewn in different shapes according to content and purpose in fine leather with fine stitching and worn or carried as one wears the crucifix or the image of the Virgin. One healer I saw in action wore about a hundred bound on thongs around his arms, legs, waist and in his hair. Those were the ones in sight. The number of fetishes worn is not only a sign of strength and protection from harm, but of prestige, because the operation of their making costs something.

There is also in my garden in Senegal to distract me from my Haitian recollections a sacred rooster who has been told many of my most personal hopes and desires, who has doubled his size on the good food from our kitchen, and who stares at me balefully when I talk to him and who crows five times from prayer time at four in the morning until noon prayer time, outdoing the muezzin in the minaret of the Grande Mosquée in force and purity of voice. All these things have been a temptation, but when Julio, my Cuban blood brother, wrote that Rosita was disturbed by my trafficking with African gods (I had written neither of them any of these things) I answered that if I were to examine things from all sides, really believe in something or anything at all, it was all the same thing and the believing that counted. I didn't try to go into the origin and distribution of black people in the New World; that seemed too obvious. I thought of trying to tell Julio and Rosita about Erich Fromm's "non-theistic-mysticism," but that was too complicated for my limited Spanish. I hope one day to examine further the Cuban gods, and perhaps even bring some reconciliation into these wandering, jealous siblings of different nations but of the same ancestors.

In all, I have decided that the gods of Haiti have been very kind to the present owners of Leclerc. I can now say "master" and "mistress" because until the malediction dating from before General Rochambeau had been thoroughly exorcized I felt full responsibility for any unsuccess in the lives of my immediate family, and ran the place most of the time singlehanded. Now that all springs have been cleansed and all hiding places of troublesome souls forever sealed and the souls themselves sent back to sleep peacefully in 'Nan Guinée, I shall see what it feels like to be mistress of Leclerc and leave the maintaining of order to the master, my husband.

Dakar, Senegal

Glossary

Action de grâce   Act of grace, generosity; clemency, pardon.

Affaires   Affair; what one has to do or has to do with. Used vaguely of any proceeding which it is not desired to be precise about.

Arada-Dahomey   (Rada-) Two West African kingdoms from which a large number of slaves were exported. Vaudun cult of which Damballa, snake god, and his mistress and wife, Erzulie and Freda, are rulers.

Ason   Sacred rattle of priest or priestess, dried gourd with trade beads of different colors strung on the outside; may also be strung with dried snakes' vertebrae.

Asotor   Tallest drum of Arada-Dahomey cult, at times approximating nine feet, cut from a single tree trunk, hollowed.

Bacalou   (Bakulou) An evil and mischievous demon; werewolf; an evil spirit nourished by human flesh.

Bamboche   Formerly (nineteenth century) a tall marionnette; (eighteenth century) burlesque painting. A get-together; popular dance gathering; as verb, to have a good time.

Banda   A hip-grinding, sexually cathartic dance dedicated to Guedé and Baron Samedi, gods of death and cemeteries. Dance at times associated with funeral rites also danced during carnival and during "rest" periods of ceremonies.

Béguine   National popular dance of Martinique.

Bocor   Cult priest who practices divining and/or magic in addition to working with the loa and the dead.

Bosalle   Wild, untamed; unclean spirit; one not yet inducted into the vaudun. A slave newly arrived from Africa and not apt in the colonial systems of manners.

Boubou   West African wide sacklike garment used as outer wearing apparel by both men and women.

Boula   Smallest of three Arada-Dahomey ceremonial drums. Sometimes called "bébé" (baby).

Boumrab   Assistant priestess or servitor in Senegalese curing ceremony, the N'Dop.

"Breaks" or feints   Convulsive movements and sharp temporary changes in a ceremonial Haitian cult rhythm to keep it from becoming too hypnotic.

Caboclo   Indian or metis of the Brazilian forests.

Caco   Bandit or mercenary soldier known in Haiti for guerrilla resistance to Marine Occupation, and specifically used here in reference to that Occupation.

Caille   Creole word for hut or small house; cabin.

Calebasse   (Calabash) The name of various gourds or pumpkins dried for use as rattles, serving bowls, or other utensils. The hollow shell of the gourd.

Camionnette   Wagonette. Small truck carrying passengers. An omnibus usually constructed of gaily painted wood mounted on a truck chassis.

Canaris   Earthen vessels for storing or transporting water.

Canzo   Ceremony to effect the second degree of vaudun hounci; rank of hounci whose loa have been "tamed" or controlled. The person who has passed the test of fire.

Case   Cabin, house, dwelling.

Chairo pié   A shuffling dance of a crowd traveling from village to village during carnival or "combite" work sessions.

Chandelle   Spiny plant, candelabra-shaped; of the cactus family. The milky sap is mildly poisonous. Frequently planted for barricades.

Charros   Mexican army or police regiment horseman; élite of ranch horsemen in northern Mexico.

Cigouaves   Demons of the lycanthrope family, frightful creatures of the night with wolf body and human head. They especially tear out men's genitals.

Ciseaux   Scissors; dance step where feet are crossed imitating cutting movement of scissors.

Clairin   Raw or unrefined white rum.

Cocomacaque   "Monkey coco" or dwarf coco tree from which club of same name is cut.

Combite   An organized community work effort—building, harvesting, road repair, etc.; work groups of friends and neighbors; formal song and dance accompany formalized work movements.

Couleuvre   Nonvenomous serpent; in Haiti the cult representation of Damballa.

Couzin   Creole for cousin; friendly and familiar term used by the god Asaka, god of the mountains, in greeting.

Daudine   Cane rocking chair approximately eighteenth-century Viennese; samples still found in Haiti.

Diablesse   Female devil spirit.

Durian   Eastern Asiatic fruit, ill-smelling but appetizing to the taste. Much prized for aphrodisiac effect.

Échappée   A ballet movement in which feet are moved from fifth position into second on point or half point and returned to fifth.

Engagement   Commitment or engagement, a compact with demon or god.

Fêtes   Festivals, holidays.

Fetishes   Magical charm, gris-gris, talisman, mascot. Any object used as an amulet or means of enchantment, or regarded with dread.

Feuilles   Leaves; medical herbs, leaves gathered for medicine or magic.

Figuier   Giant tropical tree of fig family; banyan tree.

Fromager   Large tropical tree of cottonwood family; kapok tree.

Genii   Secular spirits of animistic Moslem belief; often evil-doing, some are beneficent. The *anima* as distinct from the physical self.

Gérant   Manager, overseer.

Gourde   Haitian money; one gourde equals twenty American cents or one fifth of one dollar.

Grande robe   National feminine dress of Martinique; traditionally patterned on the Empire dresses of the early nineteenth century; similar to dresses of Joséphine Beauharnais Bonaparte.

Griffon   Approximately two fifths white blood, three fifths Negro. Darker than mulatto. The offspring of a mulatto and a Negro, three parts black.

Grillot   Succulent bits of deep-fried pork. Typical meat dish for peasant and élite alike.

Gris-gris   Fetish; talisman, magical charm; bird used in making charm.

Gros-bouzain   Dance characterized by haunch-grinding circular movement. Chiefly danced during carnival or parties where prostitutes may be participating.

Grouillère   Swarming, grinding, hip-winding crowd dance. A vaudun and adapted social dance characterized by lascivious pelvic movements.

Guajira   A social dance in six-eight rhythm of Spanish American origin.

Guru   Mentor, leader, teacher of the Buddhist or Zen faiths; holy man. Hindu religious teacher.

Hiatus   Lapse; pause. A break in continuity.

Horse   Person "mounted" by or possessed by god or loa.

Hounci canzo   An acolyte to the vaudun; servitor of the gods or loa who has been "tamed" or controlled. May be male or female.

Houngenicon   Male assistant to male priest or houngan, serves houngan during ceremony. Acts as a sort of chief of the main body of devotees.

Houngfor   The vaudun or voodoo temple, structure dedicated to the Haitian loa or gods for permanent housing and ceremonial offerings; repository of artifacts associated with and of the mystic spirit of the gods.

Kata   Smallest of a set of three ceremonial drums. Also *boula* and *bébé*. Designates also the rhythm of sticks on sides of drums.

Kébiosilie   Kebiosili (Kebiosu), deity of Arada-Yoruba of West African origin.

Kola   A bottled artificial fruit drink, very sweet; similar to soda pop.

Laillé   The play, the movements, swirling of skirts in a dance.

Lalawa-di   See *Lalwadi*.

La loi di   See *Lalwadi*.

Lalwadi   *La loi dit*: literally translated, "the law says." May also be lalawa-di, lawalwadi. King of lalwadi, leader of dances during Rara or post Mardi Gras season.

Langage   Language of the "mystères" or loa; mysterious tongues, recognizable as African in origin; spoken by priests or possessed persons during vaudun rites.

La place   Chief assistant of the houngan. Assumes responsibility for running the houngfor in the absence of his chief.

Lares   Household gods. The tutelary deities of a house. Hence, the home. Often coupled with "penates."

Likembe   An African thumb piano also known as sansa.

Loa The spirit or god who possesses people or a person during cult ceremonies. The loa, originally from Africa, may take residence in the head or occupy the entire body. Services to the loa are the chief means of perpetuating practices brought from Africa by the ancestors, the slaves.

Loup garou Classically known as werewolf: creature part man, part wolf.

Macumbera Priestess of the macumba, Brazilian equivalent of the vaudun; equivalent to mambo in Haiti.

Mait' tête The spirit residing in and master of the head. One may be born with, inherit, or acquire, through ritual offerings, this spirit.

Major-domo Leader of a carnival or Rara (Easter) dance group or band of dancers.

Malaise Uneasiness, discomfort.

Mama The largest of a set of three ceremonial drums.

Mambo Officiating priestess of the vaudun.

Mambo caille High priestess of house or tonnelle.

Mana Intrinsic power in an object because of dedication or cumulative use.

Mange' moun' "Mange' monde' "—Eats people; cannibalistic.

Mapou Very large uncommon tree found near springs. Of the cottonwood family.

Marabou Depends on context. Africa: Moslem holy man. Haiti: a much admired type of female beauty with black skin and straight or curly hair.

Maracas Pairs of rattles made of small gourds filled with pellets. Cuban in origin.

Marasta Twins; spirit or loa of the twins. Sacred in some cults, feared magically in others.

Marimboula Large version of the African thumb piano; mounted in a box large enough to be sat upon and played between the legs; tones regulated by curved iron thongs placed in relative tensions.

Mazouk West Indian adaptation of the mazurka, a lively Polish dance resembling the polka.

Méringue Haitian national social dance. There is also a Dominican merengue more influenced by Spanish music.

Negritude Doctrine advanced by Aimée Césaire, poet and playwright, and Léopold Sédar Senghor, President of Senegal and poet, that humanism may be approached through appreciation of black culture.

Ogan   A metal percussion device that accompanies Arada drums. Traditionally a forged iron bell.

Orgeat   Syrupy drink, almond liquid base. Frequently a part of offerings to Damballa and his pantheon.

Ouanga   Aggressive magic; charm; spell.

Oxun   Important African god in the Brazilian Macuba cult. The god of iron and lightning. Sometimes identified with Ogun in Haiti, Oxun in Cuba, Shango in Trinidad and Cuba.

Penates   The guardian deities of the household and of the state, who were worshipped in the interior of every house; often coupled with "lares": household gods.

Pièce de résistance   Principal portion, highlight.

Placée   "Placed" or living with man or woman as husband or wife without legal ceremony. Most Haitian peasants are "placées" even if otherwise legally married. Second or third wife. Also a woman who wishes to protect her legal inheritance by not being married.

Poteau mitan   Central post of the tonnelle around which most rites occur. Loa who descend upon the service enter by way of this pole.

Pot tête   A covered china pot in which loa and spirits are kept in the houngfor. Small remnants of personal baptismal sacrifices are in pots têtes and are considered to contain the mana or spirit essence of the owner.

Pouin   A potent defensive charm which is the product of ritual magic within the cult temple. A form of protective magic. A gris-gris.

Prête savant   (Pret' savan') Bush priest, learned priest of any of the sects. "Savant" also means "savanne" or plains, though it is used indiscriminately for all bush or interior regions. The functionary who reads or recites Catholic prayers in a vaudun service.

Prix-des-yeux   "Prize of eyes," or "price of eyes;" clairvoyance. Highest degree of vaudun initiates.

Rab   Spirit entering the body of the possessed in the animistic-Islamic religions of French West Africa.

Rara bands   A cohesive unit of dancing revelers during the carnival season.

Régisseur   Director, stage manager.

Rites de passage   The collection of ceremonies which accompany major life transitions—birth, puberty, marriage, death.

Roi   King; here means leader.

Sablier   A tree which at maturity develops a tough armature of spines on trunk and lower branches, commonly used for protective property barriers in Haiti; named after the tusked hog.

Sansa   Another name for likembe, an African thumb piano.

Santera   A Cuban cult priestess.

Seconde   Middle size of a set of three vaudun drums.

Services   A ceremony petitioning favors or in repayment for favors previously received or a promise of future ceremonies; ritual honoring the gods or the ancestors.

'ti Malice   Folk-tale figure, a spider personification, humorous as well as cunning. An African survival, he has a character much like Br'er Rabbit. Also a peppery sauce into which grillot is dipped.

Tonnelle   Roofed area of the houngfor court or patio, generally thatched with palm fronds.

Valse créole   Creole or West Indian adaptation of the waltz.

Vaudun   Animistic cult or religious belief probably originating in Arada-Dahomey kingdoms of West Africa. The hierarchy of gods governing the belief.

Vedette   French word for theatrical star.

Vévé   Ceremonial drawing made of meal or flour on the ground by the houngan.

Yonvalou   The Arada-Dahomey vaudun cult rhythm and dance.

'Zepaules   "Les épaules"—A ceremonial dance with accent on shoulder movements.

Zin   A pot used in second-degree initiation into the vaudun, the canzo. Originally of iron and transported from Africa to the Caribbean, the pots may currently be of clay.